Praise for *Deciphering Data Architectures*

In *Deciphering Data Architectures*, James Serra does a wonderful job explaining the evolution of leading data architectures and the trade-offs between them. This book should be required reading for current and aspiring data architects.

—*Bill Anton, Data Geek, Opifex Solutions*

James has condensed over 30 years of data architecture knowledge and wisdom into this comprehensive and very readable book. For those who must do the hard work of delivering analytics rather than singing its praises, this is a must-read.

—*Dr. Barry Devlin, Founder and Principal, 9sight Consulting*

This reference should be on every data architect's bookshelf. With clear and insightful descriptions of the current and planned technologies, readers will gain a good sense of how to steer their companies to meet the challenges of the emerging data landscape. This is an invaluable reference for new starters and veteran data architects alike.

—*Mike Fung, Master Principal Cloud Solution Architect, Oracle*

Marketing buzz and industry thought-leader chatter have sown much confusion about data architecture patterns. With his depth of experience and skill as a communicator, James Serra cuts through the noise and provides clarity on both long-established data architecture patterns and cutting-edge industry methods. that will aid data practitioners and data leaders alike. Put it on your desk—you'll reference it often.

—*Sawyer Nyquist, Owner, Writer, and Consultant,*
The Data Shop

The world of data architectures is complex and full of noise. This book provides a fresh, practical perspective born of decades of experience. Whether you're a beginner or an expert, everyone with an interest in data must read this book!

—*Piethein Strengholt, author of* Data Management at Scale

An educational gem! *Deciphering Data Architectures* strikes a perfect balance between simplicity and depth, ensuring that technology professionals at all levels can grasp key data concepts and understand the essential trade-off decisions that really matter when planning a data journey.

—*Ben Reyes, Cofounder and Managing Partner, ZetaMinusOne LLC*

I recommend *Deciphering Data Architectures* as a resource that provides the knowledge to understand and navigate the available options when developing a data architecture.

—*Mike Shelton, Cloud Solution Architect, Microsoft*

Data management is critical to the success of every business. *Deciphering Data Architectures* breaks down the buzzwords into simple and understandable concepts and practical solutions to help you get to the right architecture for your dataset.

—*Matt Usher, Director, Pure Storage*

As a consultant and community leader, I often direct people to James Serra's blog for up-to-date and in-depth coverage of modern data architectures. This book is a great collection, condensing Serra's wealth of vendor-neutral knowledge. My favorite is Part III, where James discusses the pros and cons of each architecture design. I believe this book will immensely benefit any organization that plans to modernize its data estate.

—*Teo Lachev, Consultant, Prologika*

James's blog has been my go-to resource for demystifying architectural concepts, understanding technical terminology, and navigating the life of a solution architect or data engineer. His ability to transform complex technical concepts into clear, easy-to-grasp explanations is truly remarkable. This book is an invaluable collection of his work, serving as a comprehensive reference guide for designing and comprehending architectures.

—*Annie Xu, Senior Data Customer Engineer, Google*

James's superpower has always been taking complex subjects and explaining them in a simple way. In this book, he hits all the key points to help you choose the right data architecture and avoid common (and costly!) mistakes.

—Rod Colledge, Senior Technical Specialist (Data and AI), Microsoft

This book represents a great milestone in the evolution of how we handle data in the technology industry, and how we have handled it over several decades, or what is easily the equivalent of a career for most. The content offers great insights for the next generation of data professionals in terms of what they need to think about when designing future solutions. 'deciphering' is certainly an excellent choice of wording for this, as deciphering is exactly when it is needed when turning requirements into data products.

—Paul Andrew, CTO, Cloud Formations Consulting

A fantastic guide for data architects, this book is packed with experience and insights. Its comprehensive coverage of evolving trends and diverse approaches makes it an essential reference for anyone looking to broaden their understanding of the field.

—Simon Whiteley, CTO, Advancing Analytics Limited

There is no one whose knowledge of data architectures and data processes I trust more than James Serra. This book not only provides a comprehensive and clear description of key architectural principles, approaches, and pitfalls, it also addresses the all-important people, cultural, and organizational issues that too often imperil data projects before they get going. This book is destined to become an industry primer studied by college students and business professionals alike who encounter data for the first time (and maybe the second and third time as well)!

—Wayne Eckerson, President of Eckerson Group

Deciphering Data Architectures is an indispensable vendor-neutral guide for today's data professionals. It insightfully compares historical and modern architectures, emphasizing key trade-offs and decision-making nuances in choosing an appropriate architecture for the evolving data-driven landscape.

—Stacia Varga, author and Data Analytics Consultant, Data Inspirations

Deep, practitioner wisdom within, the latest scenarios in the market today have vendor specific skew, latest terminology, and sales options. James takes his many years of expertise to give agnostic, cross cloud, vendor, vertical approaches from small to large.

—*Jordan Martz, Senior Sales Engineer, Fivetran*

Data Lake, Data Lakehouse, Data Fabric, Data Mesh … It isn't easy sorting the nuggets from the noise. James Serra's knowledge and experience is a great resource for everyone with data architecture responsibilities.

—*Dave Wells, Industry Analyst, eLearningcurve*

Too often books are "how-to" with no background or logic – this book solves that. With a comprehensive view of why data is arranged in a certain way, you'll learn more about the right way to implement the "how."

—*Buck Woody, Principal Data Scientist, Microsoft*

Deciphering Data Architectures is not only thorough and detailed, but it also provides a critical perspective on what works, and perhaps more importantly, what may not work well. Whether discussing older data approaches or newer ones such as Data Mesh, the book offers words of wisdom and lessons learned that will help any data practitioner accelerate their data journey.

—*Eric Broda, Entrepreneur, Data Consultant, author of* Implementing Data Mesh *(O'Reilly)*

No other book I know explains so comprehensively about data lake, warehouse, mesh, fabric and lakehouse! It is a must have book for all data architects and engineers.

—*Vincent Rainardi, Data Architect and author*

Deciphering Data Architectures

Choosing Between a Modern Data Warehouse, Data Fabric, Data Lakehouse, and Data Mesh

James Serra

Beijing · Boston · Farnham · Sebastopol · Tokyo   

Deciphering Data Architectures

by James Serra

Published by O'Reilly Media, Inc., 1005 Gravenstein Highway North, Sebastopol, CA 95472.

O'Reilly books may be purchased for educational, business, or sales promotional use. Online editions are also available for most titles (*http://oreilly.com*). For more information, contact our corporate/institutional sales department: 800-998-9938 or *corporate@oreilly.com*.

Acquisitions Editor: Aaron Black
Development Editor: Sarah Grey
Production Editor: Katherine Tozer
Copyeditor: Paula L. Fleming
Proofreader: Tove Innis

Indexer: WordCo Indexing Services, Inc.
Interior Designer: David Futato
Cover Designer: Karen Montgomery
Illustrator: Kate Dullea

February 2024:   First Edition

Revision History for the First Release
2024-02-06:   First Release
2024-03-29:   Second Release

See *http://oreilly.com/catalog/errata.csp?isbn=9781098150761* for release details.

978-1-098-15076-1

[LSI]

To the loving memory of my grandparents—Dolly, Bill, Martha, and Bert

Table of Contents

Part IV. People, Processes, and Technology

Foreword

Never in the history of the modern, technology-enabled enterprise has the data landscape evolved so quickly. As the pace of change continues to accelerate, the data ecosystem becomes far more complex—especially the value chains that connect suppliers and customers to organizations. Data seems to flow everywhere. It has become one of any organization's most strategic assets, fundamentally underpinning digital transformation, automation, artificial intelligence, innovation, and more.

This increasing tempo of change intensifies the importance of optimizing your organization's data architecture to ensure ongoing adaptability, interoperability and maintainability. In this book, James Serra lays out a clear set of choices for the data architect, whether you are seeking to create a resilient design or simply reduce technical debt.

It seems every knowledge worker has a story of a meeting with data engineers and architects that felt like a Dilbert cartoon, where nobody seemed to speak the same language and the decisions were too complicated and murky. By defining concepts, addressing concerns, dispelling myths, and proposing workarounds for pitfalls, James gives the reader a working knowledge of data architectures and the confidence to make informed decisions. As a leader, I have been pleased with how well the book's contents help to strengthen my data teams' alignment by providing them with a common vocabulary and references.

When I met James around 15 years ago, he was considering expanding his expertise beyond database administration to business intelligence and analytics. His insatiable desire to learn new things and share what he was learning to serve the greater good left a strong impression on me. It still drives him today. The countless blog posts, presentations, and speaking engagements through which he shares the depth of his experience now culminate in this expansive resource. This book will benefit all of us who handle data as we navigate an uncertain future.

Understanding the core principles of data architecture allows you to ride the waves of change as new data platforms, technology providers, and innovations emerge. Thankfully, James has created a foundational resource for all of us. This book will help you to see the bigger picture and design a bright future where your data creates the competitive advantage that you seek.

— Sean McCall
Chief Data Officer, Oceaneering International
Houston, December 2023

Preface

I've been in information technology (IT) for nearly 40 years. I've worked at companies of all different sizes, I've worked as a consultant, and I've owned my own company. For the last 9 years, I have been at Microsoft as a data architect, and for the last 15 years, I have been involved with data warehousing. I've spoken about data thousands of times, to customers and groups.

During my career, I have seen many data architectures come and go. I've seen too many companies argue over the best approach and end up building the wrong data architecture—a mistake that can cost them millions of dollars and months of time, putting them well behind their competitors.

What's more, data architectures are complex. I've seen firsthand that most people are unclear on the concepts involved, if they're aware of them at all. Everyone seems to be throwing around terms like *data mesh*, *data warehouse*, and *data lakehouse*—but if you ask 10 people what a data mesh is, you will get 11 different answers.

Where do you even start? Are these just buzzwords with a lot of hype but little substance, or are they viable approaches? They may sound great in theory, but how practical are they? What are the pros and cons of each architecture?

None of the architectures discussed in this book is "wrong." They all have a place, but only in certain use cases. No one architecture applies to every situation, so this book is not about convincing you to choose one architecture over the others. Instead, you will get honest opinions on the pros and cons of each architecture. Everything has trade-offs, and it's important to understand what those are and not just go with an architecture that is hyped more than the others. And there is much to learn from each architecture, even if you don't use it. For example, understanding how a data mesh works will get you thinking about data ownership, a concept that can apply to any architecture.

This book provides a basic grounding in common data architecture concepts. There are *so* many concepts out there, and figuring out which to choose and how to implement them can be intimidating. I'm here to help you to understand all these concepts and architectures at a high level so you get a sense of the options and can see which one is the most appropriate for your situation. The goal of the book is to allow you to talk intelligently about data concepts and architectures, then dig deeper into any that are relevant to the solution you are building.

There are no standard definitions of data concepts and architectures. If there were, this book would not be needed. My hope is to provide standard definitions that help everyone get onto the same page, to make discussions easier. I'm under no illusion that my definitions will be universally accepted, but I'd like to give us all a starting point for conversations about how to adjust those definitions.

I have written this book for anyone with an interest in getting value out of data, whether you're a database developer or administrator, a data architect, a CTO or CIO, or even someone in a role outside of IT. You could be early in your career or a seasoned veteran. The only skills you need are a little familiarity with data from your work and a sense of curiosity.

For readers with less experience with these topics, I provide an overview of big data (Chapter 1) and data architectures (Chapter 2), as well as basic data concepts (Part II). If you've been in the data game for a while but need to understand new architectures, you might find a lot of value in Part III, which dives into the details of particular data architectures, as well as in reviewing some of the basics. For you, this will be a quick cover-to-cover read; feel free to skip over the sections with material that you already know well. Also note that although the focus is on big data, the concepts and architectures apply even if you have "small" data.

This is a vendor-neutral book. You should be able to apply the architectures and concepts you learn here with any cloud provider. I'll also note here that I am employed by Microsoft. However, the opinions expressed here are mine alone and do not reflect the views of my employer.

I wrote this book because I have an innate curiosity that drives me to comprehend and then share things in a way that everyone can understand. This book is the culmination of my life's work. I hope you find it valuable.

Conventions Used in This Book

The following typographical conventions are used in this book:

Italic
> Indicates new terms, URLs, email addresses, filenames, and file extensions.

`Constant width`
> Used for program listings, as well as within paragraphs to refer to program elements such as variable or function names, databases, data types, environment variables, statements, and keywords.

> This element signifies a tip or suggestion.

> This element signifies a general note.

O'Reilly Online Learning

For more than 40 years, *O'Reilly Media* has provided technology and business training, knowledge, and insight to help companies succeed.

Our unique network of experts and innovators share their knowledge and expertise through books, articles, and our online learning platform. O'Reilly's online learning platform gives you on-demand access to live training courses, in-depth learning paths, interactive coding environments, and a vast collection of text and video from O'Reilly and 200+ other publishers. For more information, visit *https://oreilly.com*.

How to Contact Us

Please address comments and questions concerning this book to the publisher:

O'Reilly Media, Inc.
1005 Gravenstein Highway North
Sebastopol, CA 95472
800-889-8969 (in the United States or Canada)
707-827-7019 (international or local)
707-829-0104 (fax)
support@oreilly.com
https://www.oreilly.com/about/contact.html

We have a web page for this book, where we list errata, examples, and any additional information. You can access this page at *https://oreil.ly/deciphering-data-architectures*.

For news and information about our books and courses, visit *https://oreilly.com*.

Find us on LinkedIn: *https://linkedin.com/company/oreilly-media*.

Watch us on YouTube: *https://youtube.com/oreillymedia*.

Acknowledgments

This book would not have been possible without the unwavering support and patience of my wife, Mary. Her encouragement was instrumental during those long nights spent writing, even when it meant missing out on card games with family and friends. Her presence was a constant source of comfort and motivation.

My journey has been enriched by the support of my family: my parents, Jim and Lorraine; my sisters, Denise, Michele, and Nicole; and my now-adult children, Lauren, RaeAnn, and James, who have been a source of inspiration despite having no idea what the book is about!

A heartfelt thank you goes to my mentors and colleagues from my years at Microsoft. Individuals like Steve Busby, Eduardo Kassner, and Martin Lee helped shape my career, offering wisdom that often found its way into these pages.

Gratitude is due to those who lent their critical eye and constructive feedback, notably Piethein Strengholt, Barry Devlin, Bill Inmon, and Mike Shelton. Your insights were invaluable.

I am particularly grateful to Sean McCall, not only for introducing me to the world of data warehousing many years ago but also for being a steadfast friend and agreeing to pen the forward for this book.

Finally, I want to thank all the amazing people at O'Reilly who made this book possible: Sarah Grey, whose amazing editing and suggestions make this book so much better than if I went at it alone; Aaron Black, for helping me to create and the book abstract and get it approved; Paula Fleming, for her exceptional copyediting; Katie Tozer, for managing the production of the book; Kristen Brown, for keeping everything running smoothly; and Suzanne Huston, for her wonderful marketing of the book.

I'd like to express my deep appreciation to you, the reader, whose interest and engagement in this work makes the countless hours of writing not just worthwhile but deeply fulfilling.

As I close this chapter of my life and look forward to the new horizons ahead, I am profoundly grateful for the journey this book has taken me on and the incredible people who have been a part of it.

Foundation

In Part I of this book, I will lay the foundation for deciphering data architectures. Chapter 1 starts with a description of big data, while Chapter 2 provides an overview of the types of data architectures and their evolution. Chapter 3 shows how you can conduct an architecture design session to help determine the best data architecture to use for your project.

This part of the book will give you a good starting point to understand the value of big data and the history of the architectures that captured that data. The later chapters will then dig into the details.

Big Data

The number of companies building data architectures has exploded in the 2020s. That growth is unlikely to slow down anytime soon, in large part because more data is available than ever before: from social media, Internet of Things (IoT) devices, home-grown applications, and third-party software, to name just a few sources. According to a 2023 BCG study (*https://oreil.ly/hpOPt*), "the volume of data generated approximately doubled from 2018 to 2021 to about 84 ZB, a rate of growth that is expected to continue." The researchers "estimate that the volume of data generated will rise at a compound annual growth rate (CAGR) of 21% from 2021 to 2024, reaching 149 ZB." Companies know that they can save millions of dollars and increase revenue by gathering this data and using it to analyze the past and present and make predictions about the future—but to do that, they need a way to store all that data.

Throughout the business world, the rush is on to build data architectures as quickly as possible. Those architectures need to be ready to handle any future data—no matter its size, speed, or type—and to maintain its accuracy. And those of us who work with data architectures need a clear understanding of how they work and what the options are. That's where this book comes in. I have seen firsthand the result of not properly understanding data architecture concepts. One company I know of built a data architecture at the cost of $100 million over two years, only to discover that the architecture used the wrong technology, was too difficult to use, and was not flexible enough to handle certain types of data. It had to be scraped and restarted from scratch. Don't let this happen to you!

It's all about getting the right information to the right people at the right time in the right format. To do that, you need a data architecture to ingest, store, transform, and model the data (big data processing) so it can be accurately and easily used. You need an architecture that allows any end user, even one with very little technical knowledge, to analyze the data and generate reports and dashboards, instead of relying on people in IT with deep technical knowledge to do it for them.

Chapter 1 begins by introducing big data and some of its fundamental ideas. I then discuss how companies are using their data, with an emphasis on business intelligence and how this usage grows as a company's data architecture matures.

What Is Big Data, and How Can It Help You?

Even though the term *big* is used in *big data*, it's not just about the size of the data. It's also about all the data, big or small, within your company and all the data outside your company that would be helpful to you. The data can be in any format and can be collected with any degree of regularity. So the best way to define *big data* is to think of it as *all* data, no matter its size (volume), speed (velocity), or type (variety). In addition to those criteria, there are three more factors you can use to describe data: veracity, variability, and value. Together, they're commonly known as the "six *Vs*" of big data, as shown in Figure 1-1.

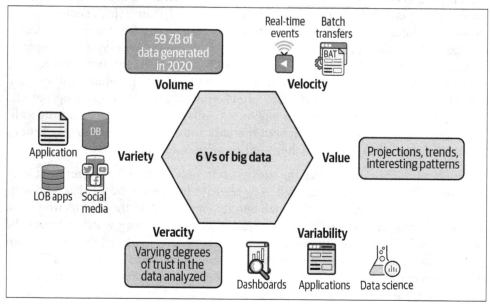

Figure 1-1. The six Vs of big data (source: The Cloud Data Lake *by Rukmani Gopalan [O'Reilly, 2023]).*

Let's take a closer look at each one:

Volume

> *Volume* is the sheer amount of data generated and stored. This can be anywhere from terabytes to petabytes of data, and it can come from a wide range of sources

including social media, ecommerce transactions, scientific experiments, sensor data from IoT devices, and much more. For example, data from an order entry system might amount to a couple of terabytes a day, while IoT devices can stream millions of events per minute and generate hundreds of terabytes of data a day.

Variety

Variety refers to the wide range of data sources and formats. These can be further broken down into *structured data* (from relational databases), *semi-structured data* (such as logs and CSV, XML, and JSON formats), *unstructured data* (like emails, documents, and PDFs), and *binary data* (images, audio, video). For example, data from an order entry system would be structured data because it comes from a relational database, while data from an IoT device would likely be in JSON format.

Velocity

Velocity refers to the speed at which data is generated and processed. Collecting data infrequently is often called *batch processing*; for example, each night the orders for the day are collected and processed. Data can also be collected *very* frequently or even in real time, especially if it's generated at a high velocity such as data from social media, IoT devices, and mobile applications.

Veracity

Veracity is about the accuracy and reliability of data. Big data comes from a huge variety of sources. Unreliable or incomplete sources can damage the quality of the data. For example, if data is coming from an IoT device, such as an outdoor security camera located at the front of your house that is pointing to the driveway, and it sends you a text message when it detects a person, it's possible that environmental factors, such as weather, have made the device falsely detect a person, corrupting the data. Thus, the data needs to be validated when received.

Variability

Variability refers to the consistency (or inconsistency) of data in terms of its format, quality, and meaning. Processing and analyzing structured, semi-structured, and unstructured data formats require different tools and techniques. For example, the type, frequency, and quality of sensor data from IoT devices can vary greatly. Temperature and humidity sensors might generate data points at regular intervals, while motion sensors might generate data only when they detect motion.

Value

Value, the most important *V*, relates to the usefulness and relevance of data. Companies use big data to gain insights and make decisions that can lead to business value, such as increased efficiency, cost savings, or new revenue streams. For example, by analyzing customer data, organizations can better understand their customers' behaviors, preferences, and needs. They can use this information to develop better targeted marketing campaigns, improve customer experiences, and drive sales.

Collecting big data allows companies to gain insights that help them make better business decisions. *Predictive analysis* is a type of data analysis that involves using statistical algorithms and machine learning to analyze historical data and make predictions about future events and trends. This allows businesses to be proactive, not just reactive.

You'll hear many companies calling data "the new oil," because it has become an incredibly valuable resource in today's digital economy, much like oil was in the industrial economy. Data is like oil in a number of ways:

- It's a raw material that needs to be extracted, refined, and processed in order to be useful. In the case of data, that involves collecting, storing, and analyzing it in order to gain insights that can drive business decisions.

- It's incredibly valuable. Companies that collect and analyze large amounts of data can use it to improve their products and services, make better business decisions, and gain a competitive advantage.

- It can be used in a variety of ways. For example, if you use data to train machine learning algorithms, you can then use those algorithms to automate tasks, identify patterns, and make predictions.

- It's a powerful resource with a transformative effect on society. The widespread use of oil powered the growth of industries and enabled new technologies, while data has led to advances in fields like artificial intelligence, machine learning, and predictive analytics.

- It can be a source of power and influence, thanks to all of the preceding factors.

For example, you can use big data to generate reports and dashboards that tell you where sales are lagging and take steps "after the fact" to improve those sales. You can also use machine learning to predict where sales will drop in the future and take proactive steps to prevent that drop. This is called *business intelligence* (BI): the process of collecting, analyzing, and using data to help businesses make more informed decisions.

As Figure 1-2 shows, I can collect data from new sources, such as IoT devices, web logs, and social media, as well as older sources, such as line-of-business, enterprise resource planning (ERP), and customer relationship management (CRM) applications. This data can be in multiple formats, such as CSV files, JSON files, and Parquet files. It can come over in batches, say once an hour, or it can be streamed in multiple times a second (this is called *real-time streaming*).

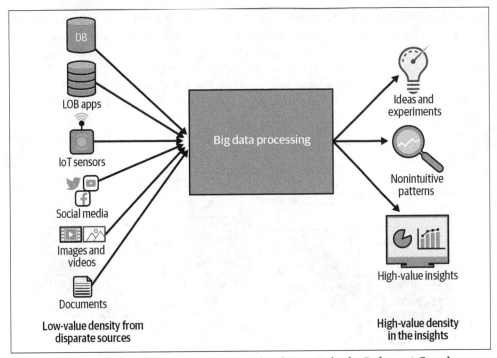

Figure 1-2. Big data processing (source: The Cloud Data Lake *by Rukmani Gopalan [O'Reilly, 2023])*

It's important for companies to understand where they are in their journey to use data compared to other companies. This is called *data maturity*, and the next section shows the stages of the data maturity journey so you can understand where your company is.

Data Maturity

You may have heard many in the IT industry use the term *digital transformation*, which refers to how companies embed technologies across their business to drive fundamental change in the way they get value out of data and in how they operate and deliver value to customers. The process involves shifting away from traditional, manual, or paper-based processes to digital ones, leveraging the power of technology to improve efficiency, productivity, and innovation. A big part of this transformation is usually using data to improve a company's business, which could mean creating a customer 360 profile (*https://oreil.ly/rSF6P*) to improve customer experience or using machine learning to improve the speed and accuracy of manufacturing lines.

This digital transformation can be broken into four stages, called the *enterprise data maturity* stages, illustrated in Figure 1-3. While this term is used widely in the IT industry, I have my own take on what those stages look like. They describe the level of development and sophistication an organization has reached in managing, utilizing, and deriving value from its data. This model is a way to assess an organization's data management capabilities and readiness for advanced analytics, artificial intelligence, and other data-driven initiatives. Each stage represents a step forward in leveraging data for business value and decision making. The remainder of this section describes each stage.

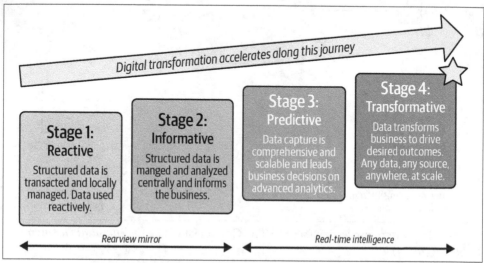

Figure 1-3. Enterprise data maturity stages

Stage 1: Reactive

In, the first stage, a company has data scattered all over, likely in a bunch of Excel spreadsheets and/or desktop databases on many different filesystems, being emailed all over the place. Data architects call this a *spreadmart* (short for "spreadsheet data mart"): an informal, decentralized collection of data often found within an organization that uses spreadsheets to store, manage, and analyze data. Individuals or teams typically create and maintain spreadmarts independently of the organization's centralized data management system or official data warehouse. Spreadmarts suffer from data inconsistency, lack of governance, limited scalability, and inefficiency (since they often result in a lot of duplicated effort).

Stage 2: Informative

Companies reach the second maturity stage when they start to centralize their data, making analysis and reporting much easier. Stages 1 and 2 are for *historical reporting*, or seeing trends and patterns from the past, so Figure 1-3 calls them the "rearview mirror." In these stages, you are reacting to what's already happened.

At stage 2, the solution built to gather the data is usually not very scalable. Generally, the size and types of data it can handle are limited, and it can ingest data only infrequently (every night, for example). Most companies are at stage 2, especially if their infrastructure is still on-prem.[1]

Stage 3: Predictive

By stage 3, companies have moved to the cloud and have built a system that can handle larger quantities of data, different types of data, and data that is ingested more frequently (hourly or streaming). They have also improved their decision making by incorporating machine learning (advanced analytics) to make decisions in real time. For example, while a user is in an online bookstore, the system might recommend additional books on the checkout page based on the user's prior purchases.

Stage 4: Transformative

Finally, at stage 4, the company has built a solution that can handle any data, no matter its size, speed, or type. It is easy to onboard new data with a shortened lead time because the architecture can handle it and has the infrastructure capacity to support it. This is a solution that lets nontechnical end users easily create reports and dashboards with the tools of their choice.

Stages 3 and 4 are the focus of this book. In particular, when end users are doing their own reporting, this activity is called *self-service business intelligence*, which is the subject of the next section.

Self-Service Business Intelligence

For many years, if an end user within an organization needed a report or dashboard, they had to gather all their requirements (the source data needed, plus a description of what the report or dashboard should look like), fill out an IT request form, and wait. IT then built the report, which involved extracting the data, loading it into the data warehouse, building a data model, and then finally creating the report or dashboard. The end user would review it and either approve it or request changes. This often resulted in a long queue of IT requests so that IT ended up becoming a huge bottleneck. It took days, weeks, or even months for end users to get value out of the

---

1 Being on-prem, short for *on-premises*, refers to an organization's hosting and managing its IT infrastructure—such as servers, storage, and networking equipment—within its own physical facilities, usually called data centers. This contrasts with cloud-based services, where these resources are hosted and managed by third-party providers such as Azure, Amazon Web Services (AWS), or Google Cloud Platform (GCP) in remote data centers. I'll discuss the benefits of moving from on-prem to the cloud in Chapter 16, but for now, know that transitioning from on-prem servers to cloud is a huge part of most enterprises' digital transformations.

data. This process is now called "traditional BI," because in recent years something better has developed: self-service BI.

The goal of any data architecture solution you build should be to make it quick and easy for any end user, no matter what their technical skills are, to query the data and to create reports and dashboards. They should not have to get IT involved to perform any of those tasks—they should be able to do it all on their own.

This goal requires more up-front work; IT will have to contact all the end users to find out what data they need, then build the data architecture with their needs in mind. But it will be well worth it for the time savings in creating the reports. This approach eliminates the queue and the back-and-forth with IT, whose team members generally have little understanding of the data. Instead, the end user, who knows the data best, accesses the data directly, prepares it, builds the data model, creates the reports, and validates that the reports are correct. This workflow is much more productive.

Creating that easy-to-consume data solution results in self-service BI. Creating a report should be as easy as dragging fields around in a workspace. End users shouldn't have to understand how to join data from different tables or worry about a report running too slowly. When you are creating a data solution, always be asking: *How easy will it be for people to build their own reports?*

Summary

In this chapter, you learned what big data is and how it can help you and your organization make better business decisions, especially when combined with machine learning. You saw how to describe big data using the six Vs, and you learned what data maturity means and how to identify its stages. Finally, you learned the difference between traditional and self-service BI, where the goal is for everyone to be able to use the data to create reports and identify insights quickly and easily.

Let me now give you an idea of what to expect in the following chapters. In Chapter 2, I will go into what a data architecture is and provide a high-level overview of how the types of data architectures have changed over the years. Chapter 3 is where I show you how to conduct an architecture design session to help determine the best data architecture to use.

Part II, "Common Data Architecture Concepts," gets into more detail about various architectures. In Chapter 4, I cover what a data warehouse is and what it is not, as well as why you would want to use one. I'll discuss the "top-down approach," ask if the relational data warehouse is dead, and cover ways to populate a data warehouse. Chapter 5 describes what a data lake is and why you would want to use one. It also discusses the bottom-up approach and then dives into data lake design and when to use multiple data lakes.

Chapter 6 is about common data architecture concepts related to data stores, including data marts, operational data stores, master data management, and data virtualization. Chapter 7 covers common data architecture concepts related to design, including OLTP versus OLAP, operational versus analytical data, SMP versus MPP, Lambda architecture, Kappa architecture, and polyglot persistence. Chapter 8 is all about data modeling, including relational and dimensional modeling, the Kimball versus Inmon debate, the common data model, and data vaults. And in Chapter 9, you will read about data ingestion, with sections on ETL versus ELT, reverse ELT, batch versus real-time processing, and data governance.

Part III focuses on specific data architectures. Chapter 10 describes the modern data warehouse and the five stages of building one. Chapter 11 covers the data fabric architecture and its use cases. Chapter 12 goes over the data lakehouse architecture and the trade-offs of not using a relational data warehouse.

Chapters 13 and 14 are both about data mesh architectures—there's a lot to talk about! Chapter 13 focuses on the data mesh's decentralized approach and the four principles of a data mesh, and it describes what data domains and data products are. Chapter 14 gets into the concerns and challenges of building a data mesh and tackles some common myths of data mesh. It'll help you check if you are ready to adopt a data mesh. It finishes with what the future of the data mesh might look like.

Chapter 15 looks at why projects succeed and why they fail, and it describes the team organization you'll need for building a data architecture. Finally, Chapter 16 is a discussion of open source, the benefits of the cloud, the major cloud providers, being multi-cloud, and software frameworks.

Now I'm about to revolutionize your data world. Are you ready?

CHAPTER 2

Types of Data Architectures

It's absolutely vital to invest time up front designing and building the right data architecture. I found this out the hard way early in my career. I was so excited to start building my solution that I breezed over important decisions about the design of the architecture and what products to use. Three months into the project, I realized the architecture would not support some of the required data sources. We essentially had to restart the project from scratch and come up with another architecture and different products, wasting a ton of money and time. Without the right planning, end users won't get value out of your solution, they'll be angry about the missed deadlines, and your company risks falling farther and farther behind its competitors.

When building a data solution, you need a well-thought-out blueprint to follow. That is where a data architecture comes into play. A *data architecture* defines a high-level architectural approach and concept to follow, outlines a set of technologies to use, and states the flow of data that will be used to build your data solution to capture big data. Deciding on a data architecture can be very challenging, as there is no one-size-fits-all architecture. You can't flip through a book to find a stock list of architecture approaches with corresponding products to use. There's no simple flowchart to follow with decision trees that will lead you to the perfect architecture. Your architectural approach and the technologies you use will vary greatly from customer to customer, use case to use case.

The major types of high-level architectural approaches and concepts are exactly what this book is about. It's not a stock list, but it will give you a sense of what they're all about. Although it's useful to separate data architectures into types based on their characteristics, which I will do in this book, that's not the same thing as choosing from a bunch of predefined one-size-fits-all templates. Each data architecture is unique and requires a customized approach to meet specific business needs.

Data architecture refers to the overall design and organization of data within an information system. Predefined templates for data architectures can seem like an easy way to set up a new system quickly. However, data architecture templates often fail to account for the specific requirements and constraints of the system to which they are being applied, which can lead to issues with data quality, system performance, and maintenance. Additionally, the organization's needs and data systems are likely to change over time, requiring updates and adjustments to the data architecture. A standardized template may not be flexible enough to accommodate these changes, which can introduce inefficiencies and limitations in the system.

This chapter gives a brief guided tour of the major types the book will cover: relational data warehouse, data lake, modern data warehouse, data fabric, data lakehouse, and data mesh. Each type will get its own chapter with plenty of detail later in the book.

Evolution of Data Architectures

A *relational database* stores data in a structured manner, with relationships between the data elements defined by keys. The data is typically organized into tables, with each table consisting of rows and columns. Each row represents a single instance of data, while each column represents a specific attribute of the data.

Relational databases are designed to handle structured data, and they provide a framework for creating, modifying, and querying data using a standardized language known as Structured Query Language, or SQL. The relational model was first proposed by Edgar F. Codd in 1970,[1] and since the mid-'70s it has become the dominant model for database management systems. Most operational applications need to permanently store data, and a relational database is the tool of choice for a large majority.

In relational databases, where consistency and data integrity are of primary importance, data is usually organized with an approach called *schema-on-write*. Schema refers to the formal structure that defines the organization of—and relationships between—tables, fields, data types, and constraints. It serves as a blueprint for storing and managing data and ensures consistency, integrity, and efficient organization within the database. Relational databases (and relational data warehouses) require a bit of up-front work before data can land in them. You must create the database and its tables, fields, and schema, then write the code to transfer the data into the database. With a *schema-on-write* approach, the data schema is defined and enforced when data is written or ingested into the database. Data must adhere to the

---

1 E. F. Codd, "Derivability, Redundancy, and Consistency of Relations Stored in Large Data Banks," *Communications of the ACM*, 13, no. 6 (1970): 377–87, available at A Relational Model of Data for Large Shared Data Banks (*https://oreil.ly/vJwgQ*).

predefined schema, including data types, constraints, and relationships, before it can be stored.

By contrast, in a *schema-on-read* approach, the schema is applied when data is read or accessed, rather than when it is written. Data can be ingested into the storage system without conforming to a strict schema, and the structure is defined only when data is queried or consumed. This approach offers more flexibility in storing unstructured or semi-structured data, and it is commonly used in data lakes, discussed later in this chapter.

At a high level, data architectures provide a framework for organizing and managing data in a way that supports the needs of an organization. This involves defining how data is collected, stored, processed, and accessed, as well as maintaining data quality, security, and privacy. While data architectures can take many different forms, some common elements include:

Data storage
> All data architectures need to specify how data is stored, including the physical storage medium (such as hard drives or cloud storage) and the data structures used to organize the data.

Data processing
> Data architectures need to define how data is processed, including any transformations or calculations that are performed on the data before it is stored or analyzed.

Data access
> Data architectures need to provide mechanisms for accessing data, including user interfaces and application program interfaces (APIs) that enable data to be queried and analyzed.

Data security and privacy
> Data architectures need to incorporate mechanisms for ensuring the security and privacy of data, such as access controls, encryption, and data masking.

Data governance
> Data architectures need to provide frameworks for managing data, including quality standards, lineage tracking, and retention policies.

Overall, the main goal of a data architecture is to enable an organization to manage and leverage its data assets effectively in order to support its business objectives and decision-making processes.

Table 2-1, which provides a high-level comparison of the characteristics of the data architectures I cover in this book, should give you a starting point to determine which architecture may be the best fit for your use case.

Table 2-1. Comparison of data architectures

Characteristic	Relational data warehouse	Data lake	Modern data warehouse	Data fabric	Data lakehouse	Data mesh
Year introduced	1984	2010	2011	2016	2020	2019
Centralized/decentralized	Centralized	Centralized	Centralized	Centralized	Centralized	Decentralized
Storage type	Relational	Object	Relational and object	Relational and object	Object	Domain-specific
Schema type	Schema-on-write	Schema-on-read	Schema-on-read and schema-on-write	Schema-on-read and schema-on-write	Schema-on-read	Domain-specific
Data security	High	Low to medium	Medium to high	High	Medium	Domain-specific
Data latency	Low	High	Low to high	Low to high	Medium to high	Domain-specific
Time to value	Medium	Low	Low	Low	Low	High
Total cost of solution	High	Low	Medium	Medium to high	Low to medium	High
Supported use cases	Low	Low to medium	Medium	Medium to high	High	High
Difficulty of development	Low	Medium	Medium	Medium	Medium to high	High
Maturity of technology	High	Medium	Medium to high	Medium to high	Medium to high	Low
Company skill set needed	Low	Low to medium	Medium	Medium to high	Medium to high	High

Relational Data Warehouse

Relational databases were the mainstay of data storage for several decades. The first relational data warehouse used in production was the Teradata system, developed at Stanford University by Dr. Jack E. Shemer, who founded the Teradata Corporation in 1979. Wells Fargo Bank installed the first Teradata system in 1983 (*https://oreil.ly/BMbzc*) and used it to analyze financial data.

As organizations began generating ever more vast amounts of data, it was increasingly challenging to process and analyze that data without a long delay. The limitations of relational databases led to the development of relational data warehouses,[2] which became more widely popular in the late 1980s,[3] about 15 years after relational databases had come along. A *relational data warehouse* (RDW) is a specific type of relational database that is designed for data warehousing and business intelligence applications, with optimized query performance and support for large-scale data analysis. While both relational data warehouses and transactional processing use the relational model to organize data, a relational data warehouse is typically larger in scale and is optimized for analytical queries.

RDWs have both a compute engine and storage. The compute engine is the processing power used to query the data. The storage is *relational storage*, which holds data that is structured via tables, rows, and columns. The RDW's compute power can be used only on its relational storage—they are tied together.

Some of the most important features of RDWs include transaction support (ensuring that data is processed reliably and consistently), audit trails (keeping a record of all activity performed on the data in the system), and schema enforcement (ensuring that data is organized and structured in a predefined way).

In the 1970s and 1980s, organizations were using relational databases for operational applications like order entry and inventory management. These applications are called *online transaction processing* (OLTP) systems. OLTP systems can make create, read, update, and delete changes to data in a database, or *CRUD operations*. CRUD operations form the foundation of data manipulation and management in data architectures. They're essential to designing and implementing data storage systems and user interfaces that interact with data.

CRUD operations require fast response times from the application so that end users don't get frustrated at how long it takes to update data. You can run queries and generate reports on a relational database that's in use by an operational application, but doing so uses a lot of resources and can conflict with other CRUD operations running at the same time. That can slow everything down.

RDWs were invented in part to solve this problem. The data from the relational database is copied into a data warehouse, and users can run queries and reports against the data warehouse instead of the relational database. This way, they're not taxing the system that houses the relational database and slowing the application for end users. RDWs also centralize data from multiple applications in order to improve reporting, as pictured in Figure 2-1.

Chapter 4 will discuss RDWs in more detail.

---

2 A note on language: You might see people refer to the relational data warehouse architecture as a *traditional data warehouse*. In this book, I mostly use *relational data warehouse* (RDW), sometimes shortening it to *data warehouse*. These terms all refer to the same thing.

3 RDW's popularity increased thanks largely to both Barry Devlin and Bill Inmon, which I discuss in Chapter 8.

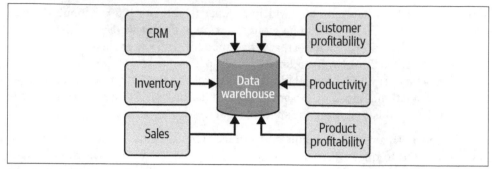

Figure 2-1. Data warehousing

Data Lake

The data lake is a more recent concept, first appearing around 2010. You can think of a data lake as a glorified filesystem, not very different from the filesystem on your laptop. A *data lake* is simply storage—unlike a relational data warehouse, there is no compute engine associated with it. Fortunately, there are many compute engines that can work with data lakes, so compute power is usually cheaper for a data lake than for a relational data warehouse. Another difference is that while RDWs use relational storage, data lakes use *object storage*, which does not need the data to be structured into rows and columns.

Data lake storage technology started with the Apache Hadoop Distributed File System (HDFS), a free open source technology hosted almost exclusively on-prem that was very popular in the early 2010s.[4] HDFS is a scalable, fault-tolerant distributed-storage system designed to run on commodity hardware. It is a core component of the Apache Hadoop ecosystem, which I discuss more in Chapter 16. As cloud computing continued to grow in importance, data lakes were built in the cloud using a different type of storage, and most data lakes now exist in the cloud.

In contrast to a relational data warehouse, a data lake is schema-on-read, meaning that no up-front work is needed to put data in the data lake: it can be as simple as copying files into it, like you would with folders on your laptop. The data in a data lake is stored in its natural (or raw) format, meaning it can go from its source system into the data lake without being transformed into another format. For example, if you export data from a relational database into a file in raw CSV format, you could store it unaltered in a data lake. If you wanted to store it in a relational data warehouse, however, you'd have to transform it to fit into the rows and columns of a table.

---

4 *Open source* (*https://opensource.org*) refers to software whose source code is made available for free to the public for use, modification, and distribution.

When you copy a data file into a data lake, its schema might not be copied along with it or might be in a different file. So you must define the schema by creating it or pulling it from the separate file—hence the term *schema-on-read*. As Figure 2-2 shows, data from source systems such as operational application databases, sensor data, and social media data can all land in the data lake. These files could hold data that is structured (like data from relational databases), semi-structured (like CSV, logs, XML, or JSON files), or unstructured (such as from emails, documents, and PDFs). They can even hold binary data (like images, audio, and video).

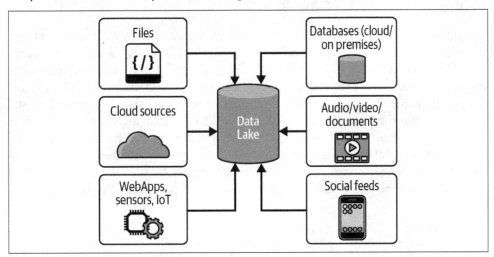

Figure 2-2. Data lake

Data lakes started out as the solution to all the problems with relational data warehouses, including high cost, limited scalability, poor performance, data preparation overhead, and limited support for complex data types. Companies selling Hadoop and data lakes, such as Cloudera, Hortonworks, and MapR, hyped them as if they were filled with unicorns and rainbows that would copy and clean data and make it available to end users with magical ease. They claimed that data lakes could replace relational data warehouses entirely, in a "one technology to do everything" approach. More than a few companies decided to save money by using free open source tools for all their technology.

The problem was that querying data lakes isn't actually that easy: it requires some fairly advanced skill sets. IT would tell end users, "Hey, we copied all the data you need into this data lake. Just go and open a Jupyter notebook and use Hive and Python to build your reports with the files in these folders." This failed miserably, since most end users did not have anywhere near the skills needed to do all that. Companies found out the hard way that these complex, difficult-to-use solutions wound up actually being more expensive because of hardware and support costs, production delays, and lost productivity. In addition, data lakes did not have some of the features people liked about data warehouses, like transaction support, schema enforcement, and audit trails. This resulted in two of the three top data lake suppliers, Hortonworks and MapR, going out of business.

But the data lake did not go away. Instead, its purpose morphed into a different, but very useful, one: staging and preparing data. Chapter 5 will discuss data lakes in detail.

Modern Data Warehouse

Relational data warehouses and data lakes, on their own, are simplistic architectures. They use only one technology to centralize the data, with few to no supporting products. When you use more technologies and products to support relational data warehouses or data lakes, they evolve into the architectures discussed in this and the following chapters. Data lakes failed to replace relational data warehouses but still offered benefits for staging and preparing data. Why not have the advantages of both? Around 2011, many companies started building architectures that place data lakes side by side with relational data warehouses to form the data architecture we now call the *modern data warehouse* (MDW), shown in Figure 2-3. The *modern* in *modern data warehouse* refers to the use of newer technologies and approaches to data warehousing.

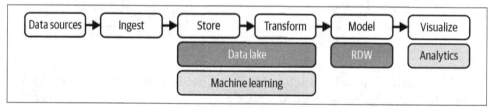

Figure 2-3. Modern data warehouse (MDW)

It's a "best of both worlds" approach: the data lake is for staging and preparing data, and data scientists use it to build machine learning models; the data warehouse is for serving, security, and compliance, and business users do their querying and reporting with it. Chapter 10 will provide much more detail on modern data warehouse architectures.

Data Fabric

Data fabrics started to appear around 2016. You could think of the *data fabric* architecture as an evolution of the modern data warehouse architecture, with more technology added to source more data, secure it, and make it available. Also, improvements have been made to how the system ingests data, transforms, queries, searches, and access data, as Figure 2-4 shows. With all those additions, the system becomes a "fabric"—a large framework that can ingest any sort of data. Chapter 11 will go into this in more detail.

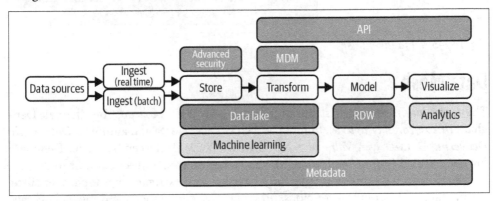

Figure 2-4. Data fabric

Data Lakehouse

The term *data lakehouse* is a portmanteau (blend) of *data lake* and *data warehouse*. Data lakehouse architectures became popular around 2020, when the company Databricks started using the term. The concept of a lakehouse is to get rid of the relational data warehouse and use just one repository, a data lake, in your data architecture. All types of data—structured, semi-structured, and unstructured—are ingested into the data lake, and all queries and reports are done from the data lake.

I know what you're thinking: "Wait a minute. You said that data lakes took this same approach when they first appeared, and it failed miserably! What changed?" The answer, as shown in Figure 2-5, is a transactional storage software layer called Delta Lake that runs on top of an existing data lake and makes it work more like a relational database. The competing open source options for this layer include Delta Lake, Apache Iceberg, and Apache Hudi. All of this will be covered in more detail in Chapter 12.

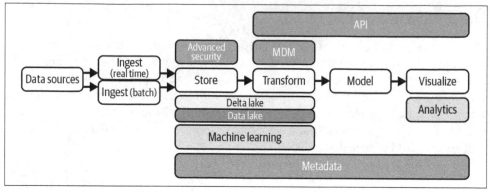

Figure 2-5. Data lakehouse

Data Mesh

The term *data mesh* was first introduced in a May 2019 blog post by Zhamak Deh-ghani (*https://oreil.ly/nvu79*), founder and CEO of Nextdata and author of *Data Mesh: Delivering Data-Driven Value at Scale* (O'Reilly, 2022). In December 2020, Dehghani further clarified (*https://oreil.ly/trtvm*) what a data mesh is and set out four underpinning principles. Data mesh architectures have been an extremely hot topic ever since, getting talked about in tons of blogs, presentations, conferences, and media coverage and even appearing in the Gartner Hype Cycle for data management (*https://oreil.ly/n4Lzr*). There is a lot to like about data mesh architecture, but despite the hype, it is only a fit for a small number of use cases.

The modern data warehouse, data fabric, and data lakehouse architectures all involve *centralizing* data: copying operational data into a central location owned by IT under an architecture that IT controls, where IT then creates analytical data (the left side of Figure 2-6). This centralized approach brings three main challenges: data ownership, data quality, and organizational/technical scaling. The aim of the data mesh is to solve these challenges.

In a data mesh, data is kept within several domains within a company, such as manufacturing, sales, and suppliers (the right side of Figure 2-6). Each domain has its own mini IT team that owns its data, cleans it, creates the analytical data, and makes it available. Each domain also has its own compute and storage infrastructure. This results in a *decentralized* architecture where data, people, and infrastructure are scaled out—the more domains you have, the more people and infrastructure you get. The system can handle more data, and IT is no longer a bottleneck.

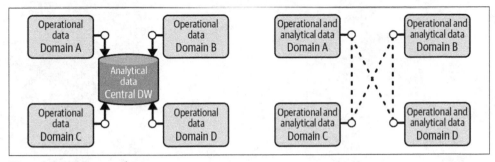

Figure 2-6. Data mesh

It is important to understand that data mesh is a *concept*, not a technology. There is no "data mesh in a box" that you can buy. Implementing data mesh involves a very big organizational and cultural shift that very few companies are ready for. (Indeed, most companies aren't even large enough to be considered for a data mesh architecture: this is very much an enterprise approach.) Building it requires determining which pieces of existing technology you can repurpose for it and which pieces you will have to create. Each domain gets to determine what technologies it will use to build out its part of the data mesh, which could include building a modern data warehouse, data fabric, or data lakehouse. There is much to discuss regarding data mesh architectures, and I'll do that in Chapters 13 and 14.

Summary

Now that you have a high-level understanding of the types of data architectures, the next chapter will talk about how to determine the best data architecture to use: a process called an *architecture design session*.

CHAPTER 3

The Architecture Design Session

I have conducted hundreds of architecture design sessions and have found them to be vital to building a successful data solution. This chapter walks you through how to hold a successful architecture design session that puts your data solution on the right path.

What Is an ADS?

An *architecture design session* (ADS) is a structured discussion with business and technical stakeholders that's driven by technical experts and focused on defining and planning the high-level design of a solution to collect data for specific business opportunities. The first ADS is the start of the architecture process and will lead to many more discussions (including, quite possibly, other ADSs) to support the data solution project. The ADS should produce two deliverables:

- An architecture (or "blueprint") that can serve as a starting point for the data solution
- A high-level plan of action, which may include follow-on demonstrations, proofs of concept, and product discussions

An ADS is not a technical workshop, a technical training, a tech demonstration, nor a low-level requirements session.

Why Hold an ADS?

There are many reasons to hold an ADS. First, it often brings together multiple stakeholders from the same organization, including some who have never met face-to-face. Even just the act of getting together in person or virtually can foster creativity and problem solving. Further, it may include stakeholders who understand their business very well and who can describe in great detail the specific use cases they are looking to solve.

The ADS also differentiates projects with a solid business case from "science projects" meant to test some technology or product. It flushes out the reasons for the project and, if it is indeed a science project, limits the resources devoted to it.

What's more, an ADS provides a structured framework for "thinking big, starting small." As noted, this involves coming up with a high-level architecture, but should also involve discussing how you can start small to get quick wins. For example, the architecture may ultimately involve ingesting data from dozens of sources, but the ADS might choose a low-risk, high-reward approach, such as starting with two or three high-value data sources that require fewer estimated work hours to complete.

You can also include your organization's customers and/or partner organizations in an ADS. When I was about to hold my first ADS, another Microsoft architect described the process as "business therapy." I quickly found out what he meant. We had about a dozen attendees from a customer company, most of whom had never met. We started discussing their current environment, and a few brought up some pain points that were blocking progress. To my surprise, another attendee from that organization chimed in with advice on how to solve the blocker. Then they solved two more blockers while I sat back and listened. (Of course, my coworkers and I often help with removing blockers, too, but it was enlightening to be quiet and allow the others to work it out among themselves.)

You'll learn from your customer in other ways, too, especially if your account team hasn't been as thorough as they might have been. You can dig into any questions you have about their current environment, their pain points, their goals, and other information you'll need.

A customer ADS also gives your account team many ways to follow up, such as demos, proofs of concept, and answers to technical questions. It's a great way to kickstart an account that hasn't been getting much traction and accelerate the sales cycle. And if you're working with a partner, such as a consulting firm, consider bringing them into the ADS alongside the customer in order to educate them both on how to use the technology. Make sure to clear this with the customer first, especially if you'll be discussing sensitive information.

Before the ADS

In this section, I'll assume that you are the architect who will be leading the ADS. Even if you're not, I recommend you read this section before participating in an ADS.

Preparing

Set aside at least a day to prepare for an ADS workshop. You'll need to prepare for the logistics of the meeting. Is it physical or virtual? If physical, do you have a big enough room? If virtual, what platform will you use? Does it have the necessary equipment, such as a whiteboard, audio/video, and other supplies? Who will take care of lunch?

If the ADS will be in person, and especially if a large group is traveling to get there, I usually set aside a full seven- to eight-hour day, since logistics may make it difficult to get everyone in the same room again. If much of the technology is new to the customer, however, six or seven hours is often enough. If you notice that participants are feeling overwhelmed, end the ADS early, because at that point anything else you cover will be forgotten.

For remote ADSs, two four-hour days is usually better than one full day. I try to hold the two four-hour sessions on back-to-back days or, at least, within a week of each other.

Make sure you find out the project budget and timeline and identify the decision maker. This is important whether the meeting is internal or not, but if you have a long list of customers who want to hold an ADS, this information can help you focus on your best prospects. If the ADS is for a customer, read their latest corporate report for insight on their wider interests and concerns.

I also recommend you hold a pre-call to speak with the account team in your company that is supporting the customer. You'll likely want to discuss the following:

- Details about the customer and the project's background and context
- The customer's problems with their current architecture
- How you can help the customer
- The account team's goals and the outcome they want from the meeting (for example, do they want the customer to request a proof of concept?)
- How well the customer knows your products
- How you will run the ADS and what you expect from the account team

The deliverables from this meeting will be an email to the account team that recaps the call, a draft agenda that they can send to the customer, a seating chart (if the ADS will be held in person), and a reminder for the account team to set up a pre-call with the customer.

Make sure to tell the customer the main reason for the pre-call with them is to help you all prepare as much as possible for the ADS. The information surfaced will allow you to brush up on topics as needed or bring in subject matter experts (SMEs) to help with areas that you are not familiar with. You'll also share the agenda, and together you can make sure it does not include any off-topic items. For example, if the focus of the ADS is on data architectures, discussions of security or DevOps are best taken care of outside the ADS.

The customer pre-call should include a few things:

Here's what I understand so far...
> First, recap your understanding of the problem or opportunity so the customer has a chance to correct any misperceptions.

Tell me about the attendees...
> Determine who will be in attendance and what roles they play in the organization. This will help you determine how deep or high-level to make the technology discussion.

Here's what will happen...
> Provide an agenda and go over it with the customer, but assure them that the discussion can pivot if needed. Explain the approach you will take in running the ADS and set their expectations accordingly. For example, it's a good idea to tell them to be 100% focused—no phones or emails for anyone involved, including you.

What do you have for us to look at?
> This is the discovery phase. Encourage them to send you any architecture diagrams for their current solution, any architectures they may have drafted for their future solution, and any documents describing their current solution and future plans.

What would a successful ADS look like to you?
> Ask, "Is there anything else that I should be aware of?" This question can surface questions or goals that might otherwise be missed.

Figure 3-1 shows a sample ADS agenda.

Make sure to include scheduled breaks in the agenda—and don't skip them. It may be tempting to bypass a break if you are in a groove with the discussion, but that's usually a mistake. Ask someone on your account team to remind you to take a break in case you forget.

Your Company Name

Architecture Design Session
Modern Data Warehouse
Agenda

9:00 – 9:15	Welcome and Introductions	Architect name
	Review and outline the goals and outcomes that COMPANY X is looking to drive as part of this strategy briefing	
9:15 – 10:30	Background / Discovery / Current State Review	All
	Review current data platform and capture future state vision	
10:30 – 12:00	Modern Data Warehouse Overview	Architect name
	High-level discussion of the modern data warehouse architecture. Ingest, Store, Transform, Model, Visualize.	
12:00 – 12:30	Lunch	
12:30 – 2:00	Data Lake Concept	Architect name
	How to organize the data lake and data governance	
2:00 – 3:45	Product use case discussion	Architect name
	What products to use, their use cases, and what would the solution look like	
3:45 – 4:00	Wrap Up Day	All
	Summarize discussions and capture action items	

* Breaks will be added as needed

Figure 3-1. Sample agenda for an ADS about a modern data warehouse project

Set aside some time beforehand to get to know the ins and outs of any tools you will use to whiteboard (for example, a Surface Hub) so you aren't figuring things out during the ADS. Pretend you are in an ADS and use the whiteboard to write down goals, pain points, and follow-ups and to draw the architecture, based on your guesses as to how the customer will answer your questions. You can even ask a coworker to role-play as the customer to help you out.

Inviting Participants

The people who should participate in the ADS will vary a bit depending on whether the customer is internal (a group within your company) or external (an outside company you do business with).

From the customer side (or if it's an internal ADS, from the group for which you are doing the ADS), attendees should include:

- The sponsors (at least one from business and one from IT)
- Business representatives
- Technical representatives
- Project manager
- Advisors, architects, developers, and infrastructure or operations people, as necessary

From your team, include:

- An architect to facilitate the session and make sure the ADS meets its objectives
- From the account team, an account executive, account specialist, and/or cloud solution architect
- Subject matter experts (SMEs) to provide in-depth knowledge on specific topics
- At least one person to take notes (possibly a member of the account team)

If the customer wants to talk about a subject area that you are not familiar with, in most cases it's better to bring in a SME instead of trying to learn the topic yourself, especially if your time is limited. Make sure to thank the SME and send their manager a nice email afterward. When a SME attends the ADS, everyone wins: the customer is happy to get expert advice, the account team is happy because the customer is satisfied, and you can learn from the SME.

If you're new to facilitating, you might also want to ask a mentor to participate, to back you up during the ADS (by answering questions that you can't answer), and to give you feedback afterward on what you did well and what you could do better.

Sometimes I arrange the agenda to allow people to attend only part of the day. For example, I might plan for the morning to be more about business and discovery, saving the technical side for the afternoon when we'll delve into the proposed architecture and technologies. In this example, the C-level executives would likely attend the morning session, and the technical people would attend in the afternoon. However, anyone who wanted to could attend for the whole day—maybe some C-level people would be interested in the technical discussion, while some technical people would be interested in discovery.

Conducting the ADS

Remember, you're in charge, so it's up to you to set the tone and keep the meeting on course. If someone brings up an off-topic point, say that you can discuss it offline; then write it on the whiteboard for follow-up. Similarly, if you or someone else agrees to follow up on a specific item, add it to the whiteboard. Let the account team take notes—you need to focus on talking with the customer and whiteboarding.

At the halfway point, check the agenda and goals. If you are behind, mention to the customer that the meeting will need to stay on track to get through all the goals. If it seems you will not have time to cover all the goals, ask the customer to reprioritize the goals so that any goals that don't get discussed are the lowest priority.

Introductions

At the start of the ADS, have everyone introduce themselves, stating their name, role, and what (if anything) they know about the technology you will discuss. Then, perhaps most important, ask what they want to get out of the ADS (their learning goals). Write the goals on the whiteboard and prioritize them as a group. If some attendees were not on the pre-call, make clear what the ADS will cover.

Use this time to explain how and why the ADS has been arranged and set ground rules for the rest of the day. For instance, you might tell them that you'll send them a copy of the final whiteboard so they don't need to take pictures of it, that it will be an interactive session and you encourage lots of questions, that the agenda is just a recommendation and the group can cover other topics they feel would be valuable, and that you can have follow-up meetings to cover additional topics if you run out of time (there's no need to rush through important conversations).

Discovery

Discovery is where you spend an hour or two at the beginning of the ADS asking questions about things like:

- The customer's current pain points
- Their current technology and architecture
- Their future architecture (if any has been discussed)
- Any decisions they've already made about technologies, products, or tools they use or plan to use
- Current and future use cases
- Details on their business

The customer should be doing most of the talking, especially early on in the ADS. You won't learn anything about them if you do all the talking. I always start out asking a ton of questions and getting answers before I go into "education mode," where I start talking for long periods. Even then, I always make sure to pause for questions. You may want to let them know early on that you will stop periodically for questions.

A good architect asks lots of questions. As the saying goes, "You don't know what you don't know." Experienced architects are aware of all the available architectures, techniques, and tools and keep up with the constantly changing landscape of technologies and products. They have the expertise to ask questions that will help them choose the right technologies and products. Discovery is the best way to narrow down the product options to a workable number that you can consider. Then you can come up with the best architecture and products for the particular use case.

By way of analogy, say you're selling medical instruments out of a van filled with a thousand instruments. (It doesn't usually work that way, but bear with me.) You wouldn't just walk up to a doctor, point to your van, and have them look at all the instruments to find the ones they like. Instead, you would ask the doctor a bunch of questions—about their practice area, instruments, and budget—and based on their answers, you would pull out only a small number of instruments for the doctor to look at. Architects do the same thing, and the discovery phase of the ADS is a great opportunity to ask your questions while the appropriate people are in the room.

I'll pass on another great bit of advice I received early in my career: as you start asking questions, make sure to stay away from the solution. That is, *don't* talk about architectures or products until you are done asking all the discovery questions. When I first started running ADSs, as soon as the customer mentioned they wanted to build a data warehouse, I would jump right into demonstrating a Microsoft product. I should have waited and asked all of my questions to make sure I was clear on what the customer was trying to accomplish. Instead, I sometimes discovered that the customer really didn't need a data warehouse at all, which meant my efforts to educate them about the data warehouse product were wasted.

ADS Questionnaire

As you plan your ADS, take a look at this list of questions, which I developed over the course of numerous ADSs I have conducted. I spend an hour or two at the beginning of the meeting doing "discovery." You'll notice that none of the questions is about any specific product. This is so you can begin creating an architecture in a vendor-neutral way. Later on in the ADS, you can ask what products the customer currently uses and what cloud provider they prefer and then apply products to the architecture.

Is your business using the cloud?

Nowadays, the answer is almost always yes. If not, evaluate why and see if you can overcome whatever the source of resistance is. Many such customers just

---

need to better understand the benefits of the cloud (see Chapter 16). Others have outdated reasons for not using the cloud, like "not enough security," that have long been taken care of.

Is the data architecture you're considering a new solution or a migration?
If this is a migration, then part of the conversation will need to be about how to migrate the existing solution to the new solution.

What are the skill sets of the engineers?
Knowing what products and technologies the data engineers are familiar with heavily influences the products I recommend. If they are already familiar with the tool, they'll need less training time, which will likely save costs.

Will you use nonrelational data?
In other words, what kind of variety will the data have? If nonrelational data is coming from any of the sources, the customer will definitely need a data lake, so this is a good time to introduce them to data lake technologies and design.

How much data do you need to store?
What volume of storage is needed? The size of the data will heavily influence performance, so if there's a large volume of data, you'll need to discuss how to design the architecture (for example, the folder structure of the data lake) to avoid performance issues such as slow queries and reports.

Will you have streaming data?
What kind of velocity is needed? Streaming data sources, such IoT devices, influence the types of products needed to support that kind of data.

Will you use dashboards and/or ad hoc queries?
Knowing how the data will be used will influence not only the types of products you recommend but also the system's performance needs. For example, with dashboards, you need millisecond response time so end users can slice and dice the data without noticeable delays.

Will you use batch and/or interactive queries?
Make sure you understand what types of queries will go against the data. This will influence the type of storage used and the compute needed to ensure acceptable performance.

How fast do the reports need to run? Are there service level agreements (SLAs) in place with specific requirements?
Whether the reports need to run in milliseconds or minutes will affect the architecture, the products used, and how many copies of the data will be needed to get to an acceptable level of performance. For example, the data may need to be aggregated.

Will you use this data in predictive analytics or machine learning?

If so, discuss the machine learning (ML) or analytics products that will be used and ways to gather the data that will facilitate training the ML models.

What are your high-availability and/or disaster recovery requirements (such as recovery time objectives and recovery point objectives)?

Most cloud providers build in all the high availability the average customer needs, but supporting any specific high-level requirements could require a change in the architecture. If disaster recovery is required, depending on the recovery point objectives (RPOs), you might need to make major additions to the architecture. Asking this question is also a good way to start the customer thinking about disaster recovery, if they have none built into their current solution.

Do you need to master the data?

Master data management (MDM) involves creating a single master record for each person, place, or thing in a business, gathered from across internal and external data sources and applications. These master records can then be used to build more accurate reports, dashboards, queries, and machine learning models. I explain MDM in detail in Chapter 6. If MDM is needed, you will have to show how it fits into the architecture and recommend products.

Are there any security limitations with storing data in the cloud (for example, defined in your customer contracts)?

This is a very important question: contracts can limit what the organization can do with its customers' data. For example, if customers keep data in certain countries and that data can't leave the country, you will need to architect a solution with multiple data lakes. Similarly, if they cannot store any personally identifiable information in the cloud, you will need to talk about how and when to anonymize that data.

Does this solution require 24/7 client access?

If so, the architecture needs to minimize or eliminate downtime for each of the components. For example, if the customer is using a relational data warehouse, the solution needs to make sure there is no need for a maintenance window to load and clean data.

How many concurrent users will be accessing the solution at peak times? And how many on average?

This is important to know because some products limit how many concurrent users they support. If the number of concurrent users is over or close to such a limit, your design should avoid those products or combine them with other products to minimize the chance of exceeding a limit.

What is the skill level of the end users?

This will determine what products you recommend. If the skill level is low, you might recommend no-code/low-code products. For example, if I mention Spark and get a blank stare from the customer, I won't even talk about Spark-type products but will instead focus on easier-to-use products. If the skill level is high, you can consider higher-code options.

What is your budget?

The project budget, of course, has a huge impact on the architecture and the products you choose. If you have a large budget, there are no constraints on the architecture—you can design whatever you wish. However, you will often run into customers with low budgets. This forces you to make trade-offs: for example, you may reduce financial costs by using less compute but at the cost of a hit to performance (as data loading and reporting will take longer).

What is your planned timeline?

If the timeline is long, which is usually the case when building a data warehouse solution, meet with the cloud provider to find out what products are in development but haven't been announced yet. Then you can educate the customer about anything worth waiting for. The last thing you want is to start building a solution with one product only to find out 4 or 5 months into development that the cloud provider is about to release a better product.

Is the source data in the cloud and/or on-prem?

If some of the data sources are on premises, you'll need a pipeline from the on-prem source to the cloud. Depending on the volume of the data, this could force architecture changes, such as using a product that allows for a bigger pipeline.

How much data needs to be imported into the solution every day?

If a lot of data needs to be uploaded each night, transferring it could take too long. Instead of uploading many large files every night, the system may need to upload data on a more frequent basis, such as hourly. Also, look into architectural changes that can speed uploading, such as doing parallel data uploads, compressing the data before uploading, or using products that perform faster file transfers.

What are your current pain points or obstacles with regard to performance? Scale? Storage? Concurrency? Query times?

You need to know these pain points so you can design an architecture that will address and overcome them. No one wants to pour time and money into building a new solution that leaves them with the same problems, so you'll have to convince the ADS attendees that the solution you're whiteboarding will solve their problems.

Do you want to use third-party and/or open source tools?

Very few customers will be completely committed to a specific cloud provider, using only that cloud provider's products. So, when you finish exploring the high-level architecture and get to the point of talking about products, you might recommend using third-party and open source tools that the engineers are already familiar with.

Are you OK with using products that are in public or private preview?

Before a product is made generally available (or GA'd), it starts out in private preview (available only to a few invited customers) and then moves to public preview (anyone can use it). This is done to make sure the product is as stable and bug-free as possible. The negatives of using a product before it is GA'd include limited functionality, potential bugs, lack of support, unpredictable changes, and uncertainty around pricing. If the company has some appetite for using private or public preview products, it can get a jump on using a new product or feature.

Some companies have strict policies forbidding the use of products before they are GA'd. However, this policy may apply only to products that the company has put into production, which means it is OK to use preview products that will be GA'd by the time the solution is put into production. (It takes a long time to build a data architecture, so this happens a lot.)

What are your security requirements? Do you need data sovereignty?

The answers to these questions can change the architecture in many ways. You might need to build in encryption or extra security features. The requirement to have multiple data lakes because data can't leave a country might apply here, too.

Is data movement a challenge?

Data movement is the process of extracting data from source systems and bringing it into the data warehouse or lake. If the data is coming from many different sources or if there's a mixture of on-prem and cloud sources, your architecture decisions will have to accommodate these various sources. For example, the system might need to use replication software to pull data from a source system into the data lake more quickly.

How much self-service BI would you like?

If the end users have limited or no technical skills but want to be able to create their own reports, then the architecture will need to go to extra lengths to put the data in an easily consumable format. This might mean a relational data warehouse (see Chapter 4) and/or a star schema (see Chapter 8). If the end users are all very technical, then a data lakehouse (see Chapter 12) may be the best architecture.

Whiteboarding

Use a whiteboard, not presentation slides. An ADS is all about discovery; there's lots of talking, and then you'll move on to whiteboarding. Too many slides and the ADS becomes just another presentation. Your whiteboard should include a rough diagram of the architecture, as well as places for goals, pain points, and items for follow-up. Figure 3-2 shows what a final whiteboard might look like for an ADS focused on a modern data warehouse.

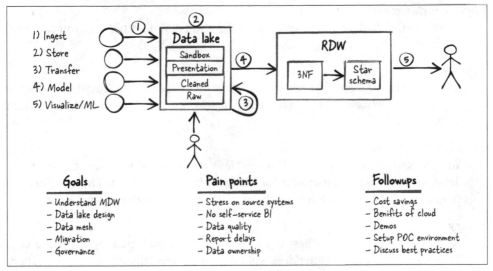

Figure 3-2. A typical whiteboard after the end of an ADS

The whiteboard contains not only the architecture but prioritized goals, pain points, and "parking lot" items and other things to follow up on.

List all the pain points on the whiteboard and make sure to check them off as you solve them. By the end of the ADS, all of the pain points should be addressed in the architecture you have laid out. If not, schedule a follow-up meeting with the customer to address missed pain points. The same applies to goals: if you can't address them all, schedule a follow-up meeting.

Reserve the last 30 minutes of the ADS to discuss follow-up items.

After the ADS

Debrief with the account team after the ADS. Ask them what went well and what you can do better. This is part of putting a growth mindset into action, and it is a great way to get feedback and improve your ADS sessions. You should also communicate the outcomes of the ADS to all stakeholders. This might include a high-level summary for upper management and a more detailed report for those directly involved in the project. Last, collect all the materials you used for the ADS into a digital folder that you can use as a reference for future ADSs. For example, I store all my previous whiteboards; I've found that they're great to review when you're planning an ADS similar to one you have done before.

Shortly after the ADS, email the customer with the following information:

Summary document
Briefly summarize the major points discussed during the ADS.

Physical architecture

> If you used a digital whiteboard, export the end result to a file that you can send to stakeholders, including the customer.

Action items

> Include any next steps that you agreed on, such as "Meet next Tuesday to discuss a proof of concept" or "Customer will email a diagram of their current architecture."

Parking lot items and follow-ups

> You tracked these on the whiteboard. Now in the email you can go into more detail and list who is responsible for following up on each item. This provides the customer with an opportunity to clarify anything you didn't get quite right.

Survey

> At an in-person ADS, it's best to hand a survey to each participant at the end. That way, most if not all attendees will fill it out—especially if you joke with them that they can't leave until they do! Consider making this request during the last break of the day, instead of at the very end of the ADS. If it's a remote ADS, you can post the link to the survey in the meeting chat shortly before the end of the session with encouragement to "copy the link before you leave the meeting so you can provide your feedback." Tell them it takes just two minutes to complete (and make sure that's the truth). You can also include a link to the survey in your follow-up email.

Tips for Conducting an ADS

While it's rare, I've had my fair share of difficult people decide to challenge me during an ADS. Sometimes a person in the room is afraid of change, afraid a new architecture will put them out of a job (especially when the ADS is about a cloud migration), or simply believes they already have all the answers. If you find yourself dealing with someone like this, don't get into an argument—even if you are right. Just reply with something that defuses the argument and gets the ADS back on track, for instance, "You have an excellent point and I'd like to dive into that further, but we'll need to do that offline at another time so that we can stay on topic."

Use humor, too. You don't need to tell jokes, but if you're comfortable, try making funny comments throughout the day to lighten the mood and keep everyone's attention engaged. An ADS can make for a long day, and laughing is the best way to boost people's energy levels.

Be humble—don't come off as a know-it-all. People don't like that. They much prefer people who admit they don't know everything. If you are asked a question you can't answer, just say you don't know but will find out and get back to them quickly. You can research the answer during the lunch break and respond that afternoon. Or find a coworker who knows the answer and invite them in to answer the question directly and to take follow-up questions. Never try to make up or fudge an answer. You might get caught, and even if you don't, that's just not the right way to treat a customer or a colleague.

Of course, customers aren't the only people who can throw things off. It's not unusual for a member of the account team to talk at length in the hope of looking good in front of the customer, without adding any value to the ADS. If that happens, pull them aside during a break for a friendly word and politely ask them to refrain from talking too much. Tell them you'll make sure to ask them pertinent questions that they can answer during the ADS so they can establish their expertise with the customer.

Read the room, too. You know who the decision makers are, so keep them focused and engaged. Pay attention to their body language: if they go from looking at you to reading their emails, they're bored. If so, switch to another topic or take a break.

Learn to adjust on the fly. It's rare that I follow an agenda completely; other topics often come up that are much more interesting and useful to the customer. The challenge will be when those topics are unfamiliar to you! Over time, you will gain the knowledge to be able to pivot and cover just about any topic. It took me about two years of doing ADSs nearly daily to get to that point, so be patient!

Finally, I recommend building up your stamina. When I first started doing full-day ADSs, I found it challenging to keep up my energy—not to mention my voice—for six to eight hours and would collapse when I got home. I talked so much more in ADSs than I was used to, and it took me a while to stop going hoarse! Expect it to take a few months before you can keep up your energy and voice the whole day. My personal favorite tips to keep up stamina and to keep your voice sharp are to get at least eight hours of sleep the day before, stay hydrated during the day by sipping water every few minutes, eat healthy snacks, and exercise regularly during the week.

When you are facilitating an ADS in a remote or hybrid environment, here are some additional tips to keep in mind:

- Turn on live captions in your communication software. Not only does this make the session more accessible for everyone, it can also help you follow the conversation and prevent you from having to ask people to repeat themselves.

- Sign into the call using two different devices: one for screensharing and whiteboarding, the other to communicate (most communication software supports this). Ideally, your communication device will be a computer with two or three large monitors. This way, you don't have to constantly minimize windows or move them around, and you can always see the customer as you are whiteboarding and speaking.

- I recommend having a back channel going with the account team (and *only* the account team) in the chat tool of whatever communication software you are using. This is a great way to communicate with your account team without the customer hearing—for instance, to ask them to research a question you can't answer, to jump in and talk when needed, or to provide details on the person who is speaking.

- I also recommend these tools:

  — If you are using Microsoft Teams, turn on Speaker Coach, a feature that listens to your audio while you present and provides private real-time feedback and suggestions for improvement, as well as a summary afterward. Only you can see its live insights, and they are not saved in recorded meetings' transcripts.

  — I also like ZoomIt (*https://oreil.ly/g8NTJ*), a screen zoom, annotation, and recording tool for technical presentations and application demonstrations. It runs unobtrusively in the tray and activates with customizable hotkeys to let you zoom in on an area of the screen, move around while zoomed, and draw on the zoomed image. It is an excellent way to call attention to specific portions of your presentation—much better than using your cursor, which can be hard to see.

Summary

An ADS is a vital part of building a data architecture. It helps you align design decisions with business goals, address potential risks and challenges, optimize costs and resources, and foster collaboration among stakeholders.

The end result of an ADS is to build a good data architecture, or even a great one. A good data architecture is robust and scalable and can effectively support data-driven initiatives. Taking a data architecture from good to *great* means meeting these needs end to end, with feedback from all users in the data value chain, so that the overall data strategy can meet the organization's goals. Building a data solution is a user-focused journey into design and feedback, and it requires the kind of strategy and planning that only an ADS can provide.

PART II

Common Data Architecture Concepts

Before diving into data architectures, it's important to make sure you understand all the data architecture concepts that could be used within an architecture. I find there tends to be a lot of confusion about many of these concepts, which I hope to clear up. Therefore, you will find discussion of over 20 such concepts in the upcoming chapters. At the very least, these chapters will be a refresher for those who may have not used these concepts in a while. I don't claim that all my definitions of these concepts are universally agreed upon by everyone, but at least these chapters will help get everyone on the same page to make it easier to discuss architectures.

I have included the relational data warehouse and the data lake under concepts instead of architectures. At one time, when they were the only products used in a solution, they could have been considered data architectures. Now, however, they are almost always combined with other products to form the solution. For example, many years ago there were relational data warehouse products that included the relational storage, compute, ETL (extract, transform, and load) software, and reporting software—basically everything you needed bundled together from one vendor. Nowadays, you will stitch together multiple products from possibly multiple vendors, with each product having a particular focus (e.g., ETL), to complete your data architecture.

CHAPTER 4

The Relational Data Warehouse

By the mid-2000s, I had used relational databases for years, but I had never been exposed to relational data warehouses. I was working as a database administrator (DBA) for a company that used an accounting software package to manage its financial transactions. The reporting from the package was limited and slow, so the company was looking to improve performance, create dashboards to slice and dice the data, and combine its financial data with data from a homegrown application to get a better understanding of the business.

My employer hired a consulting company to build this thing called a "relational data warehouse"—and, in a decision that changed the course of my career, asked me to help. We generated dashboards that saved the end users a ton of time and added business insights they'd never had before. When I saw the excitement on their faces, I knew I'd found my new passion. I changed my career to focus on data warehousing and never looked back.

What Is a Relational Data Warehouse?

A *relational data warehouse* (RDW) is where you centrally store and manage large volumes of structured data copied from multiple data sources to be used for historical and trend analysis reporting so that your company can make better business decisions. It is called *relational* because it is based on the *relational model*, a widely used approach to data representation and organization for databases. In the relational model, data is organized into tables (also known as relations, hence the name). These tables consist of rows and columns, where each row represents an entity (such as a customer or product) and each column represents an attribute of that entity (like name, price, or quantity). It is called a *data warehouse* because it collects, stores, and manages massive volumes of structured data from various sources, such as transactional databases, application systems, and external data feeds.

Not all data warehouses are based on the relational model. *Non-relational data warehouses* include types like columnar, NoSQL, and graph data warehouses. However, relational data warehouses are much more popular and widely adopted, primarily because relational databases have been the dominant data management paradigm for decades. The relational model is well suited for structured data, which is commonly found in business applications. It is also popular due to the widespread use of SQL, which has been the standard language for relational data warehouses for many years.

An RDW acts as a central repository for many subject areas and contains the *single version of truth* (SVOT). A critical concept in data warehousing, the SVOT refers to the practice of creating a unified, consistent view of an organization's data. It means that all the data within the data warehouse is stored in a standardized, structured format and represents a single, accurate version of the information. This ensures that all users have access to the same information, eliminating any discrepancies or inconsistencies and eliminating data silos. This improves decision making, collaboration, and efficiency across the organization. It also reduces the risk of errors and misunderstandings that can arise from working with disparate, inconsistent data sources.

Imagine you don't have a data warehouse and are generating reports directly from multiple source systems, and maybe even some Excel files. If a report viewer questions the accuracy of the data, what can you tell them? The "truth" can be spread out over so many source systems that it's difficult to trace where the data came from. In addition, some reports will give different results for the same data—for example, if two reports use complex logic to pull the data from multiple sources and the logic is updated incorrectly (or not at all). Having all the data in one central location means that the data warehouse is the single source of truth; any questions about the report data can be answered by the data warehouse. Maintaining a SVOT is essential for organizations looking to harness the full potential of their data.

If a data warehouse (DW) is used by the entire company, it's often called an *enterprise data warehouse* (EDW). This is a more comprehensive and robust version of a data warehouse, designed to support the needs of the entire organization. While a standard DW might support a few business units, with many DWs throughout the organization, the EDW uses a wider range of data sources and data types to support *all* business units. The EDW provides a single, unified view of all of the organization's data.

Figure 4-1 illustrates a major reason to have a data warehouse. The diagram on the left shows how challenging it is to run a report using data from multiple applications when you do not have a data warehouse. Each department runs a report that collects data from all the databases associated with each application. So many queries are being run that you're bound to have performance problems and incorrect data. It's a mess. The diagram on the right shows that, with all application data copied into the

EDW, it becomes very easy for each department to run a report without compromising performance.

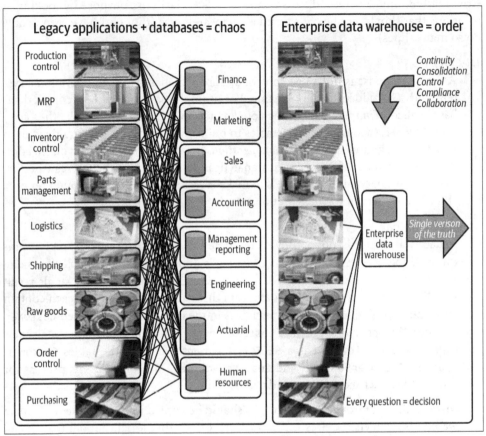

Figure 4-1. Before and after an enterprise data warehouse

Typically, to build a data warehouse, you will create data pipelines that perform three steps, called extract, transform, and load (ETL):

1. The pipeline extracts data from the source systems, such as databases and flat files.

2. The extracted data is then transformed or manipulated to fit the target systems' requirements (in this case, to fit a data warehouse). This can involve cleaning, filtering, aggregating, or combining data from multiple sources.

3. The transformed data is loaded into the data warehouse. A DBA can make the database and field names more meaningful, making it easier and faster for end users to create reports.

What a Data Warehouse Is Not

Now that you know what a data warehouse is, let's clarify its purpose by looking at solutions that should *not* be considered a data warehouse (though I have seen people do so many times):

DW prefix

A data warehouse is not a just copy of a source database from an operational system with *DW* added to the filename. For example, say you were to copy a database called *Finance* containing 50 operational tables and call the copy *DW_Finance*, then use those 50 tables to build your reports. This would result in a data warehouse designed for *operational* data when instead you need it designed for *analytical* data. With analytical data, you have better read performance and can create data models to make it easier for end users to build reports. (I'll explain more in the next section.)

Views with unions

A data warehouse is not a copy of multiple tables from various source systems unioned together in a SQL view. (*Unioning* is done via the SQL UNION statement, which combines the results of two or more SELECT statements into a single result set.) For example, if you copied data from three source systems that each contain customers, you'd end up with three tables in the data warehouse called Customer Source1, CustomerSource2, and CustomerSource3. So you'd need to create a view called CustomerView that is a SELECT statement unioning the tables Customer Source1, CustomerSource2, and CustomerSource3. You'd repeat this process for other tables, such as products and orders.

Instead, the data from the three tables should be copied into one table in the data warehouse, which requires the extra work of creating a data model that fits all three tables. You would likely want to use master data management (MDM), explained in Chapter 6, at this point to prevent duplicates and improve accessibility and performance.

Dumping ground

A data warehouse is not a dumping ground for tables. Many times, this practice arises when a company does not have a DW and an end user wants to create a report from a subset of data from a couple of source systems. To help them out quickly, a person from IT creates a DW without much thought, copying the data from those two source systems into the DW. Then other end users see the benefit the first end user got, and they want additional data from those same source systems and a few others to create their own reports. So once again the IT person quickly copies the requested data into the DW. This process repeats over and over until the DW becomes a jumbled mess of databases and tables.

So many DWs start out as one-off solutions for a couple of users, then morph into full-blown but poorly designed DWs for the entire company. There is a better way.

Instead, when that first end-user request comes in, assess your company's reporting needs. Find out if the request is really a one-off or if it should be the start of building an EDW. If it should, this is your chance to show senior leaders why your company needs a DW. If so, be adamant that you need enough up-front time to design a DW that can support many data sources and end users. (Use "Why Use a Relational Data Warehouse?" on page 49 to support your case.)

The Top-Down Approach

In an RDW, you will do a lot of work up front to get the data to where you can use it to create reports. Doing all this work beforehand is a design and implementation methodology referred to as a *top-down approach*. This approach works well for historical-type reporting, in which you're trying to determine what happened (*descriptive analytics*) and why it happened (*diagnostic analytics*). In the top-down approach, you first establish the overall planning, design, and architecture of the data warehouse first and then develop specific components. This method emphasizes the importance of defining an enterprise-wide vision and understanding the organization's strategic goals and information requirements before diving into the development of the data warehouse.

Descriptive analytics and diagnostic analytics are two important types of data analysis that are commonly used in business. *Descriptive analytics* involves analyzing data to describe past or current events, often through the use of summary statistics or data visualizations. This type of analysis is used to understand what has happened in the past and to identify patterns or trends in the data that can help with decision making.

Diagnostic analytics is used to investigate the causes of past events, typically by examining relationships between different variables or factors. This type of analysis can identify the root causes of problems or diagnose issues that may be affecting business performance.

Suppose a company wants to analyze sales data from the past year. Descriptive analytics would involve calculating summary statistics such as total sales revenue, average sales per day, and sales by product category to understand what happened. Diagnostic analytics, in contrast, would examine relationships between factors (such as sales and marketing spend, or seasonality and customer demographics) to understand why sales fluctuated throughout the year. By combining both approaches, companies can gain a deeper understanding of their data and make more informed decisions.

Figure 4-2 shows the architecture of a typical RDW. ETL is used to ingest data from multiple sources into the RDW, where reporting and other analytics can be performed.

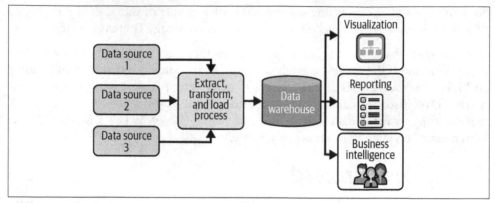

Figure 4-2. The architecture of a data warehouse

The top-down approach typically involves the following steps:

1. *Formulate some hypotheses up front.*
   Start with a clear understanding of corporate strategy. Then make sure you know what questions you want to ask of the data.

2. *Define the business requirements.*
   Identify the organization's goals, objectives, and key performance indicators (KPIs). Gather and analyze the information needs of various departments and users. You can also think of this step as defining your reporting requirements.

3. *Design the data warehouse architecture.*
   Based on the business requirements, create a high-level architecture for the data warehouse, including its structure, data models, and data integration processes. These will be your technical requirements.

4. *Develop the data model.*
   Design a detailed data model for the data warehouse, taking into account the relationships between various data entities and the granularity of the data.

5. *Build the architecture.*
   Develop the appropriate databases, schemas, tables, and fields for the data warehouse. This is the previously described approach called schema-on-write.

6. *Develop ETL.*
   Develop the ETL processes to extract data from various source systems, transform it into the desired format, and load it into the data warehouse.

7. *Develop and deploy BI tools and applications.*
   Implement BI tools and applications that allow users to access, analyze, and report on the data stored in the data warehouse.

8. *Test and refine the data warehouse.*

Perform testing to ensure data quality, performance, and reliability. Make any necessary adjustments to optimize the system.

9. *Maintain and expand the data warehouse.*

As the organization's needs evolve, update and expand the data warehouse accordingly.

The top-down approach has some advantages, such as a comprehensive view of the organization's data needs, better data consistency, and improved governance. However, it can also be time-consuming and resource intensive, taking longer to deliver value than to the bottom-up approach used by the data lake, described in Chapter 5. The modern data warehouse architecture, described in Chapter 10, combines both the top-down and bottom-up approaches.

Why Use a Relational Data Warehouse?

Having an RDW makes it so much easier to build any kind of BI solution, since BI solutions can pull data just from the RDW without having to create complex logic to pull data from multiple source systems. Also, they won't have to clean or join the data because the RDW will have already done that. The BI solution that is built from the RDW could be a data mart (which contains a subset of the RDW data for a specific group of people, as explained in Chapter 6), aggregate data to make queries and reports faster, and even be usable within Microsoft Excel. The bottom line is that with a RDW, you already have a solid foundation to build upon.

Let's look in detail at some of the major benefits you can get from using an RDW:

Reduce stress on the production system

You may have seen this problem before: an angry call from an end user complaining that inserting orders via the order entry application is taking forever. You look into it, and it turns out that another end user is running a report via the order entry application that is hogging all the resources on the server where the application resides. This situation is especially common when end users are allowed to create ad hoc queries and they come up with poorly written SQL.

By copying the order entry application database to a DW and optimizing it, you can have all reports and ad hoc queries go against the DW and avoid this problem altogether, especially if the end user needs to run a report that goes against multiple application databases.

Optimize for read access

Application databases are going to be optimized to support all the CRUD operations equally, so the reading of data will not be as fast as it could be. The data warehouse, on the other hand, is a write-once, read-many type of system, meaning it will be used mainly for the reading of data. Therefore, it can be optimized for read access, especially for the time-consuming sequential disk scans that frequently occur when reports or queries are run. There are many database techniques that can be used to speed up read access in a DW, some to the detriment of write access, which we are not concerned about.

Integrate multiple sources of data

The ability to integrate many sources of data in order to create more useful reports is one of the more important reasons to build a DW. Locating all the data in one spot instead of having it spread out over various databases not only makes report building easier but greatly improves reporting performance.

Run accurate historical reports

Without a DW, end users of applications usually run all their reports on a particular day each month (usually the last). They then save them to disk so they have copies that they can refer to in the future. For example, the user wants to look at a report from a few months ago that lists customer sales by state. However, one customer has recently moved to a different state. If the user runs a current report, it would incorrectly show that customer's sales in their new state instead of their old state (since their record in the database has been updated to their new state). Hence, the user must look back at a saved older report instead of running a current report.

A DW can take care of this by keeping track of when a customer moves (via tracking customer location history with start and end dates) as well as any other fields that need to be tracked (for example, employer or income). Now the user can run a report today but ask it to pull data as of some date in the past, and the report will be accurate. Moreover, saving report files each month is no longer required.

Restructure and rename tables

Many application databases have table and field names that are very difficult to understand, especially older ERP and CRM products (think table names such as T116 and field names like RAP16). In the data warehouse, you can copy the data from those source tables into something much easier to understand (for example, Customer instead of T116). You can also likely come up with a better data model for all the tables. End users will be able to create reports much more easily when they don't have to translate cryptic table and field names.

Protect against application upgrades

Imagine you don't have a DW and users instead create reports against an application database. Everything is running fine, and then all of a sudden, many reports start giving errors. It turns out the application went through an upgrade, installing a new version that renamed a bunch of tables and fields. So now you must go through each and every report, out of hundreds, and rename the changed tables and fields. That could take months, resulting in a lot of upset end users. Even after that, any reports that got missed might still give errors.

A DW can protect you against this. After an application upgrade, only the ETL that copies data from the application databases to the DW needs to be updated—a quick task. The reports do not have to be changed. End users won't see any new data until the ETL is fixed, but their reports don't have errors.

Reduce security concerns

Without a DW, your team would need to give each end user security access to each application database they needed to use for reporting purposes. There could be dozens; the process of providing access could take weeks, and sometimes they still might not have access to everything they need. With a DW, each end user needs access only to the appropriate tables, and providing this is much faster and easier.

Keep historical data

Many production systems limit the amount of historical data they keep (for example, data from the last three years). They do this to save space and improve performance and, in some cases, to comply with regulations. Older data is usually purged yearly or monthly. On the other hand, a DW can hold all of the history, so you never have to worry about running a report for older years and not finding any data.

Master data management (MDM)

As you collect data from multiple source systems, many times you will need to use MDM to remove duplicate records for such things as customers, products, and assets. (See Chapter 6 for a more detailed explanation of MDM.) The DW is the perfect place to perform MDM. Also, many of the MDM tools allow you to create hierarchies (for example, Company → Department → Employee), adding more value to mastering the data.

Improve data quality by plugging holes in source systems

You will find that a lot of the data you get from the various source systems needs to be cleaned, despite what the owners of the applications say (I have heard them say "Our data is clean" many times, only to be proved wrong). For example, an order entry application may require a customer's birth date, and if the person entering the data does not know the customer's birth date, they might enter a date in the future or a date more than 100 years old just to be able to complete the order. Or maybe the application does not check the accuracy of the two digits entered for a state code. There are always dozens of "holes" in the source system. You can not only clean the data in the DW, but also notify the people who maintain the applications of the holes in their systems so they can fix them. In this way, you help prevent the entry of bad data in the future.

Eliminate IT involvement in report creation

This goes back to the self-service BI mentioned in Chapter 3: building a proper DW will remove the need to get IT involved with building reports and leave this task in the hands of the end user. Without the bottleneck of limited IT resources, reports and dashboards can be built sooner. And IT will be thankful they can work on more interesting projects than creating reports!

Drawbacks to Using a Relational Data Warehouse

There are always trade-offs, and here are the drawbacks to consider when building an RDW:

Complexity

DWs can be complex and time-consuming to design, build, and maintain. The specialized skills and resources required can increase costs.

High costs

Implementing a DW can be expensive, requiring significant investments in hardware, software, and personnel. Ongoing maintenance and upgrades can also add to the cost.

Data integration challenges

Integrating data from various sources can be challenging, as it may involve dealing with different data formats, structures, and quality issues. This can result in spending time and effort on data cleaning and preprocessing. In addition, certain data, such as streaming data from IoT devices, is too challenging to ingest into an RDW and so the potential insights from this information are lost.

Time-consuming data transformation

For data to be loaded into a DW, it may need to be transformed to conform to the warehouse's data model. This process can be time-consuming, and errors in data transformation can lead to inaccurate analysis.

Data latency

Because DWs are designed to handle large volumes of data, they can be slower to process than other types of databases. This can result in data latency, where the data in the warehouse is not up-to-date with the most recent changes to the source databases.

Maintenance window

With an RDW, you usually need a maintenance window. Loading and cleaning data is very resource intensive, and if users are trying to run reports at the same time, they will experience very slow performance. So users must be locked out of the warehouse while maintenance is going on, preventing 24/7 access. If any problems occur during the maintenance window, such as a failed ETL job, you may have to extend the maintenance window. If users try to run reports and are still locked out, you'll have upset users who can't perform their jobs.

Limited flexibility
DWs are designed to support specific types of analysis, which can limit their flexibility for other types of data processing or analysis. Additional tools or systems may need to be integrated with the warehouse to meet specific needs.

Security and privacy concerns
Storing large amounts of sensitive data in a centralized location can increase the risk of data breaches and privacy violations, necessitating strong security measures.

Populating a Data Warehouse

Because the source tables that are fed into a data warehouse change over time, the DW needs to reflect those changes. This sounds simple enough, but there are many decisions to make: how often to *extract* (or pull) the data, what extract method to use, how to physically extract the data, and how to determine which data has changed since the last extraction. I'll briefly discuss each of these.

How Often to Extract the Data

How often you need to update the DW depends largely on how often the source systems are updated and how timely the end user needs the reporting to be. Often end users don't want to see data for the current day, preferring to get all data through the end of the prior day. In this case, you can run your jobs to extract the data from the source systems via ETL tools each night after the source system databases have finished updating, creating a nightly maintenance window to do all the data transfer. If the end users require updates during the day, then a more frequent extract, say hourly, will be required.

One thing to consider is the size of the data for each extract. If it is very large, updating the DW may take too long, so you might want to split the update into smaller chunks and do more frequent extracts and updates (for example, hourly instead of daily). Also, it may take too long to transfer large amounts of data from the source systems to the data warehouse, especially if the source data is on-prem and you don't have a large pipeline from the source system to the internet. This is another reason why you may want to go from a large nightly transfer to smaller hourly transfers during the day.

Extraction Methods

There are two methods for extracting data from source systems. Let's look at each:

Full extraction
> In a full extraction, all the data is extracted completely from one or more tables in the source system. This works best for smaller tables. Because this extraction reflects all the data currently available on the source system, there is no need to keep track of changes, making this method very easy to build. The source data is provided as is, and you don't need any additional information (for example, timestamps).

Incremental extraction
> In incremental extraction, you're pulling only the data that has changed since a specified time (such as the last extraction or the end of a fiscal period) instead of the whole table. This works best for large tables, and it works only when it's possible to identify all the changed information (discussed below).

With most source systems, you'll use a combination of these two methods.

Whether you're doing a full or an incremental extraction, there are two ways to extract the data: online and offline.

In online extraction, the extraction process can connect directly to the source system to access the source tables, or it may connect to an intermediate system that stores changes to the data in a preconfigured manner (for example, in transaction logs or change tables).

However, direct access to the source system is not always available. In such cases, the data is staged outside the original source system and is created by an extraction routine originating from the source system (for example, a mainframe performs an extract routine on a table and deposits the data in a folder in a filesystem). The extracted data is usually placed in a flat file that is in a defined, generic format (for example, CSV or JSON).

How to Determine What Data Has Changed Since the Last Extraction

Unfortunately, it can be difficult for many source systems to identify the recently modified data and do an incremental extract. Following are several techniques for identifying recently modified data and implementing incremental extraction from source systems. These techniques can work in conjunction with the data extraction methods discussed. Some techniques are based on the characteristics of the source systems; others may require modifications to the source systems. The source system's owners should carefully evaluate any technique prior to implementation:

Timestamps

Timestamps are the most preferable option and the easiest to implement. The tables in some operational systems have timestamp columns with the time and date that a given row was last modified, making it easy to identify the latest data. In relational databases, the timestamp column is often given the data type `time stamp` or `datetime`, along with a column name like `Timestamp` or `Last Modified`. The source application will then populate this column. If not, you can set up the relational database to default to the current date when the record is saved, or you can add database triggers to populate the column.

Change data capture

Most relational databases support *change data capture* (CDC), which records the `INSERT`s, `UPDATE`s, and `DELETE`s applied to database tables and makes a table record available of what changed, where, and when based on the relational database's transaction log. If you need near-real-time data warehousing, where you can see changes to the source system reflected in the data warehouse within a few seconds, CDC can be the key enabling technology.

Partitioning

Some source systems use range partitioning, in which the source tables are partitioned along a date key, which makes it easy to identify new data. For example, if you are extracting from an orders table partitioned by day, it is easy to identify the current or previous day's data.

Database triggers

You can add a trigger for `INSERT`, `UPDATE`, and `DELETE` on a single table and have those triggers write the information about the record change to a "change table." This is similar to change data capture, so use CDC if your database product supports it; otherwise, use triggers.

`MERGE` *statement*

The least preferable option is to do a full extraction from the source system to a staging area in the DW, then compare this table with a previous full extract from the source system using a `MERGE` statement to identify the changed data. You will need to compare all source fields with all destination fields (or use a hash function). This approach likely won't have a significant impact on the source system, but it can place a considerable burden on the DW, particularly if the data volumes are large. This option is usually the last resort if no other options are possible.

The Death of the Relational Data Warehouse Has Been Greatly Exaggerated

Around the early 2010s, people in IT started questioning whether the relational data warehouse was needed anymore, asking, "Is the relational data warehouse dead?" Many people understood this as asking if businesses still need DWs. They do, as this chapter points out. But the question is really about the data warehouse architecture—can you just use a data lake, or should you use both a data lake and an RDW?

When data lakes first appeared, they were built on Apache Hadoop technology, and it was largely Hadoop vendors pronouncing the RDW dead. "Just put all your data in the data lake and get rid of your RDW," they advised. As mentioned in Chapter 2, the projects that attempted to do that all failed.

For many years, I had felt that RDWs would always be needed because data lakes were all Hadoop based and there were just too many limitations. But once solutions like Delta lake (see Chapter 12) had become available and data lakes began using better, easier-to-use products than Hadoop (see Chapter 16), I started to see some use cases where a solution could work without an RDW. That type of solution is a data lakehouse architecture, which will be covered in Chapter 12.

However, there are still plenty of use cases where an RDW is needed. And while data lake technologies will continue to improve, thereby reducing or eliminating the concerns about bypassing an RDW (see Chapter 12), we will never completely do away with RDWs. I think there are three reasons for this. First, it's still harder to report off a data lake than from a DW. Second, RDWs continue to meet the information needs of users and provide value. Third, many people use, depend on, and trust DWs and don't want to replace them with data lakes.

Data lakes offer a rich source of data for data scientists and self-service data consumers ("power users"), and they serve the needs of analytics and big data well. But not all data and information workers want to become power users. The majority continue to need well-integrated, systematically cleansed, easy-to-access relational data that includes a historical log that captures how things have evolved or progressed over a period of time. These people are best served with a data warehouse.

Summary

This chapter covered the first widely used technology solution to centralize data from multiple sources and report on it: the relational data warehouse. The RDW revolutionized the way businesses and organizations manage their data by providing a centralized repository for data storage and retrieval, enabling more efficient data management and analysis. With the ability to store and organize data in a structured manner, RDWs allow users to generate complex queries and reports quickly and easily, providing valuable insights and supporting critical decision making.

Today, the relational data warehouse remains a fundamental component of many data architectures and can be seen in a wide range of industries, from finance and healthcare to retail and manufacturing. The following chapter discusses the next technology to become a major factor in centralizing and reporting on data: the data lake.

CHAPTER 5

Data Lake

Big data started appearing in unprecedented volumes in the early 2010s due to an increase in sources that output semistructured and unstructured data, such as sensors, videos, and social media. Semi-structured and unstructured data hold a phenomenal amount of value—think of the insights contained in years' worth of customer emails! However, relational data warehouses at that time could only handle structured data. They also had trouble handling large amounts of data or data that needed to be ingested often, so they were not an option for storing these types of data. This forced the industry to come up with a solution: data lakes. Data lakes can easily handle semi-structured and unstructured data and manage data that is ingested often.

Years ago, I spoke with analysts from a large retail chain who wanted to ingest data from Twitter to see what customers thought about their stores. They knew customers would hesitate to bring up complaints to store employees but would be quick to put them on Twitter. I helped them to ingest the Twitter data into a data lake and assess the sentiment of the customer comments, categorizing them as positive, neutral, or negative. When they read the negative comments, they found an unusually large number of complaints about dressing rooms—they were too small, too crowded, and not private enough. As an experiment, the company decided to remodel the dressing rooms in one store. A month after the remodel, the analysts found an overwhelming number of positive comments about the dressing rooms in that store, along with a 7% increase in sales. That prompted the company to remodel the dressing rooms in all of its stores, resulting in a 6% increase in sales nationwide and millions more in profit. All thanks to a data lake!

What Is a Data Lake?

The term *data lake* is a metaphor to describe the concept of storing vast amounts of raw data in its natural format. Just as a lake holds water without changing the water's nature, a data lake holds data without the need to structure or process it first. Also, just as lakes hold various wildlife and plant species, a data lake holds different types of data (structured, semi-structured, and unstructured). Contrast that with the data warehouse, where data is more structured and processed, like bottled or packaged goods in a warehouse.

Once the data is in a data lake, it must be cleaned, joined, and possibly aggregated in order to make it useful. This is where some type of *compute* (that is, the processing power required to manage, manipulate, and analyze data) must connect to the data lake, take and transform the data, then put it back into the data lake.

Why Use a Data Lake?

There are many reasons for using a data lake, especially alongside an RDW. As mentioned, you can quickly store data in a data lake with no up-front work—an approach called schema-on-read (see Chapter 2). This enables you to access the data much faster, which can allow power users to run reports quickly (for faster return on investment, or ROI) and give data scientists quick access to data to train a machine learning model. It's also useful for investigating data. If an end user asks you to copy source data into a DW, you can quickly copy the source data to the data lake and investigate it to make sure it has value before you put forth the effort of creating the schema in the data warehouse and writing the ETL.

I mentioned in Chapter 4 that typically, with a DW, you have a maintenance window at night where you kick the end users off so you can load the source data into DW staging tables. You then clean the data and copy it into the DW production tables. The problem is that if you run into problems and maintenance takes longer than expected, when end users try to access the data in the morning, they're locked out. A better option is to transform the data in the data lake instead of in the DW. The benefits of this include:

- Cost savings, since the DW compute is usually much more expensive than other types of compute that you can use on the data in the data lake.

- Extreme performance for transformations (if needed), by having multiple compute options where each compute can access different folders containing data and run in parallel (or run in parallel on the same data).

- Ability to refine the data in many more ways than with the DW because of the flexibility to use many different types of compute options on the data in the data lake. For example, you can use code libraries with prebuilt routines to do complex transformations that are very difficult or impossible to do using SQL in the DW.

- No need for a DW maintenance window, allowing 24/7 use of the DW for queries. You also avoid users competing for the same compute resources if you try to run reports while data transformations are going on. Since data transformations are resource hogs, you can really slow each other down.

A data lake is an inexpensive way to store an unlimited amount of data. Unlike on-prem storage, cloud providers have unlimited storage, so you never have to worry about running out of space in your data lake. Also, cloud storage is relatively cheap, and most cloud providers have multiple storage tiers that allow their customers to save even more money.

The data lake lets you collect any data "just in case" you might need it in the future. This *data stockpiling* is rarely done with a DW since storage in a DW is usually much more expensive than in a data lake and holding more data in the DW can affect performance. And because storage is so cheap in a data lake, data is rarely deleted unless for regulatory reasons.

Because it acts as a centralized place for all subjects of data, a data lake can be the "single version of the truth." If any and all data lands in the data lake before it is copied elsewhere, the data lake can be the place to go back to if there are questions about the accuracy of the data in any of the other places it is used, such as queries, reports, and dashboards. A data lake also makes it easy for any end user to access any data from any location and use it many times for any analytic needs and use cases they wish. When you use a data lake alongside a DW, the data lake becomes the single version of the truth instead of the DW. Furthermore, a data lake is a place to land streaming data, such as from IoT devices, which is nearly impossible to land in a DW.

The data lake also acts as an online archive. For example, you could keep the last three years of order data in the DW and order data older than three years in the data lake. Most of the technology used to build a DW will allow you to query data in a data lake using SQL, so users can still use the data in the lake in reports (with the trade-off of slower performance). This can save costs and avoid running out of storage space in the DW.

The data lake is also a place where you can back up data from the data warehouse in case you need to restore data to the DW due to accidental deletion, corruption, an incorrect WHERE clause on an UPDATE query, and so on.

In addition, you can integrate differently structured data into a data lake: everything from CSV and JSON files to Word documents and media files. Data can be extracted from those files to give you more value.

With a DW, the raw data that is copied from a source system into staging tables in the DW, then transformed and loaded into the production tables is usually deleted after a day or two to save space in the limited relational storage. A problem arises if an ETL error is discovered from an ETL run many days ago; if the ETL needs to be rerun but the raw data has been deleted, you have to go back to the source system and possibly affect its performance. By doing the transformation in the data lake, where storage is cheaper, you can keep a long history of the raw data and never have to go back to the source system.

Bottom-Up Approach

Because a data lake is schema-on-read, little up-front work needs to be done to start using the data. This works really well if you don't know what questions to ask of the data yet—you can quickly explore the data to surface the relevant questions. This results in what is referred to as a *bottom-up approach*, as seen in Figure 5-2, where you collect data up front before generating any theories or hypotheses. This is very different from the top-down approach of a relational data warehouse, as seen in Figure 5-1.

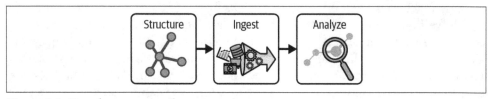

Figure 5-1. Top-down approach

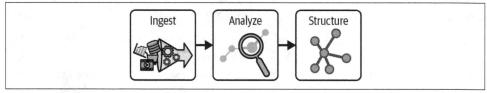

Figure 5-2. Bottom-up approach

This allows data scientists, who typically use software that prefers data in files, to use machine learning on the data in the data lake to determine what will happen (predictive analytics) and how can people make it happen (prescriptive analytics).

Predictive analytics makes use of data, statistical algorithms, and machine learning techniques to predict future outcomes based on historical data. It includes a variety of statistical techniques, such as data mining, predictive modeling, and machine learning, to analyze current and historical facts to make predictions about future or otherwise unknown events. This allows you to be proactive, not just reactive. For instance, predictive analytics can be used in healthcare to forecast patient readmission rates, in retail to predict future sales, or in banking to predict loan defaults.

Prescriptive analytics goes a step further than predictive analytics. It utilizes optimization and simulation algorithms to advise on possible outcomes. Prescriptive analytics not only predicts what will happen in the future but also suggests actions to take to affect those outcomes. The goal is to provide advice based on predicted future scenarios to optimize decision making. Prescriptive analytics can suggest decision options on how to take advantage of a future opportunity or mitigate a future risk, and it can illustrate the implications of each decision option. For example, in logistics, prescriptive analytics can be used to find the best routes for delivery and even suggest alternate routes in case of unexpected road closures.

Data lakes were used mainly for predictive and prescriptive analytics at first to avoid the difficulties of trying to perform advanced analytics with the traditional data warehouse. But now data lakes are used for much more, as indicated in "Why Use a Data Lake?" on page 60.

If you find valuable data in the data lake when exploring and you want to make it easily accessible to end users, you can always model it later by copying it to an RDW. *Data modeling* is like creating a blueprint for organizing and understanding data. It helps define what data is important, how it's related, and how it should be stored and used in an RDW. Data lakes have limited tools for data modeling, while DWs have had modeling tools for years.

Best Practices for Data Lake Design

Designing a data lake should be a time-consuming process. I often find that companies don't spend enough time thinking through all their use cases when designing their data lakes and later have to redesign and rebuild them. So make sure you think through all the sources of data you use now and will use in the future, and that you understand the size, type, and speed of the data. Then absorb all the information you can find on data lake design and choose the appropriate design for your situation.

A data lake generally doesn't enforce a specific structure on the data it ingests; in fact, this is one of its key characteristics. This is different from a traditional database or data warehouse, which requires data to be structured or modeled beforehand. However, to make data usable and prevent the data lake from becoming a "data swamp" (an unorganized and unmanageable collection of data), it's important to apply some organization and governance practices. This section introduces some best practices to get you started.

The first best practice is to logically divide the data lake into multiple layers (also called zones) corresponding to increasing levels of data quality, as shown in

Figure 5-3. Otherwise, you would have all your files in one folder, greatly affecting performance, manageability, and security.

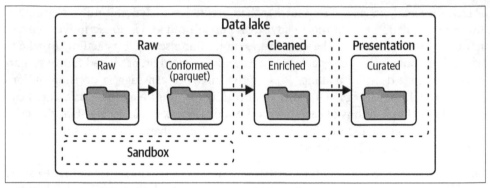

Figure 5-3. Data lake layers

To better understand the structure and function of a data lake, let's delve into its various layers, each representing a step in the enhancement of data quality and usability. These layers are arranged in a hierarchy, progressing from raw, unprocessed data to highly refined and business-ready information. Here's a closer look at each layer:

Raw layer

Raw events, stored for historical reference, are usually kept forever (immutable). Think of the raw layer as a reservoir that holds data in its natural and original state (no transformations applied). It's unfiltered and unpurified. This layer is also called the *bronze layer*, *staging layer*, or *landing area*.

Conformed layer

Many times, the data in the raw layer will be stored as different types, such as CSV, JSON, and Parquet (a common storage file format optimized for efficient big data processing). The conformed layer is where all the file types are converted to one format, usually Parquet. Think of the lake as having two reservoirs, one of saltwater and one of freshwater, and using desalination to turn the saltwater into freshwater. This layer is also called the *base* or *standardized layer*.

Cleansed layer

Here, raw events are transformed (data is cleaned, integrated, and consolidated) into directly consumable datasets. Think of the cleansed layer as a filtration layer. It removes impurities and may also enrich the data. The aim is to make the stored files uniform in terms of encoding, schema, format, data types, and content (such as strings and integers). This layer is also called the *silver, transformed, refined, integrated, processed*, or *enriched layer*.

Presentation layer

Business logic is applied to the cleansed data to produce data ready to be consumed by end users or applications, typically in a format that's easy to understand and use. Transformation might involve aggregations or summaries, or it may mean putting files into a specific layout for use in reporting tools (such as a star schema, discussed in Chapter 8), often including information about the data (metadata) within each file. This layer is also called the *application, workspace, trusted, gold, secure, production ready, governed, curated, serving, analytics,* or *consumption layer.*

Sandbox layer

This optional layer is used to "play" in. Generally the sandbox is used by data scientists. It is usually a copy of the raw layer where data can not only be read, but also modified. You might create multiple sandbox layers. This layer is also called the *exploration layer, development layer,* or *data science workspace.*

This is just one way of setting up the layers in your data lake. I have seen many other excellent designs that include additional layers or combine some layers, such as the conformed and cleansed layers.

For an example using the layers in Figure 5-3, let's consider a retail company that has different data sources like point-of-sale (POS) systems, online sales, customer feedback, and inventory systems. The four layers would contain data of different quality as follows:

- Raw layer
  - Raw logs from the POS system, including every transaction detail (such as timestamp, items purchased, quantities, prices, total amount, cashier ID, and store location)
  - Online sales data from the website or app, such as user ID, items purchased, quantities, prices, total amount, and timestamps
  - Inventory data from various warehouses and stores, including items, quantities, and restock dates
  - Raw customer feedback collected through surveys, reviews, and ratings
- Conformed layer
  - All POS, online sales, inventory, and customer feedback files are converted to Parquet format if they are not already in this format.
- Cleaned layer
  - POS and online sales data with any errors removed or corrected (such as inconsistencies in how items are named, errors in quantities, and missing timestamps). Data has also been transformed into a common schema (for

example, common naming conventions and formats for items, common time format, or common store ID system).

— Inventory data with standardization in item naming and with errors or inconsistencies corrected. Data has also been transformed to align with the common item names and store IDs used in the sales data.

— Customer feedback data that has been cleaned to remove irrelevant or erroneous responses, given standardized formats, and so forth. Data has also been transformed into a common format, aligning with the common store ID system and perhaps with common elements extracted from the feedback for analysis.

- Presentation layer

— A consolidated sales report showing total sales per store, per region, or per day/month/year, and perhaps sales broken down by item or category

— An inventory report showing current stock levels for each item in each store or warehouse, as well as restocking schedules

— A customer feedback report summarizing the feedback, maybe with a sentiment analysis score for each store or product

Another best practice is to create a folder structure, usually a different one for each layer that can be divided up in many different ways for different reasons. Here are some examples:

Data segregation
Organizing data based on source, business unit, or data type makes it easier for data scientists and analysts to locate and use the relevant data.

Access control
Different teams or individuals within an organization may have different levels of access to data. By structuring folders based on user roles or departments, organizations can implement fine-grained access control policies.

Performance optimization
Organizing data in a specific way can lead to improved performance. For instance, certain data processing or querying operations may be faster if the data is grouped based on specific characteristics.

Data lifecycle management
Data often has a lifecycle, from ingestion to archival or deletion. Different folders might be used to segregate data based on its stage in the lifecycle.

Metadata management
Folders can be used to manage and segregate metadata from the raw data. This segregation can simplify metadata management and speed up data discovery.

Compliance requirements

In many industries, compliance requirements dictate that certain types of data be stored and managed in specific ways. Different folder structures can help organizations meet these requirements.

Backup and disaster recovery

Having different folder structures can assist in creating a strategic backup and disaster recovery plan. Certain folders might be backed up more frequently or retained for longer based on their importance.

Data versioning

Different folders might be used to manage different versions of the same dataset.

Data partitioning

Data can be partitioned by key attributes for quicker query performance.

Ingestion and processing needs

Based on the source, data might need different processing pipelines. Different folders can help manage and streamline these processes.

To satisfy one or more of the reasons above, you may divide the folders up in one or more of these ways:

- Time partitioning (year/month/day/hour/minute), such as when the data was copied into the data lake
- Subject area
- Source of the data
- Object, such as a source table
- Security boundaries, such as department or business area
- Downstream app or purpose
- Type of data, such as detail or summary
- Data retention policy, such as temporary and permanent data, applicable period, or project lifetime
- Business impact or criticality, such as high, medium, or low
- Owner/steward/SME
- Probability of data access, such as for recent or current data versus historical data
- Confidential classification, such as public information, internal use only, supplier/partner confidential, personally identifiable information, or sensitive information

Figure 5-4 shows an example folder structure for the raw and cleaned zones.

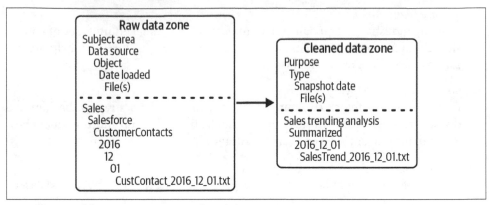

Figure 5-4. Folder structure in two data lake zones

Most times, all these layers are under one cloud subscription. There are some exceptions, such as if you have specific requirements for billing, if you'll hit some subscription limit, or if you want separate subscriptions for development, testing, and production. (See the next section for more exceptions.)

Most customers create a storage account for each layer (so three layers means three storage accounts), all within a single *resource group* (a container that holds related resources for a solution). This isolates the layers to help make performance more predictable and allows for different features and functionality at the storage account level.

Typical features that are set at each storage account level are available through most cloud providers (I'm being specific to Azure in this section) include lifecycle management, which allows you to reduce costs by automating data management tasks (like transitioning data across different storage tiers or deleting data when it's no longer needed). You can also set firewall rules to only allow access to certain trusted groups or individuals, or to prevent hitting an account's storage or throughput limit.

Most data lakes use cloud storage access tiers, with the raw and conformed layers using the archive tier, the cleansed layer using the cold tier, and the presentation and sandbox layers using the hot tier. Each tier offers a different balance of storage cost and access costs, with the hot tier being the most expensive for storage and the archive tier having the highest retrieval cost.

I recommend putting auditing or integrity checks in place to make sure the data is accurate as it moves through the layers. For example, if working with finance data, you might create a query that sums the day's orders (row count and sales total) and compares the values to the source data to make sure that those values are equal in all the data layers. If they are not equal, that indicates a problem with the pipelines you created to move and transform the data. You'll need to fix the problem and rerun the pipelines.

Multiple Data Lakes

Ideally, you'd just create one large data lake and use it for all your data. This approach would simplify finding and combining data for queries or reports. But there are many reasons you might need to create multiple physically separate data lakes (as shown in Figure 5-5) instead of just dividing one data lake into different sections. Most of the use cases I discuss next aren't possible (or are at least much less convenient) unless the data lakes are physically separate.

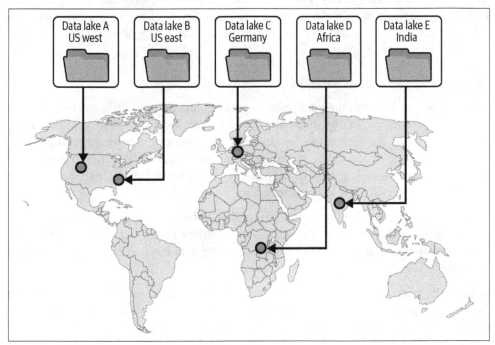

Figure 5-5. Separate data lakes across the world

Advantages

I've grouped the reasons for creating physically separate data lakes into five sections, after which I'll discuss the disadvantages of having multiple data lakes.

Organizational structure and ownership

Maintaining multiple data lakes can be advantageous for many reasons, most of which relate to organization structure and ownership. For example, the company's organizational structure may encourage or require each organizational unit to retain ownership of its own data, a feature typically associated with a data mesh (see Chapter 13).

Another reason is that different teams or departments may require their own distinct data lakes for specific use cases or projects.

Further, a company may benefit from having a source-aligned data lake as well as a consumer-aligned data lake. Data from a particular source can be collected into a data lake with minimal transformations. This works well for users who understand the source data, such as those in manufacturing when the data is sourced from a manufacturing process; however, those outside of manufacturing may find the data difficult to understand. In such cases, you might copy the data to a consumer-aligned data lake and transform it to make it more understandable. Thus, having separate data lakes for source-aligned and consumer-aligned data instead of one data lake can simplify the data-handling process.

Compliance, governance, and security

The decision to have multiple data lakes instead of just one is significantly influenced by a variety of factors falling under the broad categories of compliance, governance, and security. For instance, multi-regional deployments can necessitate multiple data lakes when data residency or sovereignty requirements vary across regions. For example, data originating from China cannot be exported outside the country, so it requires a unique data lake within the region.

Another crucial consideration is that multiple data lakes allow you to separate sensitive or confidential data from less sensitive data. More restrictive and stringent security controls can be applied specifically to sensitive data lakes, enhancing overall data security.

If some individuals have elevated access privileges, separate data lakes allow you to limit the scope of those privileges, confining them to the particular data lake in which the individual is working. This promotes a more secure data environment.

Finally, diverse governance and compliance requirements can be a driving force for having multiple data lakes. Regulations such as the General Data Protection Regulation (GDPR) and the Health Insurance Portability and Accountability Act (HIPAA) necessitate unique data management standards and practices. With multiple data lakes, organizations can manage their data according to the specific governance and compliance requirements that apply to each dataset, a practice that is particularly vital in highly regulated sectors.

Cloud subscription, service limits, and policies

Having multiple data lakes can also be advantageous for reasons primarily associated with cloud subscription, service limits, and policies. For example, having multiple lakes can help circumvent cloud providers' subscription or service limits, quotas, and constraints, such as a cap on the maximum number of storage accounts per subscription. In such scenarios, if you were to operate with only a single data lake, your needs could exceed those limits.

Moreover, multiple data lakes allow you to implement distinct cloud policies. Cloud providers typically offer hundreds of different policy options, which can be tailored individually for each data lake. This flexibility helps ensure compliance with company policies. An example might be a specification that some storage accounts have infrastructure encryption, a rule that varies from one data lake to another within your operation.

Finally, it can be more straightforward to track costs for billing purposes when you maintain separate data lakes, each with its own cloud subscription. This level of granularity in cost tracking offers a clear advantage over alternative methods provided by cloud services, such as using tags for each resource.

Performance, availability, and disaster recovery

Performance, availability, and disaster recovery also provide numerous reasons to consider employing multiple data lakes. One such reason is improved latency. If a set of global end users are accessing a single data lake, those who are far away may find the service quite slow. By situating a data lake in the same region as the end user or application querying the data, you can significantly decrease the time it takes to access data.

Maintaining multiple data lakes with copies of the data in different regions also significantly enhances disaster recovery capabilities. If a data lake in one region becomes inaccessible, end users can be redirected to an alternate region holding identical data.

Having multiple data lakes also provides the flexibility to implement different data recovery and disaster recovery strategies for different types of data. Critical data that demands constant availability could be hosted in a data lake whose data is replicated across multiple lakes in different regions, while less critical data that can withstand periods of inaccessibility could be stored in a single data lake for significant cost savings.

Finally, with multiple data lakes, you can implement different service levels for distinct types of data. For instance, you could dedicate one data lake to storing and processing high-priority data, which requires low-latency access and high availability, and dedicate another data lake to lower-priority data where higher latencies and lower availability are tolerable. This strategy optimizes the cost and performance of your data management infrastructure by allowing you to use less expensive storage and processing resources for lower-priority data.

Data retention and environment management

Multiple data lakes can make data retention and environment management more efficient. For instance, by segregating the data lakes dedicated to development, testing, and production environments, organizations can ensure that each environment has its own isolated space for data storage and processing. This minimizes the risk of interference or conflicts between different stages of the data lifecycle.

Another advantage of having multiple data lakes is that you can implement distinct data retention policies. Legal or regulatory requirements often dictate the need to retain data for specific periods. If you have separate data lakes for different types of data, you can easily enforce diverse retention policies tailored to those categories. This approach allows for efficient management of data retention, ensuring compliance with various regulations while optimizing storage resources.

Disadvantages

Using multiple data lakes can increase the complexity and cost of your data management infrastructure and require more resources and more expertise to maintain, so if you have a choice, it's important to weigh the benefits against the costs. However, in some cases, you will have no choice; for example, if you're designing around a need for data sovereignty, you'll have to have multiple data lakes.

Properly transferring data between multiple data lakes while maintaining its consistency may require additional integration and management tools (such as Azure Data Factory, Informatica, or Apache NiFi). Finally, having multiple data lakes adds the performance challenge of combining the data when a query or report needs data from multiple lakes. If the lakes are physically located very far apart, possibly even in different parts of the world, it can be time consuming to copy all the data into one location.

Summary

This chapter provided a comprehensive exploration of the data lake, a large-scale data storage and management solution capable of holding raw data in its native format. I discussed the data lake's role and design principles, as well as why you might consider maintaining more than one data lake in certain contexts. Unlike relational data warehouses, data lakes allow quick data storage without any up-front preparation or transformation. This ensures a rapid and effortless data ingestion process, particularly useful in today's era of big data.

I discussed the benefits of using a data lake, emphasizing the flexibility and speed it offers for data storage. This aspect, along with its ability to accommodate a diverse range of data types (structured, semi-structured, and unstructured) is a key advantage, especially in situations where quick, scalable, and diverse data collection is crucial.

The chapter also introduced the bottom-up approach, an important methodology in which you collect data collection before generating any theories or hypotheses. Contrary to the traditional top-down strategy, this approach fosters a more agile, data-centric decision-making process.

A substantial part of the chapter focused on the design of a data lake, introducing the concept of logically dividing a data lake into multiple layers. This layering structure helps to manage data in an organized manner, paving the way for efficient data retrieval and analytics, and it can also aid in security, access control, and data lifecycle management.

The chapter concluded by exploring reasons why an organization might choose to have multiple data lakes. The potential benefits include increased security, improved regulatory compliance, and better data management across distinct business units or specific use cases.

In Chapter 6, we'll move on to looking at data stores.

Data Storage Solutions and Processes

In the digital age, data has become the lifeblood of organizations. But, as any seasoned data professional knows, simply having data isn't enough. The real value lies in how effectively this data is managed, stored, and processed. That's why this chapter is a comprehensive guide to navigating the intricate world of data management. I'll take an in-depth look at how data storage solutions and processes operate within diverse data architectures.

The components of data management are like gears in a complex machine; each fulfills a unique role, yet they all work synchronously to achieve a common goal. I'll start with some of the most practical storage solutions: data marts, operational data stores, and data hubs. The second half of the chapter, "Data Processes", reveals the broad spectrum of processes involved in managing and leveraging data effectively, examining concepts like master data management, data virtualization, data catalogs, and data marketplaces.

For instance, while data marts provide department-specific views of data, operational data stores offer a broader, real-time view of business operations. On the other hand, master data management ensures the consistency and reliability of data, with data virtualization providing a unified, abstracted view of data from various sources. The data catalog serves as the reference guide, making data discovery a breeze, while the data marketplace opens doors for data sharing or even monetizing. Meanwhile, the data hub acts as the system's data epicenter, organizing and managing data from different sources for unified access. Each of these components can stand alone in its function; however, when integrated, they can form a powerful, holistic data strategy, driving your business toward informed decision making, enhanced operational efficiency, and improved competitive advantage.

Whether you're a seasoned data scientist, an aspiring data professional, or a strategic decision maker, understanding these key components and learning to orchestrate them in harmony can unlock the true potential of your organization's data.

Data Storage Solutions

Let's dive in, shall we? This isn't just about storing and processing data—it's about setting the stage for data-driven transformation.

Data Marts

A *data mart*, as shown in Figure 6-1, is a subset of the data warehouse. It is usually designed as a focused repository of data that is optimized to meet the specific needs of a department or a business line within an organization (like finance, human resources, or marketing). Because of its narrower scope, a data mart can provide users with a more streamlined and accessible view of information than a DW can.

It can be challenging for users to navigate large and complex data warehouses that house vast amounts of data. Data marts address this challenge by extracting and consolidating relevant data from the DW and presenting it in a more user-friendly manner. This way, users within a department can easily locate and retrieve the data they need.

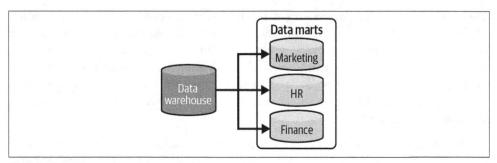

Figure 6-1. Data marts

One of the key advantages of data marts is that they can be created and maintained by individual departments, rather than relying solely on the IT department. Also, each data mart can be structured differently to accommodate the needs of the department it serves. This allows business users more control over the data; they can tailor it to their unique requirements and use the data structures that are most relevant to their domain.

Department-specific data marts provide users quicker, easier access to the data they need for their day-to-day operations and decision-making processes. They can perform analytical queries, generate reports, and gain insights into their department's performance without having to navigate the entire DW.

Moreover, data marts promote data governance and security. Each department can define and enforce access policies for its data mart, ensuring that only authorized individuals have access to specific datasets. This helps to protect sensitive information and ensure compliance with data privacy regulations.

Having delved into data marts, with their targeted, department-specific insights, we now shift our attention to operational data stores.

Operational Data Stores

The *operational data store* (ODS) has a broader scope than a data mart, providing an enterprise-wide, real-time view of data. While data marts offer valuable, in-depth insights into specific areas, the ODS presents a comprehensive look at the organization's operational data. Each tool offers a different perspective; if a data mart lets you look at your data through a microscope, the ODS lets you view it through a wide-angle lens.

The purpose of an ODS is to integrate corporate data from different sources to enable operational reporting in (or near) real time. It is not a data warehouse. As its name implies, it stores operational data, not analytical data. It provides data much faster than a DW can: every few minutes, instead of daily.

An ODS might be a good fit for your organization if the data you're currently using for reporting in the source systems is too limited or if you want a better and more powerful reporting tool than what the source systems offer. If only a few people have the security clearance needed to access the source systems but you want to allow others to generate reports, an ODS may be a good solution.

Usually, data in an ODS is structured similarly to its structure in the source systems. During integration, however, the ODS solution can clean, normalize, and apply business rules to the data to ensure data integrity. This integration happens quite frequently throughout the day, at the lowest level of granularity. Normally, you won't need to optimize an ODS for historical and trend analysis, since this is done in the data warehouse.

The data in the ODS is closer to real time than the data required by the data warehouse. You can use an ODS as one of the staging areas for the DW, at least for the data that it maintains (see Figure 6-2). I recommend that you first reconcile and cleanse that data, populating the ODS in near real time to provide value to the operational and tactical decision makers who need it. You can then also use it to populate the data warehouse, which typically has less demanding load cycles. You will still need the staging area for DW-required data that is not hosted in the ODS, but in following this recommendation, you reduce the number of ETL flows and staging-area sizes. That helps improve performance without sacrificing value or function.

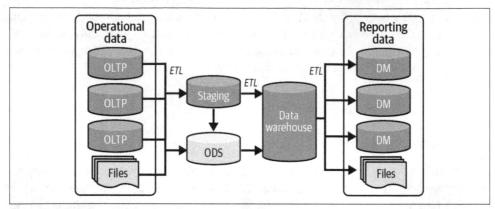

Figure 6-2. An operational data store

Table 6-1 summarizes the most important differences between an ODS and a data warehouse.

Table 6-1. Differences between an ODS and a data warehouse

	Operational data store	Data warehouse
Best suited for	Granular, low-level queries against detailed operational data	Complex queries against summary or aggregated analytical data
Purpose	Operational reporting; current or near real-time reporting	Historical and trend analysis reporting on a large volume of data
Data duration	Contains a short window of data	Contains the entire history of the organization's data
Decision making	Supports operational and tactical decisions on current or near real-time data	Provides feedback on strategic decisions, leading to overall system improvements
Data load frequency	Might load data every few minutes or hourly	Might load data daily, weekly, monthly, or quarterly

Use case

Let's say you're running inventory reports for a fictional retail chain called ShoesFor-Less. If you had only one retail store with one database to track orders, you could just run the inventory report against that database. But since you have many retail stores, each of which tracks orders in its own database, the only way to get up-to-the-minute accurate inventory reports is to combine the order data from those databases. This is important for letting customers know which items are out of stock, as well as restocking items quickly when supply is low. A data warehouse would not be real-time enough for that situation.

Now suppose a customer service representative gets a call from a customer asking whether a particular style and size of shoe is available. The representative queries the ODS to retrieve real-time data on availability for that type of shoe (for example, "men's running shoe, size 10") and return the current stock level.

On the other hand, if the store's marketing manager wants to understand sales trends for that shoe style over the past year, they can use the DW. They run an aggregated query that sums the sales of "men's running shoe" for each month within the past year. This provides a high-level view of trends that can inform strategic marketing and inventory decisions.

Data Hubs

A *data hub* is a centralized data storage and management system that helps an organization collect, integrate, store, organize, and share data from various sources and provides easy access to analytics, reporting, and decision-making tools. Most significantly, data hubs eliminate the need to use hundreds or thousands of point-to-point interfaces to exchange data between systems. While data warehouses and data lakes have the primary (and often exclusive) goal of serving data for analytics, data hubs are also valuable as a means of communication and data exchange among operational systems (Figure 6-3).

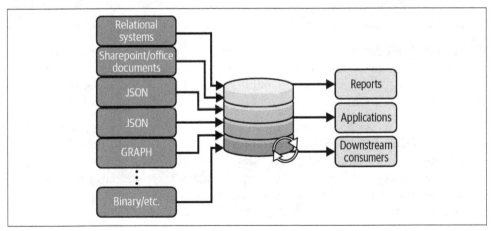

Figure 6-3. Data hub

Data hubs are often used in conjunction with data lakes and warehouses to create a comprehensive data management infrastructure. As you learned in Chapters 4 and 5, data lakes store large volumes of raw, unprocessed data, while data warehouses store structured, processed data optimized for analytical processing. A data hub complements these systems by acting as an intermediary for data exchange, collaboration, and governance. To clarify, let's look at how the data hub interacts with and compares to the other approaches in this chapter. (Table 6-2 summarizes this comparison.)

Table 6-2. Comparison of data solution features

Feature	Data hub	Data lake	Relational data warehouse	Data catalog	Data marketplace
Primary focus	Data storage, integration, distribution	Data storage, processing, analytics	Data storage, processing, analytics	Metadata management, data discovery	Data buying, selling, sharing
Data storage	Raw or lightly processed data	Raw and processed data	Highly structured, processed data	Metadata only	Various formats, provider-dependent
Data structure	Structured, semi-structured, unstructured	Structured, semi-structured, unstructured	Structured	Metadata only	Structured, semi-structured, unstructured
Data processing	Limited processing, mainly integration and distribution	On-demand processing, analytics	Extensive ETL, complex queries	None	Provider dependent
Data sharing	Built-in	Third party	Third party	None	Built-in
Data ownership	Within organization or related groups	Within organization or related groups	Within organization or related groups	Within organization or related groups	Multiple organizations
Use cases	Data ingestion, integration, distribution	Big data analytics, machine learning, artificial intelligence	Complex analytics, reporting, decision making	Data discovery, data lineage, enforcing data governance policies	Monetizing data, acquiring new datasets, data discovery

A data hub stores copies of source data and is focused on managing and distributing, whereas a data catalog does not store actual data and is primarily concerned with metadata management, data lineage, enforcement of data governance policies, and facilitation of data discovery.

A data hub can serve as a source for a data marketplace, which does not store data. The hub is focused on managing and distributing data within an organization, not the commercial transactions of a data marketplace. It is a central platform that uses more storage systems than a data lake or an RDW. Data lakes typically use object storage to store data, while RDWs use relational storage; data hubs can combine storage systems like relational databases, NoSQL databases, and data lakes.

Like a data lake, a data hub supports structured, semi-structured, and unstructured data, as shown in Figure 6-3, whereas an RDW supports only structured data. Data hubs are more likely to provide built-in mechanisms for data cataloging, lineage, and access controls, where a data lake often integrates third-party tools or custom solutions instead.

In terms of processing, a data lake uses compute to clean data and land it back in the data lake. RDWs do extensive data processing, including ETL operations, to clean, normalize, and structure data for analytical purposes. With a data hub, however, data is usually transformed and analyzed outside the hub using external tools or applications.

In summary, a data hub is a flexible and versatile solution for ingesting, managing, integrating, and distributing data from a wide variety of types and sources. By contrast, a data lake is focused on storing and processing large volumes of raw data for use in analytics and machine learning, and a data warehouse is optimized for structured data storage for use in complex analytics, reporting, and decision making.

Data Processes

This chapter has explored the landscape of data storage solutions and how they provide versatile, efficient ways to organize and access data. However, storing data is only one piece of the puzzle. To truly leverage the potential of data, we must also understand how to effectively manage it. So, we now transition from storage solutions to the intricacies of data processes, where we will discover the strategies and techniques that help us manipulate, govern, and capitalize on our data assets.

Master Data Management

Master data management (MDM) is a set of technology, tools, and processes that enables users to create and maintain consistent and accurate lists of master data (such as customer, product, and supplier lists). It involves creating a single master record for each person, place, or thing in a business from across internal and external data sources and applications. You can then use these master records to build more accurate reports, dashboards, queries, and machine learning models.

Most MDM products have very sophisticated tools to clean, transform, merge, and validate the data to enforce data standards. They also allow you to build hierarchies (for example, Company → Department → Employee), which you can use to improve reporting and dashboards. The first step is that you copy the data you want to master into the MDM product. The product then cleans and standardizes the data and creates a master record for each entity (say, a customer) that you are trying to master. It removes most duplicates automatically, but some of the work will have to be done manually, with someone reviewing the records that might be duplicates. The master records are then copied back into the data lake or DW. This master record is also known as a "golden source" or "best version of the truth."

If you are creating a star schema (see Chapter 8), the mastered records would be your dimension tables, which would then be joined to your fact tables (which are not mastered).

Use case

Let's go back to ShoesForLess, the retail chain where each store has its own customer database. The company collects the customer data from all of those databases into a data warehouse. Because some customers have purchased items from more than one retail location, the DW will include duplicates of some customer records.

If the customer's name is spelled exactly the same in both records, you can easily filter out duplicates. But if the name is misspelled or entered differently in one record (for example, if it contains a middle initial, a hyphen, or a suffix like *Junior* or *Senior* in one record but not the other), the filter will not recognize the names as duplicates. (These are called *near-duplicates*.)

If you don't implement MDM, the first time the end user receives a report from the DW, they will see the same customers showing up multiple times and will likely question the report's accuracy. You will have already lost their trust—and once you do, it is very difficult to win it back. MDM is the solution!

Data Virtualization and Data Federation

Data virtualization goes by several names; you might see it referred to as a *logical data warehouse*, *virtual data warehouse*, or *decentralized data warehouse*. It is a technology that allows you to access and combine data from various sources and formats by creating a logical view of the data without replicating or moving the actual data. It provides a single access point for all data, enabling real-time data integration and reducing the time and costs associated with traditional data integration approaches such as ETL or ELT (see Chapter 9).

Data federation and *data virtualization* are very similar terms that are often used interchangeably, and you are unlikely to get into trouble if you mix them up. However, there are subtle differences between the two. *Data federation* involves an umbrella organization consisting of smaller, fully or partially autonomous subset organizations that control all or part of their operations. (The US system of federal and state governments is a good example of a federation.) Like data virtualization, data federation creates a united view of data from multiple data sources. Data virtualization, however, is a broader concept that encompasses data federation as well as data transformation, caching, security, and governance.

The better data virtualization tools provide features that help with performance, such as query optimization, query pushdown, and caching. You may see tools with these features called *data virtualization* and tools without them called *data federation*.

Data virtualization can replace a data warehouse (see Chapter 4) or ETL/data movement. Let's look at how.

Virtualization as a replacement for the data warehouse

In some cases, especially when there are many data sources or they are changing constantly, data virtualization can be an alternative to a data warehouse. When you use this approach, there is no copying and storing of the data in a central location.

Figure 6-4 shows how most data virtualization products work. The grid (step 1) represents an end user's query results: a list of addresses. When the end user scrolls through the grid to see more data, the grid requests items that are currently not loaded from the data virtualization engine (step 2). If the engine has a cache of data available, it returns the cache immediately, and the grid simply updates to display the data. If you request data from outside the cache, the data virtualization engine passes the request to the remote data source (step 3), where it is processed. The newly fetched data is returned to the engine (step 4) and then passed to the grid. In both situations, the grid always remains completely responsive.

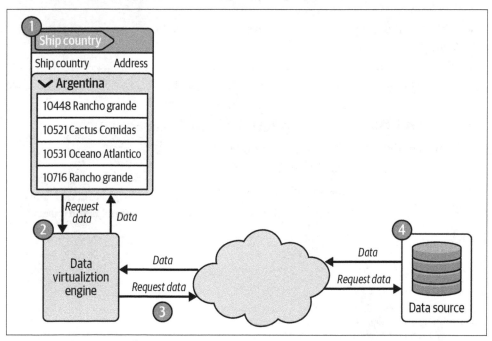

Figure 6-4. Data virtualization

The main advantage of a data virtualization solution is that it optimizes for speed to market. It can be built in a fraction of the time it takes to build a data warehouse, because you don't need to design and build a DW and ETL to copy the data into it and you don't need to spend as much time testing it. Copying the data (as with a DW) means higher storage and governance costs, more ETL flows to build and maintain, and more data inconsistencies, so using virtualization can save you a lot of money.

Data virtualization supports *federated queries,* in which you can issue a single query that retrieves data from multiple sources and formats and combines the results into a single result set.[1]

However, there are some major drawbacks to data virtualization and federated queries. If you're considering a data virtualization solution to replace your DW, I recommend you ask the following questions:

- What level of performance do I need? Is this a solution I could use for a dashboard that needs sub-second response times, or is it more for operational reporting?
- How much will the data virtualization solution affect the performance of the source system? Will my query run slowly if another end user runs a query against the same data source that consumes all the resources of the server? Does it push down the query?[2]
- Will I need to install something on every server that contains a data source I want to use?
- Does the solution use the index of each technology on the data source, or does it create its own indexes?[3] Does it use the database statistics from each data source for queries?[4]
- Can I restrict which users can access each data source for security purposes?
- How does the solution handle near-duplicates?
- Where and how will the data be cleaned?
- Will reports break if the source system is changed?
- What is the cost of the virtualization software, and how complex is it to use?

---

1 The difference between data federation and federated queries is that data federation is more about the system's architecture, while federated queries are the mechanism used to extract information from this system. In practice, if you have a data federation system in place, you are using federated queries to retrieve your data.

2 In data virtualization, the term *push-down query* refers to the capability to push certain parts of a query, such as filtering or aggregation, to the data sources themselves. This allows the data virtualization layer to offload processing tasks and retrieve only the relevant results. The benefits include enhancing performance and minimizing data transfer; the trade-off is that it uses compute resources on the server where the data source resides.

3 *Database indexes* are a type of data structure that improves the speed of data retrieval operations on a database table. They work much like book indexes, providing users a quick way to access the data they're seeking.

4 *Database statistics* are a set of information that a *database management system* (DBMS) maintains about the data stored in a database. These statistics help the DBMS optimize query performance by informing how it determines the most efficient way to execute a given query.

In addition to reasons uncovered with these questions, there are other valid rationales for using a physical data warehouse, as discussed in Chapter 4, such as a need to run accurate historical reports, rename tables, and keep historical data.

Virtualization as a replacement for ETL or data movement

If you're building a data warehouse, should you move all the source data into the data warehouse, or is it better to keep the source data where it is and create a virtualization layer on top of some of it?

The most common reason to move data is if you plan to aggregate or transform it once and then query the results many times. Another is if you will frequently be joining datasets from multiple sources and need super-fast performance. In these scenarios, I generally recommend data warehouse solutions.

However, at times, you might have ad hoc queries that don't need to be super fast. And you could certainly have a DW that uses data movement for some tables and data virtualization for others. Table 6-3 compares data movement and virtualization.

Table 6-3. Comparison of data movement and data virtualization

	Development and operations costs	Time to solution	Security	Data freshness and quality	Compliance
Data movement	Costly to build and maintain ELT jobs; duplicate data storage costs	Takes time to build and run jobs	Creating copies of the data makes it more vulnerable to hackers	ETL pipelines make the data "stale"; ETL can introduce data errors	Moving data in and out of compliance boundaries can cause data governance issues
Data virtualization	Reduces ongoing maintenance and change management; minimizes storage costs	Allows for rapid iterations and prototyping	Data is kept in one secure place, minimizing the attack surface	Data being queried is always "fresh" and accurate from the source	Having few copies of data and less movement helps meet compliance requirements

Data virtualization offers several benefits. First, it provides a comprehensive data lineage, ensuring you can clearly understand the data's path from its source to the presentation layer. Second, including additional data sources becomes seamless, eliminating the need to modify transformation packages or staging tables. Last, data virtualization software presents all data through a unified SQL interface. This allows users easy access regardless of the source, which could be flat files, spreadsheets, mainframes, relational databases, or other types of data repositories.

While Table 6-3 shows the benefits of data virtualization over data movement, those benefits may not be enough to overcome the sacrifice in performance and other drawbacks of not using a relational data warehouse, listed in Chapter 4. Also, keep in mind that the virtualization tool you choose may not support *all* of your data sources.

Here are some reasons you might choose data virtualization:

There are regulatory constraints on moving data
As you learned in "Compliance, governance, and security" in Chapter 5, Chinese data sovereignty regulations hold that data located in China has to stay in China and can only be queried by a person currently located there. But say you're in the United States and try to query customer data in China from your application. The application can retrieve metadata *about* the customer data in China, but it can't ingest that data. You could use virtualization software to keep the data within the country by letting only a person inside the country query it. Anyone outside China trying to query the data would either get an error message or just not see any results.

An end user outside the company wants to access customer data
Instead of you sending the user a copy of the data, they can use virtualization software to query it. This lets you control who accesses what data and know how much they've accessed.

There is reference data in a database outside the DW that changes frequently
Instead of copying that data into the DW again and again, you could use virtualization to query it when you're joining the external database's data with the DW data.

You want to query data from different data stores and join it together
Virtualization software usually supports many data sources (say, a data lake, relational database, and NoSQL database) and can handle this.

You want your users to do self-service analytics via a virtual sandbox
A *virtual sandbox* is a secure and isolated environment where users can explore, analyze, and manipulate data without affecting the underlying production data or systems. For example, say you're using a virtual sandbox to analyze both customer data and third-party data. Instead of copying that data into the virtual sandbox, you could use virtualization to query it *within* the virtual sandbox. This minimizes the number of copies made of the data, and you avoid having to create ETL.

You want to build a solution quickly to move source data
Instead of using a traditional ETL tool to copy the source data to a central location and then creating reports from that, you can just create reports by using the virtualization software. It will run queries against the source data and do the centralization automatically. This means you can build a solution a lot faster, since you don't have to use an ETL tool (which can be very time-consuming).

Data Catalogs

A *data catalog* is a centralized repository, typically housed in the cloud, that stores and organizes metadata about all of an organization's data sources, tables, schemas, columns, and other data assets such as reports and dashboards, ETL processes, and SQL scripts. It functions as a single source of truth for users to discover, understand, and manage data that is located in application databases, data lakes, relational data warehouses, operational data stores, data marts, and any other data storage form.

A data catalog typically includes the following information about each data asset:

- Information about the source, such as location, type, and connection details
- If within an RDW, table and schema information (such as structure, relationships, and organization) and column information (such as data types, formats, descriptions, and relationships between columns)
- If within an object store such as a data lake, file properties (storage, folder name, filename)
- Data lineage (how the data arrived from its origin), including information on any transformation, aggregation, and integration the data has undergone
- Data governance and compliance details, such as data quality, ownership, and policies
- Search and discovery tools for users to search, filter, and find relevant data

A data catalog helps you manage data more effectively by providing visibility into the data landscape. This, in turn, facilitates better collaboration between teams and more informed decision making. It also helps ensure data quality, security, and compliance by making it easier to track data lineage, enforce data policies, and maintain a clear understanding of data assets.

There are many products on the market for creating data catalogs, some of which have been around for nearly a decade. The most popular products are Informatica's Enterprise Data Catalog, Collibra Data Catalog, and Microsoft Purview. These products have additional functionalities such as data governance and compliance, business glossaries, and data quality metrics.

Data Marketplaces

A *data marketplace*, sometimes called a *data exchange*, is an online platform where data providers and data consumers come together to buy, sell, and exchange datasets.[5]

---

5 Sometimes, however, a data marketplace is internal to a company and is simply used to help its users find and exchange data.

These marketplaces are designed to help data consumers (like businesses, researchers, and developers) discover, evaluate, and purchase data for purposes such as analysis, machine learning, business intelligence, and decision making. Providers usually include organizations, governments, and individuals who have collected or generated valuable datasets.

A data marketplace typically includes a data catalog. Many marketplaces assess and improve the quality of datasets to ensure they are accurate, complete, consistent, and easy to use. Some provide tools and services for cleaning, transforming, and enriching data, which can save users time and effort in preparing it for analysis. (This is particularly valuable when you're integrating data from multiple sources or dealing with incomplete or inconsistent data.) Once a consumer makes a purchase, the marketplace may offer tools to help them access the data and integrate it into their workflows, applications, or systems. Some even allow users to customize datasets by combining data from multiple sources or filtering it based on specific criteria so they can access exactly the data they need.

Data marketplaces should have robust security measures in place to protect user data, ensure compliance with data protection regulations, and maintain the confidentiality of sensitive information. Some offer ways to easily obfuscate private or sensitive data. Data marketplaces' pricing structures and licensing agreements clearly define the terms of use and ensure legal compliance for both data providers and consumers.

Many data marketplaces also offer built-in analytics and data visualization tools that allow you to analyze and visualize (or simply preview) data directly within the platform. Other common features and tools include:

- Ratings and reviews of datasets
- Recommendations for other datasets you might like
- Shopper profiles for easy reordering, favorites lists, and so on
- Collaboration and community
- Training and support

From the providers' perspective, data marketplaces offer a way to monetize data assets, generating new revenue streams. This can be particularly beneficial for organizations that collect large amounts of data but don't have the resources or expertise to analyze and monetize it themselves.

Data marketplaces have increased in popularity as the demand for data-driven insights grows and more diverse datasets continue to become available. There are not nearly as many products available for creating data marketplaces as there are for data catalogs, since marketplaces just started appearing in the early 2020s. The most popular are Snowflake Marketplace, Datarade, and Informatica's Cloud Data Marketplace. Both providers and consumers can benefit from a more efficient and transparent exchange of data, which can foster innovation of new data-driven products and services.

Summary

This chapter explored various approaches to data stores, all of which play pivotal roles in today's data-driven business environment.

I discussed data storage, including data marts, operational data stores, and data hubs, and then shifted the focus to processes. Master data management (MDM) is a crucial approach that focuses on managing core business entities to ensure data accuracy, uniformity, and consistency across multiple systems and processes. I then moved on to discuss data virtualization, data catalogs, and data marketplaces.

By understanding these different strategies and their functionalities, you can better align your data architecture to your organization's needs and drive more significant business value from your data.

CHAPTER 7

Approaches to Design

This chapter explores design approaches to handling and organizing data and how these methods help build powerful, adaptable, and reliable systems for data management. In simple terms, we'll learn about the strategies that help us decide how data should be stored, processed, and accessed to best enhance the speed and dependability of our data systems.

To clarify, let's distinguish between data design and data modeling, which is the subject of Chapter 8. Think of *data design* as like building a city. It's about deciding where the buildings go, which roads connect different parts of the city, and how traffic flows. On the other hand, *data modeling* is more like designing individual buildings— it's about arranging rooms, deciding how they connect, and defining the purpose of each room.

In this chapter, we'll look at different types of data designs. We'll compare and contrast methods like OLTP and OLAP, which are essentially different ways of processing and analyzing data. We'll also explore concepts like SMP and MPP, which are strategies to process data more efficiently. Then, we'll learn about Lambda and Kappa architectures, which are blueprints for handling large amounts of data in real time. Lastly, we'll talk about an approach called polyglot persistence, which allows us to use different types of data storage technologies within the same application.

My aim here isn't to push one approach as the best solution for every situation but to help you understand the strengths and weaknesses of each. This way, you can choose or combine the right methods based on your specific needs. By the end of this chapter, you'll have a stronger grasp of how to create efficient data systems that can adapt to changing needs and technological advancements.

Online Transaction Processing Versus Online Analytical Processing

Online transaction processing (OLTP) is a type of informational system or application that processes online create, read, update, and delete (CRUD) transactions (see Chapter 2) in a real-time environment. OLTP systems are designed to support high levels of concurrency, which means they can handle a large number of transactions at the same time. They typically use a relational model (see Chapter 8) and are optimized for low latency, which means they can process transactions very quickly. Examples include point-of-sale applications, ecommerce websites, and online banking solutions.

In an OLTP system, transactions are typically processed quickly and in a very specific way. For example, a customer's purchase at a store would be considered a transaction. The transaction would involve the customer's account being debited for the purchase amount, the store's inventory count being reduced, and the store's financial records being updated to reflect the sale. OLTP systems use a variety of DBMSs to store and manage the data, such as Microsoft SQL Server and Oracle.

OLTP systems are often contrasted with *online analytical processing* (OLAP) systems, which are used for data analysis and reporting to support business intelligence and decision making. OLAP systems are optimized for fast query performance, allowing end users to easily and quickly analyze data from multiple perspectives by slicing and dicing the data in reports and dashboards much faster than with an OLTP system. Think of an OLAP system as "write-once, read-many" (as opposed to CRUD). Often, multiple OLTP databases are used as the sources that feed into a data warehouse, which then feeds into an OLAP database, as shown in Figure 7-1. (However, sometimes you can also build an OLAP database directly from OLTP sources.)

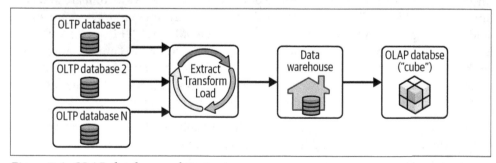

Figure 7-1. OLAP database architecture

An OLAP database is typically composed of one or more OLAP cubes. An *OLAP cube* is where data is pre-aggregated by the cube, meaning that it has already been summarized and grouped by certain dimensions; end users can quickly access it from multiple dimensions and levels of detail without having to wait for long-running queries to complete. Creating an OLAP cube generally involves using a *multidimensional model*, which uses a star or snowflake schema to represent the data. (Chapter 8 will discuss these schemas in more detail.)

For example, a retail corporation might use an OLAP database with OLAP cubes to quickly analyze sales data. This pre-aggregated data is organized by time, allowing for the analysis of sales trends, whether yearly or daily or anywhere in between. The data is also sorted by location, which facilitates geographic comparisons to look at, for example, product sales in different cities. Furthermore, the data is categorized by product, making it easier to track the performance of individual items. If a regional manager needs to quickly review how a particular product category performed in their region during the last holiday season, the OLAP cube has already prepared the data. Instead of waiting for a lengthy query to sort through each individual sale, the manager finds the relevant data—sorted by product, region, and time—is readily available, accelerating the decision-making process.

You can use another, more recent model, called a *tabular data model*, that gives similarly fast query performance as an OLAP cube. Instead of a multidimensional model, a tabular data model uses a tabular structure, similar to a relational database table, to represent the data. This makes it more flexible and simpler than a multidimensional model. This book refers to the multidimensional model as an "OLAP cube" and the tabular model as a "tabular cube," but please note that the term *cube* is used interchangeably in the industry to denote either of these models.

Table 7-1 compares the OLTP and OLAP design styles.

Table 7-1. Comparison of OLTP and OLAP systems

	OLTP	OLAP/Tabular
Processing type	Transactional	Analytical
Data nature	Operational data	Consolidation data
Orientation	Application oriented	Subject oriented
Purpose	Works on ongoing business tasks	Helps in decision making
Transaction frequency	Frequent transactions	Occasional transactions
Operation types	Short online transactions: Insert, Update, Delete	Lots of read scans
Data design	Normalized database (3NF)	Denormalized database
Common usage	Used in retail sales and other financial transactions systems	Often used in data mining, sales, and marketing
Response time	Response time is instant	Response time varies from seconds to hours
Query complexity	Simple and instant queries	Complex queries
Usage pattern	Repetitive usage	Ad hoc usage
Transaction nature	Short, simple transactions	Complex queries
Database size	Gigabyte database size	Terabyte database size

OLAP databases and data warehouses (see Chapter 4) are related but distinct concepts and are often used in conjunction. Through a multidimensional or tabular model, OLAP databases provide a way to analyze the data stored in the DW in a way that is more flexible and interactive than executing traditional SQL-based queries on a DW that contains large amounts of data. Multidimensional models and tabular models are often considered *semantic* layers or models, which means that they provide a level of abstraction over the schemas in the DW.

Operational and Analytical Data

Operational data is real-time data used to manage day-to-day operations and processes. It is captured, stored, and processed by OLTP systems. You can use it to take a "snapshot" of the current state of the business to ensure that operations are running smoothly and efficiently. Operational data tends to be high volume and helps in making decisions quickly.

Analytical data comes from collecting and transforming operational data. It is a historical view of the data maintained and used by OLAP/Tabular systems and DWs. With data analytics tools, you can perform analysis to understand trends, patterns, and relationships over time. Analytical data is optimized for creating reports and visualizations and for training machine learning models. It usually provides a view of data over a longer period than you get with operational data, often has a lower volume, and is generally consolidated and aggregated. Data is usually ingested in batches and requires more processing time than operational data.

In summary, operational data is used to monitor and control business processes in real time, while analytical data is used to gain insights and inform decision making over a longer period. Both types of data are essential for effective business management, and they complement each other to provide a complete view of an organization's operations and performance.

Think of OLTP as the technology used to implement operational data, and of OLAP/Tabular and DWs as the technology used to implement analytical data.

Symmetric Multiprocessing and Massively Parallel Processing

Some of the first relational databases used a *symmetric multiprocessing* (SMP) design, where computer processing is done by multiple processors that share disk and memory, all in one server—think SQL Server and Oracle. (This is pictured on the left side of Figure 7-2.) To get more processing power for these systems, you "scale up" by increasing the processors and memory in the server. This works well for OLTP databases but not so well for the write-once, read-many environment of a DW.

As data warehouses grew in popularity in the 1990s and started to ingest huge amounts of data, performance became a big problem. To help with that, along came a new kind of database design. In a *massively parallel processing* (MPP) design, the database has multiple servers, each with multiple processors, and (unlike in SMP) each processor has its own memory and its own disk. This allows you to "scale out" (rather than up) by adding more servers.

MPP servers distribute a portion of the data from the database to the disk on each server (whereas SMP databases keep all the data on one disk). Queries are then sent to a *control node* (also called a *name node*) that splits each query into multiple subqueries that are sent to each server (called a *compute node* or *worker node*), as shown on the right in Figure 7-2. There, the subquery is executed and the results from each compute node are sent back to the control node, mashed together, and sent back to the user. This is how solutions such as Teradata and Netezza work.

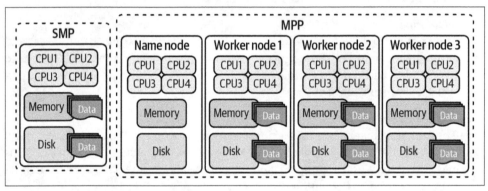

Figure 7-2. SMP and MPP database designs

By way of analogy, imagine your friend Fiona has a deck of 52 cards and is looking for the ace of hearts. It takes Fiona about 15 seconds, on average, to find the card. You can "scale up" by replacing Fiona with another friend, Max, who is faster. Using Max brings the average time down to 10 seconds—a limited improvement. This is how SMP databases work.

Now imagine you "scale out" instead of up, by replacing Fiona with 26 people, each of whom has only two cards. Now the average time to find the card is just 1 second. That's how MPP databases work.

SMP and MPP databases started as on-prem solutions, and these are still prevalent today, but there are now many equivalent solutions in the cloud.

Lambda Architecture

Lambda architecture is a data-processing architecture designed to handle massive quantities of data by using both batch and real-time stream processing methods. The idea is to get comprehensive and accurate views of the batch data and to balance latency, throughput, scaling, and fault tolerance by using batch processing, while simultaneously using real-time stream processing to provide views of online data (such as IoT devices, Twitter feeds, or computer log files). You can join the two view outputs before the presentation/serving layer.

Lambda architecture bridges the gap between the historical "single source of truth" and the highly sought after "I want it now" real-time solution by combining traditional batch processing systems with stream consumption tools to meet both needs.

The Lambda architecture has three key principles:

Dual data model
> The Lambda architecture uses one model for batch processing (batch layer) and another model for real-time processing (stream layer). This allows the system to handle both batch and real-time data and to perform both types of processing in scalable and fault-tolerant ways.

Single unified view
> The Lambda architecture uses a single unified view (called the *presentation layer*) to present the results of both batch and real-time processing to end users. This allows the user to see a complete and up-to-date view of the data, even though it's being processed by two different systems.

Decoupled processing layers
> The Lambda architecture decouples the batch and real-time processing layers so that they can be scaled independently and developed and maintained separately, allowing for flexibility and ease of development.

Figure 7-3 depicts a high-level overview of the Lambda architecture.

On the left of Figure 7-3 is the *data consumption layer*. This is where you import the data from all source systems. Some sources may be streaming the data, while others only provide data daily or hourly.

In the top middle, you see the *stream layer*, also called the *speed layer*. It provides for incremental updating, making it the more complex of the two middle layers. It trades accuracy for low latency, looking at only recent data. The data in here may be only seconds behind, but the trade-off is that it might not be clean. Data in this layer is usually stored in a data lake.

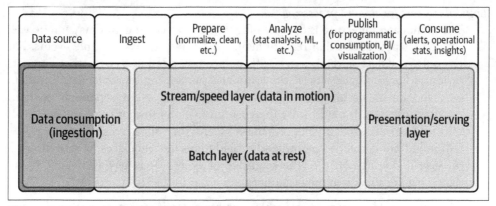

Figure 7-3. Overview of Lambda architecture

Beneath that is the *batch layer*, which looks at all the data at once and eventually corrects the data that comes into the stream layer. It is the single source of truth, the trusted layer. Here there's usually lots of ETL, and data is stored in a traditional data warehouse or data lake. This layer is built using a predefined schedule, usually daily or hourly, and including importing the data currently stored in the stream layer.

At the right of Figure 7-3 is the *presentation layer*, also called the *serving layer*. Think of it as a mediator; when it accepts queries, it decides when to use the batch layer and when to use the speed layer. It generally defaults to the batch layer, since that has the trusted data, but if you ask it for up-to-the-second data (perhaps by setting alerts for certain log messages that indicate a server is down), it will pull from the stream layer. This layer has to balance retrieving the data you can trust with retrieving the data you want right now.

The Lambda architecture is an excellent choice for building distributed systems that need to handle both batch and real-time data, like recommendation engines and fraud detection systems. However, that doesn't mean it's the best choice for every situation. Some potential drawbacks of the Lambda architecture include:

Complexity
    The Lambda architecture includes a dual data model and a single unified view. That can be more complex to implement and maintain than other architectures.

Limited real-time processing
    The Lambda architecture is designed for both batch and real-time processing, but it may not be as efficient at handling high volumes of real-time data as the Kappa architecture (discussed in the next section), which is specifically designed for real-time processing.

Limited support for stateful processing

The Lambda architecture is designed for stateless processing and may not be well suited for applications that require maintaining state across multiple events. For example, consider a retail store with a recommendation system that suggests products based on customers' browsing and purchasing patterns. If this system used a Lambda architecture, which processes each event separately without maintaining state, it could miss the customer's shopping journey and intent. If the customer browses for shoes, then socks, and then shoe polish, a stateless system might not correctly recommend related items like shoelaces or shoe storage, because it doesn't consider the sequence of events. It might also recommend items that are already in the customer's cart.

Overall, you should consider the Lambda architecture if you need to build a distributed system that can handle both batch and real-time data but needs to provide a single unified view of the data. If you need stateful processing or to handle high volumes of real-time data, you may want to consider the Kappa architecture.

Kappa Architecture

As opposed to the Lambda architecture, which is designed to handle both real-time and batch data, Kappa is designed to handle just real-time data. And like the Lambda architecture, Kappa architecture is also designed to handle high levels of concurrency and high volumes of data. Figure 7-4 provides a high-level overview of the Kappa architecture.

The three key principles of the Kappa architecture are:

Real-time processing

The Kappa architecture is designed for real-time processing, which means that events are processed as soon as they are received rather than being batch processed later. This decreases latency and enables the system to respond quickly to changing conditions.

Single event stream

The Kappa architecture uses a single event stream to store all data that flows through the system. This allows for easy scalability and fault tolerance, since the data can be distributed easily across multiple nodes.

Stateless processing

In the Kappa architecture, all processing is stateless. This means that each event is processed independently, without relying on the state of previous events. This makes it easier to scale the system, because there is no need to maintain state across multiple nodes.

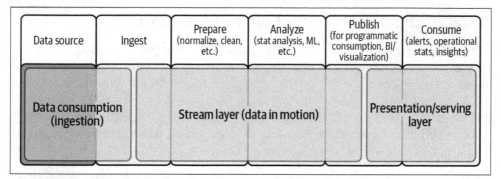

Data source	Ingest	Prepare (normalize, clean, etc.)	Analyze (stat analysis, ML, etc.)	Publish (for programmatic consumption, BI/ visualization)	Consume (alerts, operational stats, insights)
Data consumption (ingestion)		Stream layer (data in motion)			Presentation/serving layer

Figure 7-4. Overview of Kappa architecture

The layers in the Kappa architecture are exactly the same as in the Lamba architecture, except that the Kappa architecture does not have a batch layer.

Some potential drawbacks of the Kappa architecture include:

Complexity
The Kappa architecture involves a single event stream and stateless processing, which can be more complex to implement and maintain than other architectures.

Limited batch processing
The Kappa architecture is designed for real-time processing and does not easily support batch processing of historical data. If you need to perform batch processing, you may want to consider the Lambda architecture instead.

Limited support for ad-hoc queries
Because the Kappa architecture is designed for real-time processing, it may not be well suited for ad hoc queries that need to process large amounts of historical data.

Overall, the Kappa architecture is an excellent choice for building distributed systems that need to handle large amounts of data in real time and that need to be scalable, fault tolerant, and have low latency. Examples include streaming platforms and financial trading systems. However, if you need to perform batch processing or support ad hoc queries, then the Lambda architecture may be a better choice.

Note that the Lambda and Kappa architectures are high-level design patterns that can be implemented within any of the data architectures described in Part III of this book. If you use one of those architectures to build a solution that supports both batch and real-time data, then that architecture supports the Lambda architecture; if you use one of those architectures to build a solution that supports only real-time data, that architecture supports the Kappa architecture.

Polyglot Persistence and Polyglot Data Stores

Polyglot persistence is a fancy term that means using multiple data storage technologies to store different types of data *within a single application or system*, based upon how the data will be used. Different kinds of data are best kept in different data stores. In short, polyglot persistence means picking the right tool for the right use case. It's the same idea as the one behind polyglot programming (*https://oreil.ly/eowsh*), in which applications are written in a mix of languages to take advantage of different languages' strengths in tackling different problems.

By contrast, a *polyglot data store* means using multiple data stores *across an organization or enterprise*. Each data store is optimized for a specific type of data or use case. This approach allows organizations to use different data stores for different projects or business units, rather than a one-size-fits-all approach for the entire organization.

For example, say you're building an ecommerce platform that will deal with many types of data (shopping carts, inventory, completed orders, and so forth). Instead of trying to store all the different types of data in one database, which would require a lot of conversion, you could take a polyglot persistence approach and store each kind of data in the database best suited for it. So, an ecommerce platform might look like the diagram in Figure 7-5.

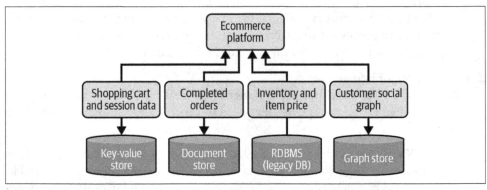

Figure 7-5. An ecommerce platform with a polyglot persistence design

This results in the best tool being used for each type of data. In Figure 7-5, you can see that the database uses a key-value store for shopping cart and session data (giving very fast retrieval), a document store for completed orders (making storing and retrieving order data fast and easy), an RDBMS for inventory and item prices (since those are best stored in a relational database due to the structured nature of the data), and a graph store for customer social graphs (since it's very difficult to store graph data in a non-graph store).

This will come at a cost in complexity, since each data storage solution means learning a new technology. But the benefits will be worth it. For instance, if you try to use relational databases for non-relational data, the design can significantly slow application development and performance; using the appropriate storage type pays off in speed.

Summary

This chapter explored the architectural concepts and design philosophies that form the basis of effective data systems.

First, you learned about the two primary types of data processing systems: online transaction processing (OLTP) and online analytical processing (OLAP). OLTP systems are designed for fast, reliable, short transactions, typically in the operational databases that power daily business operations. In contrast, OLAP systems support complex analytical queries, aggregations, and computations used for strategic decision making, typically in a data warehouse. You then learned about the differences between operational and analytical data.

You also learned the differences between symmetric multiprocessing (SMP) and massively parallel processing (MPP) architectures. We then delved into two modern big data–processing architectures: Lambda and Kappa. Last, we explored the concepts of polyglot persistence and polyglot data stores, which promote using the best-suited database technology for the specific needs and workload characteristics of the given data.

Starting with the next chapter, our focus will shift from data storage and processing to the principles and practices of data modeling: the crucial bridge between raw data and meaningful insights. The approaches to data modeling, such as relational and dimensional approaches and the common data model, serve as an underpinning structure that allows you to use and interpret data efficiently across diverse applications.

As we delve into these topics, you'll see how data modeling lets you use the storage and processing solutions we've studied efficiently, serving as a blueprint for transforming raw data into actionable insights.

CHAPTER 8

Approaches to Data Modeling

Data modeling is a high-level conceptual technique used to design a database. There are several different types of data modeling, including relational modeling and dimensional modeling. The process involves identifying the data that needs to be stored, then creating a structured representation of that data and the relationships among the data, organized into tables and columns. Think of the tables and columns as the *logical* representation of the database, where the *physical* data stored in those tables and columns can be in a relational database product or a data lake.

You can use data modeling with any type of database: relational, dimensional, NoSQL, and so on. I recommend dedicating a lot of time to data modeling to ensure that your database is logical, efficient, and easy to use. This ensures maximum performance and makes it easier to retrieve and analyze data.

Relational Modeling

Relational modeling, developed by Edgar F. Codd in 1970 (as mentioned in Chapter 2), is a detailed modeling technique used to design a database. It involves organizing the data into tables and defining the relationships between the tables. In relational databases and relational data warehouses, each table consists of rows (also called records or tuples) and columns (also called fields or attributes). Each row represents a unique instance of the data, and each column represents a specific piece of information about the data.

Keys

In relational modeling, you define relationships between tables, rows, and columns using primary keys and foreign keys. A *primary key* is a unique identifier for each record in a table, ensuring that no two rows of data have the same key value. A *foreign key* is a column in a table that refers to the primary key in another table. It's used to establish a relationship between the two tables in order to ensure the integrity of the data. For example, you might have a unique key in a product table called `ProductKey` that refers to a foreign key in a sales facts table called `ProductKey`. A *natural key* is a field that already exists in a table and is unique to each row, such as a person's Social Security number or a product's serial number. In relational modeling, a natural key is usually used as the primary key.

Entity–Relationship Diagrams

Usually, you start relational modeling with an *entity–relationship* (ER) diagram: a high-level visual structure of the database that represents the entities (data) and the relationships between them. It uses boxes for the entities and connecting lines for the relationships. Figure 8-1 shows an example of an ER diagram. Once that is complete, you can build a more detailed relational model that represents the actual tables and columns of a database.

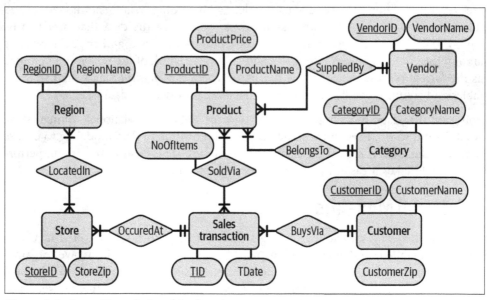

Figure 8-1. An entity–relationship diagram

Normalization Rules and Forms

Next, you apply *normalization rules*, which are a way of decomposing a complex database into smaller, simpler tables. This minimizes redundancy and dependency, improves data integrity, and makes the database more efficient and easier to maintain and manage. You do this by applying progressing levels of normalization.

A table is in *first normal form* (1NF) if it satisfies all of the following conditions:

- The table has a primary key. For example, in a `Students` table, `StudentID` could be the primary key.
- Each attribute in the table contains a single value, not a list of values. For example, in the `Students` table, each column (attribute), like `Name`, holds a single value.
- The table has no repeating groups of columns. For example, in the `Students` table, you should not have multiple "Course" columns, such as `Course1`, `Course2`, and `Course3`. Instead, each student–course pairing should have its own row.

A table is in *second normal form* (2NF) if it satisfies all of the above 1NF conditions, plus:

- Every detail (non-key attribute) in the database record must rely entirely on its unique identifier (primary key) and not on any other detail. For example, in a `Students` table with `StudentID`, `Name`, and `Major` columns, the student's `Major` (non-key attribute) must be determined solely by the `StudentID` (primary key), not by the `Name` or any other attribute in the table.

A table is in *third normal form* (3NF) if and only if it satisfies all of the above 1NF and 2NF conditions, plus:

- Every non-key detail in the table should relate directly to the main identifier (primary key) and not through another detail. For example, in a `Students` table with `StudentID`, `Major`, and `DepartmentHead` (where `DepartmentHead` is the head of the `Major`), the `DepartmentHead` should not depend on the `Major`, which in turn should not depend on the `StudentID`.

Most relational models, especially for OLTP databases (see Chapter 7), are in 3NF. That should be your ultimate goal.

A relational model uses a *normalized database schema*, in which data is stored in one place and organized into multiple tables with strictly defined relationships between them. This helps to ensure integrity, but it can also make querying more time-consuming, because the database will likely need to join multiple tables together in order to retrieve the desired data.

Figure 8-2 shows what a relational model for sales data might look like.

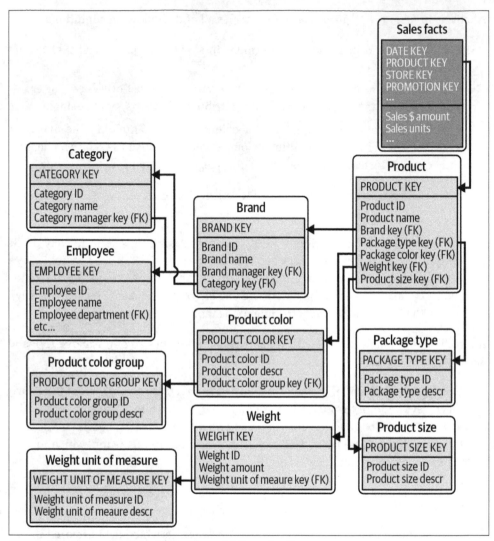

Figure 8-2. Example of a relational model for sales data

Tracking Changes

It's important to track changes to relationally modeled data over time. To maintain a record of past data and changes, history tables are often used. A *history table* is typically a copy of the original table with additional columns added to track changes, such as a date/time stamp, a user ID, and a "before" and "after" value for each column in the table. History tables can be useful for auditing, reporting, and data recovery, helping to ensure the integrity of the data and making it easier to understand how it has changed over time.

Dimensional Modeling

Dimensional modeling started in 1996 as a way to support efficient querying and analysis by organizing data into facts and dimensions. Dimensional models are needed when querying and reporting off the relational model becomes too slow or complex. Dimensional models typically use a relational model as a data source.

Facts, Dimensions, and Keys

Dimensional models use *facts* and *dimensions*:

Facts
> *Facts*, in this context, are pieces of data, typically numeric values, used to measure something, such as sales, orders, or revenue. Facts can be aggregated or summarized for performance reasons, such as by calculating averages or counting records, so that these values are already calculated and don't have to be calculated as part of running the query.

Dimensions
> *Dimensions* describe the data's characteristics, such as time, product, customer, or location. They are typically represented as hierarchies, with each level of the hierarchy providing a more detailed description of the data.

Another way to understand dimensional models is to remember that fact tables contain metrics, while dimension tables contain *attributes* of the metrics in the fact tables.

Instead of the natural keys used in relational modeling, dimensional modeling uses *surrogate keys*: artificial values created specifically (and usually automatically) to serve as the primary key for a table. A surrogate key is often used when a natural key is not available or is not suitable for use as the primary key, which happens frequently in dimensional modeling.

Natural keys are often more meaningful and easier to understand than surrogate keys, so they can make the database easier to use and maintain. However, there are also some drawbacks to using natural keys:

- They can be longer and more complex than surrogate keys and thus more challenging to work with.

- They often contain sensitive information, which can raise privacy concerns.

- They can create challenges due to potential duplication and non-standardized formats. For example, if you are using customer IDs as the natural key and your company purchases another company that uses matching customer IDs or a different format (such as characters instead of integers), conflicts can arise. The underlying principle here is that duplicates can be an issue when merging or comparing data across different systems, and inconsistency in formats can further complicate the integration process.

Tracking Changes

To track changes made to a table in dimensional modeling, you'll use *slowly changing dimensions* (SCDs), of which there are three types:

Type 1

Type 1 SCDs overwrite existing data with the new data and discard the old data. This is the simplest and most common type of SCD, and it is often used when the changes to the data are not significant or when the old data is no longer needed, such as when correcting a customer's phone number.

Type 2

Type 2 SCDs maintain multiple versions of the data: the new data and a record of the old data. Use this type of SCD when you need to track the changes to the data over time and maintain a record of the old data. For example, let's say that six months ago, a company analyzed its sales data and found New York to be its top-selling state. Now, if some customers have since moved out of New York to New Jersey, rerunning the same report without accounting for these changes would show inaccurately lower sales figures for New York. This would lead to a mistaken perception of historical data showing declining sales in New York, which could influence strategic decisions. So, if a customer moves from one US state to another, the company's Type 2 SCD would store both the old state and the new one.

Type 3

Type 3 SCDs create a new record for each change so you can maintain a complete history of the data. This type of SCD is the most complex but also the most flexible. For example, when a customer moves from one US state to another, a Type 3 SCD would store the entire old record and an entire new record, which could include dozens of fields and not just the US state field.

One key difference between history tables in relational modeling and SCDs is their level of detail. History tables track changes to the data at the level of individual records, while SCDs track changes at the dimension level. And while history tables are typically used to track changes to any type of data, SCDs are specifically for tracking changes to dimension tables in a dimensional model.

Figure 8-3 shows a dimensional model for sales, derived from the relational model in Figure 8-2.

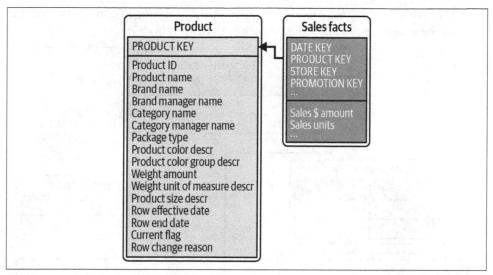

Figure 8-3. A dimensional model for sales data

Denormalization

Dimensional models use a process called *denormalization*, where you include redundant copies of the data in multiple tables. This reduces the number of tables. When you query the database, it does not need to join as many tables together, so querying is much faster. Less joining also reduces complexity for end users creating reports. However, it means that the redundant copies of data must be kept in sync to ensure integrity, and that requires careful maintenance. The redundant data also uses more storage, which may slightly increase costs.

In Figure 8-3, you can see that `CategoryName` is included in the list of product keys. As a result, the category name is repeated in all product records. By contrast, in the relational model in Figure 8-2, the product records show the `CategoryID`. In the dimensional model, if the category name were to change, you would need to change the name in multiple records in the product table; in the relational model, you would just need to change it once (in the Category table).

The more tables you have in a relational model, the more useful a dimensional model will be. If you only have a handful of tables in the relational model, you might not need a dimensional model.

A *database schema* is a logical blueprint that outlines the structure, relationships, constraints, and other elements of how data is organized and related within a database. Many types of schemas are used in dimensional modeling, such as snowflake schemas and schemas with multiple fact tables. A *star schema* is a dimensional modeling technique with a central fact table surrounded by multiple dimension tables. The diagram of the schema looks like a star (Figure 8-4), hence the name.

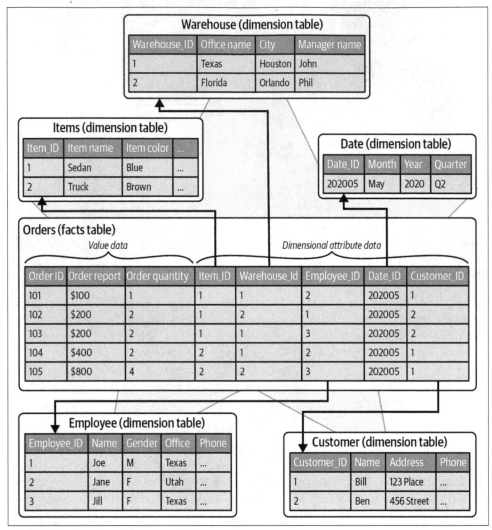

Figure 8-4. Example of a star schema

In summary, a relational model captures a business solution for how part of the business works, while a dimensional model captures the details the business needs to answer questions about how well the business is doing. The relational model is easier to build if the source system is already relational, but the dimensional model is easier for business users to employ and will generally perform better for analytic queries.

Common Data Model

A *common data model* (CDM) is a standardized structure for storing and organizing data that is typically used when building a data warehouse solution. It provides a consistent way to represent data within tables and relationships between tables, making it easy for any system or application to understand the data.

Imagine you have many source systems from which you want to import data into your DW. Some are customer relationship management (CRM) applications from different vendors that have different formats (that is, the tables and fields are different). You have to decide what table format to use in the data warehouse. Do you pick one of the CRM vendors' models? No. It's better to create a new model that can handle all those vendors' formats.

This new model (Figure 8-5) is your common data model. Building it will require a lot of work, but if you do it right, your CDM will be able to support current and future data from any CRM vendor. Fortunately, you don't have to build it from scratch. Many cloud providers and software vendors have very robust CDMs tailored for industries such as banking, healthcare, and retail. If you can customize a premade model, you'll save yourself many hours of modeling, reduce risk, and enable all the applications in your organization to access data using a common language.

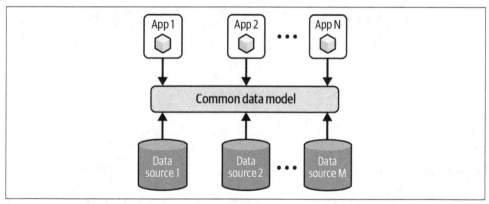

Figure 8-5. The common data model architecture

Data Vault

Created by Daniel Linstedt in 2000, *data vault modeling* is an entire methodology specifically designed for use in data warehousing and business intelligence systems. Its main goal is to provide a flexible, scalable, and standardized way to model and manage historical data.

A data vault model (shown in Figure 8-6) is built around three kinds of entities:

Hubs

Hubs are the central *business entities* in the model, representing key business concepts such as customers or products. Hubs are typically modeled as a single table with a unique identifier (such as a primary key) and a set of attributes.

Links

Links model the *relationships* between hubs, typically as a separate table. A link table contains a set of foreign keys that reference the primary keys of the related hubs.

Satellites

Satellites store *descriptive attributes* about a hub or link, such as changes to the data over time. They are typically modeled as separate tables and linked to a hub or link table through a foreign key.

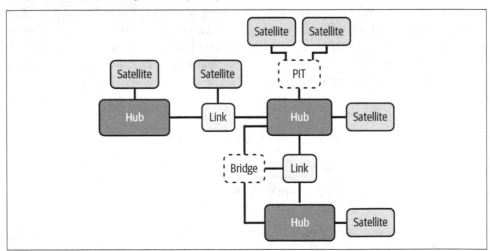

Figure 8-6. Data vault

Data vault–based models let you track data lineage, audit data, and enforce rules and standards. They are often used in conjunction with other data-modeling techniques, such as dimensional modeling, to provide a comprehensive and flexible data architecture that can be integrated easily with other systems and applications. On the spectrum of models we've looked at so far, the data vault fits somewhere between 3NF data and a star schema; it is well suited for organizations with large amounts of data and complex data relationships, while the Kimball model (discussed in "Kimball's Bottom-Up Methodology" on page 115) is better for organizations with simpler data needs.

Some of the main disadvantages of the data vault methodology include:

Complexity
> Data vault modeling can be complex to implement and maintain, especially for organizations that are not familiar with the technique. It requires a significant investment of resources and expertise, and understanding and navigating the data model can be difficult without proper documentation.

Data duplication
> Data vault modeling often leads to duplication, since data is stored at the atomic level. This can increase storage costs and make it more difficult to ensure data consistency.

Performance
> Data vault modeling can result in a large number of tables and relationships, which can degrade query performance. You may need to use more complex queries and indexing strategies to achieve acceptable performance.

Lack of standardization
> Data vault modeling is a relatively new and little-used technique, and it lacks a standardized approach. Finding engineers to build and maintain it can be challenging.

The Kimball and Inmon Data Warehousing Methodologies

Bill Inmon is considered the "father of data warehousing" because of his early pioneering work in the data warehousing field in the late 1980s. He wrote the first book on data warehousing in 1992 and played a significant role in popularizing and advancing the concept.[1] Inmon's approach to data warehousing is often characterized as a top-down approach to data marts that uses relational modeling.

---

1 Inmon likely first coined the term *data warehouse* around 1985; his *Building the Data Warehouse* (Wiley, 1992, available via the Internet Archive (*https://oreil.ly/DkEV-*)) was the first book on the topic. However, Barry Devlin and Paul Murphy published the first detailed architectural description of the data warehouse as we know it today: "An Architecture for a Business and Information System" (*https://oreil.ly/M50Xo*), *IBM Systems Journal*, 1988 (available via 9sight Consulting (*https://oreil.ly/g4NIX*)).

The terms *top-down* and *bottom-up* here have nothing to do with the top-down and bottom-up approaches for relational data warehouses and data lakes described in Chapters 4 and 5. Those approaches are related to the work done up front (or not) in building a data architecture that includes an RDW and a data lake. The Kimball and Inmon approaches are instead mainly focused on how data marts are used in building a data architecture that includes only an RDW and not a data lake (among other details).

Ralph Kimball, another early pioneer in data warehousing, popularized the star schema in data warehouse design with his first book, *The Data Warehouse Toolkit: Practical Techniques for Building Dimensional Data Warehouses* (Wiley, 1996). Kimball's approach is often characterized as a bottom-up approach, and it is also called *dimensional modeling* or the *Kimball methodology*.

Inmon's and Kimball's methodologies for building a data warehouse have sparked years of debates. This section will discuss both in more detail and dispel some common myths.

Inmon's Top-Down Methodology

Inmon's methodology emphasizes integrating data from multiple sources and presenting it in ways that aid in decision making. The top-down approach is a traditional, rigorous, and well-defined methodology, and it is often preferred in large and complex organizations that have a lot of data and value governance, data quality, and regulatory compliance. It is driven mainly by the technology department; end users participate passively.

This architecture, pictured in Figure 8-7, first pulls data from each of the OLTP source systems (see Chapter 7) into temporary relational staging tables as quickly as possible, without transforming or cleaning it.

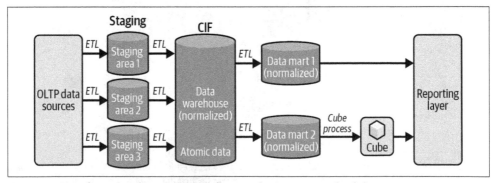

Figure 8-7. A data warehouse designed using the Inmon methodology

Transforming data can greatly increase CPU and bandwidth on source systems, so this approach avoids slowing down the source systems. Staging tables are also useful for auditing purposes, and if you need to rerun the transformations, you can pull the data from them instead of going back to the source system.

In the next step, data is copied into what Inmon calls a *corporate information factory* (CIF), where all the data is centralized and stored at the atomic level (as granular as possible) in third normal form. You can think of it as an enterprise data warehouse (EDW) that is a single version of the truth. I use the term *enterprise data warehouse* in this section over just *data warehouse*, as most solutions built in the early years of data warehousing incorporated data from all areas of an organization. Nowadays some companies will have multiple data warehouses, but more commonly solutions are built using just one "enterprise" data warehouse.

The CIF is focused on data modeling and design, with a strong emphasis on governance and data quality. From it, you can create *dependent data marts*: separate physical subsets of data, usually created to give each department the specific data it needs. The data marts are called "dependent" because they depend on data from the CIF and do not get any data from anywhere else. This is also called a *hub-and-spoke* architecture (for its shape). Users can query the data marts for reports, or query subsets— small dimensional models called *cubes* (see Chapter 7)—for specific purposes. For instance, analysts might only need to see sales volumes. The data in a cube is often aggregated.

Inmon's methodology is called "top-down" because it starts with identifying the business needs of the end users. Data modeling and design come next, then integrating and populating the data, and finally access and reporting. All data is centralized in a CIF, and then subsets are copied to subject-oriented data marts.

The CIF is off-limits to end users, who access data through the data marts or cubes. One drawback is that this means the data is permanently duplicated up to three times for the CIF, the data mart, and the cube. This results in higher storage costs, greater maintenance complexity, and the challenge of keeping all three copies synchronized.

Kimball's Bottom-Up Methodology

Kimball's "bottom-up" or "agile" methodology starts similarly to Inmon's, by pulling raw data from each of the OLTP source systems (see Chapter 7) into temporary relational staging tables with no transforming or cleaning. The Kimball methodology then moves into a phase of integrating the data and ensuring its quality, followed by phases for modeling, design, and access. Its architecture is pictured in Figure 8-8.

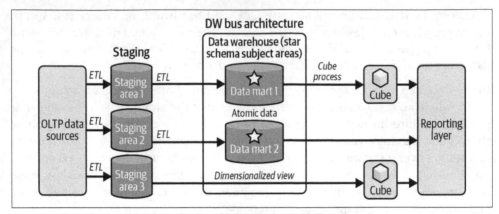

Figure 8-8. A data warehouse designed using the Kimball approach

The data from the staging tables is then copied to mission-critical *independent data marts*, which serve the analytic needs of departments. The data marts are independent because they focus on a specific subject area or business process, rather than storing and managing all data in a single central repository like Inmon's CIF. These independent data marts use a dimensional model and are stored at the atomic or summary level, depending on users' needs. The data marts are integrated for data consistency through a *DW bus* (sometimes called an *information bus*), which you can think of as a conformed data warehouse. All of the data is in a single unified view and appears to be in one database in one central physical location, but it's actually in multiple databases (and often in separate locations). These data marts are decentralized, but they do not have to be in separate physical data stores—they could be multiple databases all on the same server, or even in one database but separated by different schema names.

To provide consistency across data sources, the data marts are integrated using *conformed dimensions*, which are dimensions that have been standardized and made consistent across multiple fact tables so the data can be used and compared across fact tables without any issue. For example, if a customer dimension is used in multiple fact tables, the customer names and IDs should be the same across all the fact tables.

From the data marts, subsets of the data can be copied into cubes. You can even build a cube directly from the staging tables using a dimensionalized view if that would provide all the types of access needed. (A *dimensionalized view* is a SQL view that organizes the data into a dimensional model.) Reporting can be done from the cube or from the data mart. Kimball's methodology is business driven, and end users are active participants. Data is copied either just twice, to a data mart and to a cube, or only once if using a dimensionalized view.

Choosing a Methodology

It really boils down to two differences. First, the Inmon methodology creates a normalized DW before creating data marts, while the Kimball methodology skips the normalized DW. Second, the Inmon methodology uses a physical EDW, while the Kimball methodology uses a conformed EDW but no physical EDW. Both methodologies predate data lakes, but when data lakes started to become popular, both methodologies incorporated them. Kimball incorporates data lakes alongside data marts in the DW bus, and both Inmon and Kimball allow data lakes to replace relational staging tables.

However, there are many reasons to have a physical EDW, such as:

- A physical EDW makes it much easier to have a single version of the truth; having many data marts make up a conformed data warehouse can be difficult and confusing for users. Having the data physically in the same database is easier to understand.

- Building from lightly denormalized tables in a physical EDW is easier than building directly from the OLTP source.

- A normalized physical EDW provides enterprise-wide consistency. This makes it easier to create data marts, though with the trade-off of duplicating data.

- Physical EDWs require fewer ETL refreshes and reconciliations; with many data sources and dimensional data marts in multiple databases, you need many more daily or hourly refreshes and reconciliations to keep everything in sync.

- In a physical EDW, there is only one place to control data, so you aren't duplicating your efforts or your data.

However, if you have just a few data sources and need quick reporting, you might be better off without a physical EDW.

Which model should you use? In truth, the two models have been modified over the years and are now fairly similar. In fact, they can complement each other. You could add a normalized EDW to a Kimball-based approach or add dimensionally structured data marts to an Inmon-based approach. The bottom line is that you don't you need to choose just one approach and stick to it strictly. You should understand both approaches and pick parts from both that work for your situation. That said, no solution will be effective unless your team has solid skills in leadership, communication, planning, and interpersonal relationships (see the Chapter 15).

Hybrid Models

Let's explore the possibilities of a hybrid of the two methodologies, as pictured in Figure 8-9.

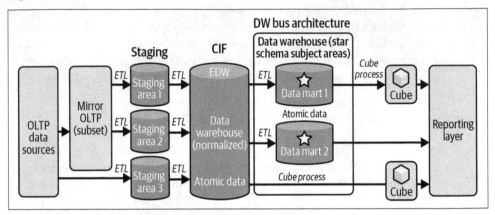

Figure 8-9. A hybrid of the Kimball and Inmon approaches

This model starts out like the other two: pulling raw data from each of the OLTP source systems directly into temporary relational staging tables. There is still no transforming or cleaning the data, but you do add a mirrored OLTP (more on that in a moment).

Next, you'll copy the data into a CIF, to be centralized and stored at the atomic level in 3NF, as in the Inmon methodology. The data from the CIF is then copied to independent, dimensional data marts. Some data marts are stored at the atomic level and others at a summary level, depending on the analytic needs of each department.

From the data marts or from the CIF, you can also copy subsets of the data into cubes. You can do reporting from a cube or a data mart, but I recommend reporting from the cube where possible. The cube's advantages include:

- It acts as a semantic layer.
- It can handle many concurrent users.
- Its data is aggregated for better performance.
- You don't have to deal with joins or relationships.
- It can contain hierarchies and KPIs.
- It has row-level security, which enhances data privacy by restricting user access to specific rows in a database.
- It offers advanced time calculations, which help you understand patterns and trends in data over time, like year-over-year sales growth.

Whether you use a Kimball, Inmon, or hybrid model, consider using database views. A *database view* is a virtual table based on the result of a SQL SELECT statement. It does not store data, only SQL code; it retrieves data from one or more tables each time it is queried. Using views in the extract, transform, and load (ETL) process makes for simpler code inside the ETL, and you don't have to see the SQL code within the view to understand what it is reading. A view makes it easier to query a database for debugging purposes, and ETL can be optimized by updating the view outside of the ETL code. Anyone can read, modify, or optimize views, not only in the ETL tool but also in other tools, and you can analyze and track dependencies in a view using third-party tools (such as the tables and fields the view uses). Views can provide default values and perform simple calculations, and you can rename fields to help you understand their flow. Views can present a star schema, even if the underlying structure is much more complex.

You can also use views in a cube. If you do, you can rename database columns to align with cube attributes, which has the advantage of exposing all the transformations to the database administrator. Using views simplifies handling fast variations and gives you full control of any joins sent to the source the cube is pulling from. And, like in the ETL, views in a cube can expose a star schema, even if the underlying structure is not a simple star schema.

I mentioned that this hybrid involves a *mirrored OLTP*, which is a duplicate of the original OLTP system that runs in parallel with it. Creating an OLTP mirror is a great strategy for several reasons. First, it means you're only using the "real" OLTP briefly, during mirroring. After that, it's freed up and available for end users or maintenance. You can modify the keys, relations, and views of a mirror, leading to simpler ETL processes that are cheaper to build and maintain. You can also build particular indexes in the OLTP mirror, meaning you don't need to do index maintenance on the original OLTP. This can improve performance on the other steps of the ETL processes. Finally, because you can mirror a subset of columns, you don't have to load all the OLTP tables. This makes the mirror much smaller and faster than the full OLTP.

Keep in mind that there is no one model that will work for every use case. There are many reasons you might need to modify your model, including security, data size, and performance. For example, you could add another layer, such as an EDW containing just star schemas, between the CIF and the DW bus architecture. This would improve performance, because star schemas are highly optimized for queries.

Methodology Myths

Because Inmon and Kimball have been so hotly debated over the years, plenty of myths have arisen about the methodologies. This section finishes the chapter by debunking some of them:

Myth: Kimball is a bottom-up approach without enterprise focus.

Kimball's approach actually incorporates both a top-down and a bottom-up methodology. The top-down aspect is demonstrated in the strategic planning and design across the enterprise. Kimball emphasizes spending significant time up front to design your solution using a tool known as the EDW bus matrix. This tool serves as an architectural blueprint of an organization's core business processes and its related dimensions, including conformed dimensions. The EDW bus matrix provides a top-down strategic perspective to ensure that data in the DW/BI environment can be integrated across the entire enterprise.

The bottom-up aspect comes into play during the execution stage. Here, Kimball's methodology focuses on one business process at a time, ensuring an agile delivery of solutions. This approach emphasizes practical implementation and demonstrates the synergy of using a top-down planning strategy along with a bottom-up execution approach.

Myth: Inmon requires you to complete a ton of design before you start building the solution, similar to the big bang or waterfall approaches.

Inmon has stated from the beginning that the way to build data warehouses is iteratively. In fact, he goes so far as to say that the absolute most critical success factor in building a data warehouse is *not* using the big bang approach.

This myth is related to the long-standing myth that it takes a long time and lots of resources to build an Inmon-style architecture. Claudia Imhoff, one of the best-known experts on the Inmon approach, and her coauthors put it this way:

> Nowhere do we recommend that you build an entire data warehouse containing all the strategic enterprise data you will ever need before building the first analytical capability (data mart). Each successive business program solved by another data mart implementation will add to the growing set of data serving as the foundation in your data warehouse. Eventually, the amount of data that must be added to the data warehouse to support a new data mart will be negligible because most of it will already be present in the data warehouse.[2]

Part of the confusion comes from people conflating Inmon's up-front design and planning approach with the architecture solution itself. Both methodologies

---

2 Claudia Imhoff, Nicholas Galemmo, and Jonathan G. Geiger, *Mastering Data Warehouse Design* (Wiley, 2003), 21.

reserve time for designing, planning, and gathering requirements before actually building anything. Both follow that with an iterative/agile approach where you build some of the solution, then do more designing and planning, then more building, in a repeating cycle.

The sliding scale shown in Figure 8-10 indicates how much design work is done before building the solution. On the far left you see the ad hoc model, where no design work is done before building the solution; on the far right is the waterfall model, where *all* design work is done first (often called the "big bang" approach). The Inmon and Kimball methodologies both fall at the mark about 25% from the left, where a decent amount of design work is done up front before building the solution.

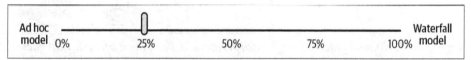

Figure 8-10. Percentage of design work done before building a solution

An analogy would be building a new city. You would design a blueprint for the city with all the neighborhoods inside it, then you would build each neighborhood and have people move in once it is completed. Throughout that process, the overall architecture of the city could be modified if needed. You wouldn't build all the neighborhoods before anyone moved in, nor would you start building neighborhoods without a good idea of what the overall city should look like.

Myth: Inmon's model does not allow star schema data marts.
    In later editions of *Building the Data Warehouse* and "A Tale of Two Architectures," Inmon argues that star schema data marts are good for giving end users direct access to data and that star schemas are good for data marts. He is not against them.

Myth: Very few companies use the Inmon method.
    Recent surveys show that more companies use the Inmon methodology than use Kimball. Many more companies use an EDW without any data marts.

Myth: The Kimball and Inmon architectures are incompatible.
    The two methods can work together to provide a better solution, as you learned in "Hybrid Models" on page 118.

Kimball also defines a development lifecycle in his books, covering such topics as project planning, business requirements definition, and maintenance (see Figure 8-11). Inmon, on the other hand, just covers the data warehouse, not how to use it.

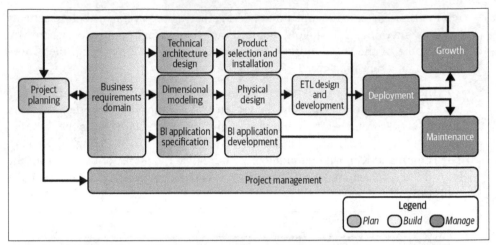

Figure 8-11. Kimball's methodology incorporates a development lifecycle that goes beyond building the data warehouse (source: Kimball, The Microsoft Data Warehouse Toolkit)

When people say they are using the Kimball methodology, often what they really mean is dimensional modeling—the two terms are commonly treated as synonymous. Kimball didn't invent the basic concepts of facts and dimensions; however, he established an extensive portfolio of dimensional techniques and vocabulary, including conformed dimensions, slowly changing dimensions, junk dimensions (*https://oreil.ly/bHoUf*), mini-dimensions (*https://oreil.ly/ZBp_W*), bridge tables (*https://oreil.ly/5TF86*), and periodic and accumulating snapshot fact tables (*https://oreil.ly/LyhQl*).

Summary

This chapter introduced you to the essential practices and methodologies behind organizing and defining data structures, relationships, and constraints for efficient data processing, storage, and retrieval. We explored the process of creating a data model, which serves as an abstract representation of the organizational data. It's a crucial initial step in managing data, since it provides a blueprint for how data is stored, consumed, and integrated within systems.

Next, we investigated relational modeling, a classic approach based on the concept of normalizing data into tables (or relations) where each row represents a record and columns represent attributes. This model is key to preventing data redundancy and enhancing data integrity, and it's at the core of most traditional relational database systems. I then discussed dimensional modeling, a methodology commonly used in data warehousing that categorizes data into facts (measurable quantities) and dimensions (contextual information); the common data model (CDM), a shared data language enabling interoperability of data across various applications and business processes; and the data vault model, a resilient hybrid approach that combines the best features of the 3NF and the star schema. The rest of the chapter made a vital comparison between two competing data warehousing philosophies. Kimball's bottom-up approach suggests building individual data marts first and then combining them into a full data warehouse, whereas Inmon's top-down approach advocates creating a comprehensive data warehouse first, then deriving data marts from it.

Understanding these methodologies can greatly help you design effective data architectures that cater to your organization's specific requirements while balancing operational efficiency with strategic analytics.

CHAPTER 9

Approaches to Data Ingestion

In our ever-growing digital world, handling and making sense of all sorts of data has become incredibly important for businesses of all types. This chapter is all about the first step in handling data—getting it into the system in the first place.

Here, we'll unravel some of the key ways data can be brought into different systems. I'll kick things off by explaining two common methods, known as ETL and ELT, in a way that is easy to understand. I'll also introduce you to a new idea called *reverse ETL* and explain how it flips the traditional methods on their head.

Since not all data needs are the same, we'll explore different techniques like batch and real-time processing. This will help you figure out what might work best based on how much data you're dealing with and how quickly you need it. Finally, we'll talk about the importance of data governance—ensuring your data is accurate, consistent, and accessible.

This chapter aims to simplify these complex ideas and show you how they all connect to the bigger picture of data handling. Whether you're a data whiz or a complete novice, I'm excited to guide you through this fascinating world of data ingestion. Welcome aboard!

ETL Versus ELT

For many years, *extract-transform-load* (ETL) was the most common method for transferring data from a source system to a relational data warehouse. But recently, *extract-load-transform* (ELT) has become popular, especially with data lakes.

The ETL process involves extracting data from outside sources, transforming and cleaning it in-flight to fit the format and structure of the destination, and then loading it into that destination (usually a data lake or RDW).

There are a few major drawbacks with ETL. First, transforming data takes time, and extraction can be a resource hog. The longer an extract is happening on the source system, the greater the likelihood that end users on that system experience performance issues. Second, if there is a bug in the ETL process and you need to rerun it, you will have to go back to the source system to extract the data again, likely affecting performance once more. Third, if there is a very large amount of data being copied, traditional ETL tools may not be able to handle it due to their limited processing power. Fourth, ETL performs transformations one record at a time, which can also be slow. Finally, some ETL tools are limited in the types of data they support.

On the plus side, ETL is often ideal for smaller datasets, where the transformation process isn't excessively complex. It offers better control over data quality, since cleaning and transforming data before loading helps minimize errors. ETL can be key for data security, as only necessary and cleaned data is loaded, reducing potential security risks. Finally, ETL is preferred when both the source and destination are relational databases, since it is typically more efficient.

ELT is similar to ETL, except the order is different. ELT also copies data from outside sources into a destination system, but the data is not transformed in-flight. Instead, it lands in the destination system in its raw form and is transformed and cleaned to fit the format and structure of the destination. You may, however, filter unneeded rows and columns as you extract data from the source so that you don't waste resources on unneeded data.

ELT is often the preferred approach for data lakes and is particularly useful when dealing with high-volume unstructured or semi-structured data. Its flexibility lies in the ability to load all raw data into the destination system first and then apply transformations as needed. Once the data is in the data lake, ELT can leverage the vast processing power of today's technology, making it efficient for handling very large amounts of data. ELT can also be faster at transformations as it processes them in batches, a notable advantage over ETL's record-by-record transformation approach. This also ensures that transformations can be altered or optimized without needing to re-extract the data. Another advantage of ELT is the wide array of tooling options available, including those designed specifically for big data platforms. This means that ELT processes can support a larger variety of data types and adapt to the evolving needs of the data environment. Additionally, the ELT approach can minimize potential performance issues on the source system, since it extracts data only once; future transformations are handled within the target system.

In conclusion, both ETL and ELT have unique strengths and are suited to different data-processing scenarios. ETL, being the older of the two methodologies, offers solid data quality control, security, and efficiency, especially when the source and destination are relational databases, making it ideal for smaller datasets. ELT, a more recent methodology, has gained popularity for use with data lakes, offering greater flexibility and scalability, especially when dealing with high-volume and unstructured data. ELT's batch processing of transformations and wide range of tooling options make it a versatile and efficient choice for big data platforms.

The choice between ETL and ELT will depend largely on the specific needs and structure of your data environment. With data technologies evolving quickly, the choice isn't a strict either–or decision; instead, it's about finding the balance that best addresses your data-processing requirements.

Reverse ETL

Reverse ETL is the process of moving data from a modern data warehouse into a third-party system or systems to make the data operational. (Figure 9-1 compares ETL, ELT, and reverse ETL.) Traditionally, data stored in a DW is used for analytical workloads and business intelligence—to identify long-term trends and influence long-term strategy—and is not copied outside the DW. However, some companies are now also using this data for operational analytics.

Operational analytics helps with day-to-day decisions and has the goal of improving efficiency and effectiveness. In simpler terms, it puts a company's data to work to help everyone make better and smarter decisions about the business. For example, say you ingest customer data into your DW and then clean and master it (ELT). You could then copy that customer data into multiple software-as-a-service (SaaS) systems, such as Salesforce, to get a consistent view of each customer across all systems. You could also copy the customer data into a customer support system and/or a sales system.

You could even identify customers who are at risk of churning (leaving the company's products or services) by surfacing usage data in a CRM.

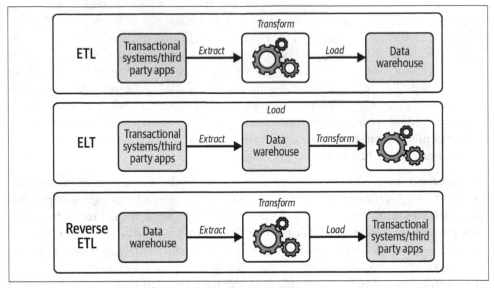

Figure 9-1. Comparison of ETL, ELT, and reverse ETL

Companies are building essential metrics in SQL on top of their data warehouses to better understand and engage with customers. These metrics might include lifetime value (a prediction of the total net profit a company expects to earn from its future relationship with a customer), product qualified lead (a potential customer who has engaged with a product and could become a paying customer), and propensity score (the likelihood that a user will buy a product), among many others.

While you could easily create reports and visualizations using this data in BI tools or SQL, the insights can be much more powerful if they drive the everyday operations of your teams in the tools they use every day. For example, you could build BI reports from the DW and train sales reps to use them—*or* operationalize their analysis by having a data analyst feed lead scores from the DW into a custom field in Salesforce. As another example, say your data science team calculates a propensity score and stores it in a DW or data lake. Using reverse ETL, you could move that propensity score to an operational production database to serve customers personalized in-app experiences in real time. In practice, this means that the company can enhance the customer's experience, providing more relevant and tailored content, recommendations, or offers based on how likely the customer is to buy a product. The app becomes more engaging and responsive to the customer's individual preferences and behaviors.

Batch Processing Versus Real-Time Processing

In ETL and ELT, you have two choices for when and how often to extract data from the source system: batch processing and real-time processing. Let's take a closer look at each:

Batch processing

   Batch processing is an efficient way to process large volumes of data. A set of similar transactions from a source system are grouped together ("batched") for a specific period of time. At regular intervals, the system automatically "runs a job," and the whole batch is copied from the source system to the destination (a data lake or warehouse), typically during non-peak business hours. The main function of a batch-processing system is to run batches at regularly scheduled times (for instance, overnight every night) or as needed.

   Your electric bill is an example of batch processing. Your electricity meter collects your consumption data over a set period (usually a month), and then the electric utility processes the whole batch in the form of your monthly bill.

Real-time processing

   Real-time data processing is a method of processing data continuously as it is collected, within a matter of seconds or milliseconds, providing near-instantaneous insights. A real-time system reacts quickly to new information in an event-based architecture. When it detects a new file or record in a source system, an event is triggered, and it copies the file or record to the destination.

   IoT devices, social media messages, and financial trading systems all use real-time processing systems. For example, if there's a suspicious credit card transaction, the bank needs to alert the cardholder without delay, which is why banks use real-time processing to detect fraud. You wouldn't want them to wait until the next day, after the overnight batch of transactions is executed!

   Traffic apps are another good example. The navigation app Waze automatically updates traffic congestion levels in real time, using information acquired from various mobile devices and road sensors in the area to suggest the optimal and shortest path to reach your destination. Obviously, if you had to wait until a nightly batch run to get the traffic info, it would be totally useless.

   Real-time processing updates the target system immediately, so reports or queries are never out-of-date. This allows quick detection of business operations that need immediate attention and updates to applications or reports that rely on real-time data.

RDWs have traditionally only used batch processing. Real-time data has become very popular in the last few years. Systems that use it mainly store their data in a data lake, which is much more suited for real-time data, since it could include millions of events per second.

Each method has its own set of advantages and trade-offs when used in data warehousing.

Batch Processing Pros and Cons

Batch processing is efficient for large volumes of data, as all data is processed at once rather than individually. This also allows batch-processing tasks to be scheduled during off-peak times, minimizing disruption to regular system use. Furthermore, batch processing poses a lower risk of system failure as failed tasks can be retried without significant repercussions.

The drawbacks to batch processing include potential delays in data availability, since it takes time to process large amounts of data at once. This could lead to underutilization of resources if not managed properly. Also, batch processing is not suitable for applications that require real-time insights, as updates are larger and less frequent and any changes in data or calculations require a complete rerun of the batch, which could impact performance.

Real-Time Processing Pros and Cons

In contrast to batch processing, real-time processing provides up-to-the-minute insights, enabling immediate action based on data. It is particularly beneficial for systems that require continuous updates and can effectively handle streaming data. Also, real-time processing is more flexible and responsive to changing business needs.

Real-time processing also has its drawbacks. It requires more system resources for continuous processing and poses a higher risk of system failure. Handling errors and recovery in real-time systems can be complex and requires robust tools. Ensuring data consistency might be more challenging due to constant updates. Moreover, the costs associated with real-time processing can be higher due to the need for continuous processing.

Deciding between batch processing and real-time processing means weighing factors such as the type of data, your processing needs, and your tolerance for latency or delay. The choice typically involves balancing the demand for instantaneous data with the system's capacity to allocate the necessary resources for real-time processing—often referred to as *latency tolerance*. If a business process or system can afford a slight delay in data access—in other words, if it has a high latency tolerance—batch processing might be the appropriate approach. Conversely, if the need for immediate data is critical and the system is equipped to manage the resources required—indicating a low latency tolerance—real-time processing could be better.

Data Governance

Data governance is the overall management of data in an organization. It involves establishing policies and procedures for collecting, storing, securing, transforming, and reporting data. In particular, it is used to ensure that the organization is complying with legal and regulatory requirements. It also includes monitoring data quality and accuracy—for instance, making sure data is properly cleaned and transformed.

Governance should include a framework that defines the people and roles responsible for managing, maintaining, and using the data within an organization. One way to do that is by creating a data governance center of excellence (CoE). The CoE serves as a hub for developing the organization's data governance policies, procedures, and standards, and defining roles, responsibilities, and decision-making processes for data-related activities.

It's important to invest time up front in defining a data governance framework and building out your CoE before building any data warehouse solution. Too often, projects fail because no one has paid enough attention to data governance.

Figure 9-2 shows a data governance maturity model I created to help you identify areas your organization should work on.

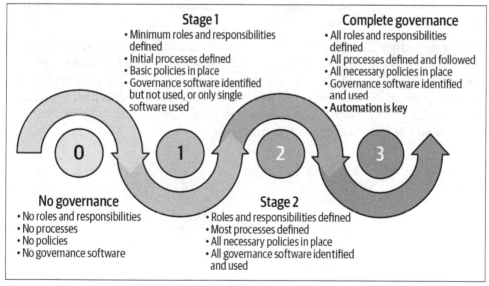

Figure 9-2. Data governance maturity model

Summary

This chapter delved into various techniques and strategies used to transport data from diverse sources into a centralized storage system, arriving ready for processing and analysis.

I compared two fundamental methods: ETL (extract, transform, load) and ELT (extract, load, transform). The ETL approach entails extracting data from sources, transforming it to fit the operational needs, and then loading it into the end system. Conversely, ELT loads data into the system before transforming it. Both methodologies have their advantages and are suited to different scenarios, depending on data volumes, complexity, performance needs, and architectural considerations.

Next, I introduced the concept of reverse ETL, a technique that allows businesses to transfer data from their data warehouse or lake back into operational systems. This process is essential for feeding insights derived from data analyses back into business applications for actionable outcomes.

You learned about two contrasting approaches to processing data: batch and real-time processing. Then we moved into the critical aspect of data governance, the discipline of managing data quality, privacy, security, and compliance. Data governance frameworks help maintain integrity and reliability throughout the data lifecycle, ensuring that data is accurate, consistent, and secure.

Choosing the right data ingestion strategy is a significant business decision that partially determines how well your organization can leverage its data for business decision making and operations. The stakes are high; the wrong strategy can lead to poor data quality, performance issues, increased costs, and even regulatory compliance breaches. So think through your approach to data ingestion carefully, not just as a technical necessity but as a business necessity.

PART III

Data Architectures

Now that you have a good understanding of the data architecture concepts, it's time to get into the meat of the book. The five chapters of Part III cover four architectures, in order of when they first appeared: the modern data warehouse, data fabric, data lakehouse, and data mesh.

These are my interpretations of the data architectures; others may have different opinions. In the end, your solution may even be a combination of these architectures.

CHAPTER 10

The Modern Data Warehouse

In Part II of this book, you learned about relational data warehouses (RDWs) and data lakes, two key components of the data management landscape. Now, let's consider the bustling world of modern business. Every day, organizations must sift through immense amounts of data to gain insights, make decisions, and drive growth. Imagine a city supermarket switching from traditional databases to a modern data warehouse (MDW). Managers can now access real-time inventory data, predict shopping trends, and streamline the shopping experience for their customers. That's the power of an MDW. It blends the best of both worlds: the structure of RDWs and the flexibility of data lakes.

Why should you care about MDWs? Because they are at the heart of our rapidly evolving data ecosystem, enabling organizations to harness the information they need to innovate and compete. In this chapter, I'll clarify what MDWs are and what you can achieve with them, and I'll show you some important considerations to keep in mind. We'll journey through the architecture, functionality, and common stepping stones to an MDW, concluding with an insightful case study. Let's dive into the world of modern data warehouses where data is more than just numbers—it's the fuel for success.

The MDW Architecture

Figure 10-1 illustrates the hybrid nature of the MDW, which combines an RDW with a data lake to create an environment that allows for flexible data manipulation and robust analytics.

As Chapter 4 detailed, an RDW operates on a top-down principle. Building one involves significant preparation in building the warehouse before you do any data loading (schema-on-write). This approach helps with historical reporting by enabling analysts to delve into descriptive analytics (unraveling *what* happened) and diagnostic analytics (probing *why* it happened).

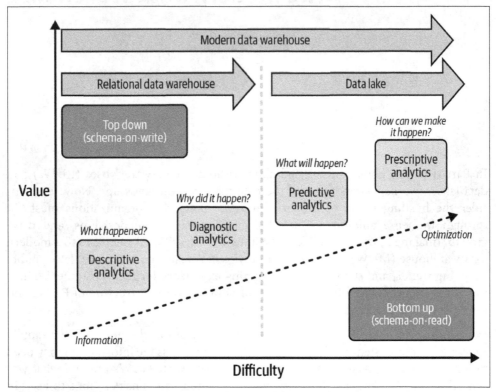

Figure 10-1. The full range of analytics facilitated by a modern data warehouse

In contrast, a data lake is defined by its bottom-up philosophy, as described in Chapter 5. Minimal up-front work is required to begin utilizing the data (schema-on-read), allowing rapid deployment of machine learning models to explore predictive analytics (forecasting what will happen) and prescriptive analytics (prescribing solutions to make desired outcomes occur).

Within an MDW architecture, a data lake is not merely a repository for storing vast amounts of information and training ML models; it's a dynamic component, responsible for data transformation and the other purposes explored in Chapter 5. It may act, for instance, as a receiving hub for streaming data, a gateway for users to do quick data exploration and reporting, and a centralized source to maintain a single version of truth.

An essential distinguishing feature of the MDW architecture is that *at least some* of its data must be replicated to an RDW. Without this duplication, it would be a data lakehouse architecture—a topic for Chapter 12.

In the mid-2010s, many organizations tried to use the data lake for all data use cases and bypass using an RDW altogether. After that approach failed, the MDW became the most popular architecture, driven by an exponential increase in data volume, variety, and velocity. Organizations in many sectors, including healthcare, finance, retail, and technology, recognized the need for a more agile and scalable approach to data storage and analysis. Their RDWs were no longer sufficient to handle the challenges of big data, but MDWs offered a flexible integration of RDWs and data lakes. Key players emerged as leading providers—Microsoft with Azure Synapse Analytics, Amazon with Redshift, Google with BigQuery, and Snowflake—revolutionizing the way businesses access and utilize their data.

As streaming data, large data, and semi-structured data became even more popular, large enterprises started to use the data fabric and data lakehouse architectures discussed in Chapters 11 and 12. However, for customers with not much data (say, under 10 terabytes), the MDW is still popular and will likely stay that way, at least until data lakes can operate as well as RDWs can.

In fact, there are still companies building cloud solutions that aren't using data lakes at all, mostly for use cases where the company has small amounts of data and is migrating from an on-prem solution that did not have a data lake. I still see this as an acceptable approach, with the caveat that the company has to be *absolutely sure* that the data warehouse will not grow much (which is very hard to say for certain). Also, if you have such a small amount of data, it may be feasible to go with a cheaper symmetric multiprocessing (SMP) solution for your RDW than a massively parallel processing (MPP) solution (see Chapter 7).

Now let's dig into the details of the MDW. Figure 10-2 shows a typical flow of data through the data lake and RDW in an MDW.

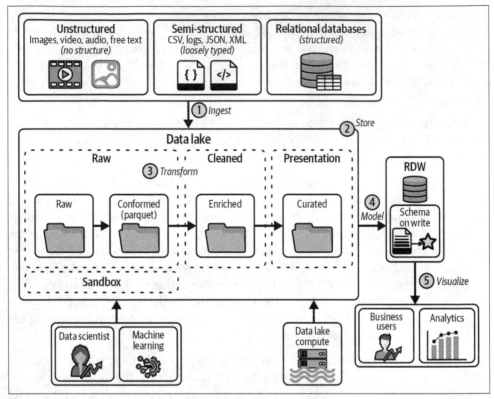

Figure 10-2. Overview of the journey that data takes through a modern data warehouse architecture

As data travels through the MDW architecture, it goes through five stages, which are numbered in Figure 10-2. Let's follow the data through each stage to give you a tour of the MDW architecture:

Step 1: Ingestion
> An MDW can handle just about any type of data, and it can come from many sources, both on-prem and in the cloud. The data may vary in size, speed, and type; it can be unstructured, semi-structured, or relational; it can come in batches or via real-time streaming; it can come in small files or massive ones. This variety can be a challenge during data ingestion.

Step 2: Storage
> Once the data is ingested, it lands in a data lake that contains all the various layers explained in Chapter 5, allowing end users to access it no matter where they are (provided they have access to the cloud). Every cloud provider offers unlimited data lake storage, and the cost is relatively very cheap. Baked into the data

lake are high availability and robust disaster recovery, along with many options for security and encryption.

Step 3: Transformation

The essence of a data lake is that it's a storage hub. However, to truly make sense of and work with the data, you need some muscle—which is where computing power comes in. A significant advantage of the MDW is its clear distinction between storing data (in the data lake) and processing it (using computing power). Keeping the two separate frees you to pick and choose from a variety of computing tools, from cloud providers or other sources. These tools, designed to fetch and understand data from the lake, can read data in various formats and then organize it into a more standardized one, like Parquet. This separation offers flexibility and enhances efficiency.

The computing tool then takes the files from the conformed layer, transforms the data (enriching and cleaning it), and stores it in the cleaned layer of the data lake. Finally, the computing tool takes the files from the enriched layer and performs more transformations for performance or ease of use (such as joining data from multiple files and aggregating it) and then writes it to the presentation layer in the data lake.

Step 4: Data modeling

Reporting directly from the data in a data lake can be slow, unsecure, and confusing for end users. Instead, you can copy all or some of the data from the data lake into a relational data warehouse. This means you will create a relational model for the data in the RDW, where the model is usually in third normal form (see Chapter 8). You may also want to copy it into a star schema within the RDW for performance reasons and simplification.

Step 5: Visualization

Once the data is in the RDW in an easy-to-understand format, business users can analyze it using familiar tools, to create such things as reports and dashboards.

For the ingestion stage, you will need to determine how often to extract data and whether to use an incremental or a full extract (see Chapter 4). Keep in mind the size and bandwidth of the pipeline from the data sources to the cloud where the data lake resides. If you need to transfer large files and your bandwidth is small, you might need to upload data multiple times a day in smaller chunks instead of in one big chunk once a day. Your cloud provider might even have options for purchasing more bandwidth to the internet.

At various steps along this journey, data scientists can use machine learning to train and build models from the data in the MDW. Depending on their needs, they can take data from the raw, cleaned, or presentation layers in the data lake, from a *sandbox layer* in the data lake (a dedicated space to do data experimentation, exploration, and preliminary analysis without affecting the other layers), or from the RDW.

There are some exceptions to the journey I've just laid out in which data flows through the MDW architecture, depending on the characteristics of the source data. For example, not all data in the presentation layer of the data lake needs to be copied to the RDW, especially with newer tools making it easier to query and report off data in a data lake. This means that in the visualization stage, the business user doesn't *have* to go to the RDW for all the data—they can access the data in the data lake that has not been copied to the RDW.

Another exception is that not all source data has to be copied to the data lake. In some cases, particularly new projects being built in the cloud, it's faster to copy data from the source right to the RDW, bypassing the data lake, especially for structured (relational) source data. For instance, reference tables that are used as dimension tables don't need to be cleaned, are full extracts, and can easily be retrieved from the source if an ETL package needed to be rerun. After all, it could be a lot of work to extract data from a relational database, copy it to the data lake (losing valuable metadata for that data, such as data types, constraints, and foreign keys), only to then import it into another relational database (the data warehouse).

This is particularly true of a typical migration from an on-prem solution that is not using a data lake and has many ETL packages that copy data from a relational database to an RDW. To reduce the migration effort, you'd need to modify the existing ETL packages only slightly—changing just the destination source. Over time, you could modify all the ETL packages to use the data lake. To get up and running quickly, however, you might only modify a few slow-running ETL packages to use the data lake and do the rest later.

Source data that bypasses the data lake would miss out on some of its benefits—in particular, being backed up, in case you need to rerun the ETL package. Bypassing can also place undue strain on the RDW, which then becomes responsible for data cleansing. Additionally, the people using the data lake will find that data missing, preventing the data lake from serving as the single source of truth.

Pros and Cons of the MDW Architecture

MDWs offer numerous benefits and some challenges. The pros include:

Integration of multiple data sources
> MDWs can handle both structured and unstructured data from various sources, including RDWs and data lakes, offering a comprehensive view of the information.

Scalability

MDWs are designed to grow with the business, easily scaling to handle increased data loads.

Real-time data analysis

MDWs facilitate real-time analytics, allowing businesses to make timely decisions based on current data.

Improved performance

By leveraging advanced technology and optimized data processing, MDWs can offer faster query performance and insights retrieval.

Flexibility

MDWs provide flexibility in data modeling, allowing for both traditional structured queries and big data processing techniques.

Enhanced security

The leading MDW providers implement strong security measures to protect sensitive data.

Some of the cons of the MDW architecture are:

Complexity

Implementing and managing an MDW can be complex, especially in hybrid architectures that combine different types of data storage and processing.

Cost

The initial setup, ongoing maintenance, and scaling can be expensive, particularly for small- to medium-sized businesses. Plus, there will be extra costs for storage and for additional data pipelines to create multiple copies of the data (for both the RDW and data lake).

Skill requirements

Utilizing an MDW to its full potential requires specialized knowledge and skills, potentially leading to hiring challenges or additional training costs.

Potential data silos

Without proper integration and governance, MDWs can lead to *data silos*, or places where information becomes isolated and difficult to access across the organization.

Compliance challenges

Meeting regulatory compliance in an environment that handles diverse data types and sources can be a challenging aspect of managing an MDW.

Vendor dependency

> If you're using a cloud-based MDW service, it may mean a dependency on a particular vendor, which could lead to potential lock-in and limit flexibility in the future.

As the data is copied within an MDW and moves through the data lake and into the RDW, it changes format and becomes easier and easier to use. This helps provide user-friendly self-service BI, where end users can build a report simply by dragging fields from a list to a workspace without joining any tables. The IT department must do some extra up-front work to make the data really easy to use, but that's often worth it, since it releases that department from being involved in (and likely a bottleneck for) all report and dashboard creation.

Combining the RDW and Data Lake

In an MDW, the data lake is used for *staging and preparing* data, while the RDW is for *serving*, *security*, and *compliance*. Let's look more closely at where the functionality resides when you're using both an RDW and data lake.

Data Lake

In a data lake, data scientists and power users—specifically those with higher technical skills—will have exclusive access, due to the complex folder-file structure and separation of metadata. Data lakes can be difficult to navigate, and access may require more sophisticated tools. The data lake's functions extend to batch processing, where data is transformed in batches, and real-time processing, which serves as the landing spot for streaming data (see Chapter 9). The data lake is also used to refine and clean data, providing a platform to use as much compute power as needed, with multiple compute options to select from. It also accommodates ELT workloads.

The data lake, in this framework, serves as a place to store older or backup data, instead of keeping it in the RDW. It's also a place to back up data from the data warehouse itself. Users can easily create copies of data in the data lake for sandbox purposes, allowing others to use and "play" in the data. The data lake also provides an opportunity to view and explore data if you're not sure what questions to ask of it; you can gauge its value before copying it to the data warehouse. It facilitates quick reporting and access to data, especially since it's schema-on-read so data can land swiftly.

Relational Data Warehouse

Business people often turn to RDWs as the place for non-technical individuals to access data, especially if they are accustomed to relational databases. These databases offer low latency, enabling much faster querying, especially if you're using MPP technology (see Chapter 7). They can handle a large number of table joins and complex queries, and they're great for running interactive ad hoc queries because of the fast performance MPP technology provides. This allows you to fine-tune queries continuously, without long waits. RDWs can also support many concurrent users running queries and reports simultaneously.

The additional security features of RDWs in the MDW context include options such as row-level and column-level security. RDWs also provide plenty of support for tools—and since they have been around for much longer than data lakes, many more tools are available. Data lakes don't have the performance to support dashboards, but you can run dashboards against RDWs, thanks to their superior performance down to the millisecond. A forced metadata layer above the data requires more up-front work but makes self-service BI much easier. Generally, when you're building out an RDW, you already know what questions you want to ask of the data and can plan for them, making the RDW a powerful and versatile tool.

Stepping Stones to the MDW

Building an MDW is a critical but long and arduous endeavor that demands considerable investment in technology, human resources, and time. It represents the evolution of data management, where integration, accessibility, security, and scalability are paramount. While that process is starting, most organizations require interim solutions to address their current data warehousing needs. These solutions, which function as stepping stones to the fully operational MDW, ensure that the organization can still derive value from its data in the meantime and remain agile and responsive to business needs. They are not merely temporary fixes but vital components in a strategic migration.

Three common types of stepping-stone architectures are:

- EDW augmentation
- Temporary data lake plus EDW
- All-in-one

Each of these approaches offers unique benefits and challenges. Their suitability as pathways to an MDW can vary depending on the organization's needs, existing infrastructure, budget, and strategic objectives. Let's look at each one more closely.

EDW Augmentation

This architecture is usually seen when a company that has had a large on-prem EDW for a long time wants to get value out of its data, but its EDW can't handle "big data" due to a lack of storage space, compute power, available time in the maintenance window for data loading, or general support for semi-structured data.

How it works

You create a data lake in the cloud and copy the big data to it. Users can query and build reports from the data lake, but the primary data remains stored in the EDW, as shown in Figure 10-3.

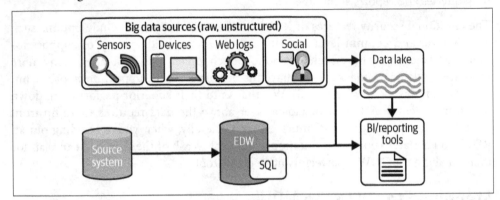

Figure 10-3. EDW augmentation architecture

Benefits

EDW augmentation architecture enhances data capacity and flexibility by leveraging a cloud data lake alongside an existing EDW. This strategy offers scalability and cost efficiency, creating opportunities for innovative analytics while maintaining current structures. It provides a balanced approach that aligns with business growth and continuity.

Challenges

This architecture does present some potential difficulties:

- If you need to combine data from the EDW with data in the data lake, you have to copy the data from the EDW to the data lake.
- Your existing query tools may not work against a data lake.
- You'll need a new form of compute to clean the data in the data lake, which may be expensive and require new skill sets.
- This architecture does not help you offload any of the EDW's workload.

Migration

This architecture can be the start of a phased approach to migrating the on-prem EDW to the cloud. After the architecture is up and running with the big data, you can begin migrating the data in the on-prem EDW to the data lake. Data from source systems goes first to the data lake and then, if needed, to a new RDW in the cloud, which is part of a true MDW.

Temporary Data Lake Plus EDW

Companies usually use a temporary data lake with an EDW when they have an EDW and need to incorporate big data, but transforming it would take too much time. These companies want to reduce the EDW maintenance window by offloading data transformations.

How it works

This architecture uses a data lake, but solely as a temporary staging and refining area. It is not used for querying or reporting; that's all done from the EDW, as Figure 10-4 shows. This limited scope means the data lake can be incorporated much faster. Sometimes you can even copy EDW data to the data lake, refine it, and move it back to the EDW.

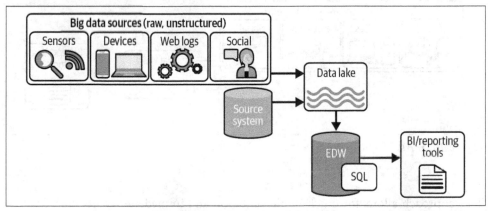

Figure 10-4. Using an EDW with a temporary data lake

Benefits

This architecture enables offloading data processing to the data lake, alleviating strain on the EDW and enhancing overall performance. Using other types of compute on the data lake can provide more speed and functionality, allowing for flexible handling of big data. This strategy offers a cost-effective solution for incorporating large data-sets without disrupting existing EDW operations, making it an agile and scalable approach.

Challenges

Although you're using a data lake, this architecture does not give you the full benefits of a data lake (discussed in Chapter 5).

Migration

With just a few modifications, this architecture can evolve into a full-blown MDW, so it's a good stepping stone.

All-in-One

All-in-one architecture is typically adopted by organizations seeking a streamlined approach to data handling, such as startups or small businesses. It may be favored to do quick prototyping or to achieve specific short-term goals. It is also a good option when the primary users are technical experts who prefer an integrated platform.

How it works

All reporting and querying are done using the data lake, as Figure 10-5 shows. No RDW is involved. (All-in-one is closely tied to the data lakehouse architecture discussed in Chapter 12.)

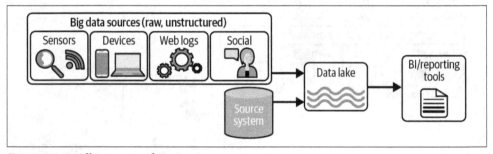

Figure 10-5. All-in-one architecture

Benefits

This approach allows for quick implementation and immediate results, benefits that are particularly attractive for technical teams aiming for rapid progress. By consolidating reporting and querying within the data lake, it simplifies the architecture, potentially reducing maintenance and integration complexities. This approach can be more agile and adaptable, accommodating various data types and fostering a more streamlined development process.

Challenges

Having no RDW involves trade-offs with respect to performance, security, referential integrity, or user friendliness.

Migration

For some companies and use cases, such as when the data in the data lake will be used only by data scientists, the data-lake-only approach may be fine. But to make it a stepping stone to an MDW, you'll need to add an RDW.

Case Study: Wilson & Gunkerk's Strategic Shift to an MDW

Wilson & Gunkerk, a fictitious midsized pharmaceutical company located in the US Midwest, had been relying on an on-prem solution to handle its data management requirements. With data volumes consistently under 1TB, the company never felt the need to transition to more advanced solutions like a data lake or an MDW.

Challenge

The company's need for actionable insights into market trends and customer behaviors became more pressing as its business environment became more competitive. The existing data system started showing its limitations, and the organization faced a dilemma: whether to upgrade to a more comprehensive data lake solution or an MDW. Another critical consideration was uncertainty about future data growth, particularly with new research and development projects in the pipeline.

Solution

After a thorough analysis, Wilson & Gunkerk decided to implement an MDW solution in the cloud. A few factors that led to this decision were:

- The existing data volume was well under 1TB, and projected growth was within 10TB.
- The migration to a cloud-based MDW offered a smoother transition from the existing on-prem solution without the need to adapt to an entirely new technology like a data lake.
- An MDW would be cost-effective. Wilson & Gunkerk opted for an SMP solution rather than a more expensive MPP option, since its data needs were modest and manageable.
- The chosen MDW provided robust performance and sufficient scalability to handle anticipated data growth within acceptable limits.

Outcome

The transition to the MDW was completed within a few months with minimal disruption to ongoing business processes. Wilson & Gunkerk realized immediate benefits:

Enhanced analytics
> The new system facilitated better data analytics, enabling more informed decision making. The company moved beyond simple historical analysis into predictive analytics. Before the MDW, insights were limited to past trends. The new system facilitated the integration of diverse data sources and the use of sophisticated data-mining algorithms. This allowed the company to create predictive models, such as forecasting drug efficacy based on patient demographics and genetic factors. The transition led to more nuanced decision making, offering a more precise approach to drug development and personalized medical solutions.

Cost savings
> The SMP solution provided excellent performance at a reduced cost compared to potential MPP solutions or a full-fledged data lake.

Future-proofing
> While keeping the door open to future transitions, the MDW allowed for gradual growth and adaptability without overinvestment in technology the company didn't immediately need.

Wilson & Gunkerk's case illustrates a balanced approach to data management solutions. For companies dealing with modest data volumes and seeking a scalable and cost-effective solution, MDWs can still present an appealing option. Each organization's needs and growth trajectory are unique, so a careful analysis of present and future requirements is vital to select the most appropriate data architecture.

Summary

This chapter started with a detailed description of the MDW and then described the five key stages of data's journey through an MDW: ingestion, storage, transformation, modeling, and visualization. These stages represent the lifecycle of data as it is initially captured, securely stored, refined for usability, modeled for insights, and finally visualized for easy interpretation and decision making.

I detailed the benefits of MDW, including aspects such as integration, scalability, real-time analysis, and security, while considering challenges like complexity, cost, and vendor dependency. We then delved into the combination of traditional RDWs with data lakes, highlighting the unique capabilities this blend provides and the enhanced flexibility it offers in dealing with various data types and structures.

I then provided a detailed exploration into three transitional architectures that companies often deploy as temporary solutions for their data-warehousing needs: enterprise data warehouse augmentation, temporary data lake plus EDW, and all-in-one. Each model serves as an interim measure while organizations work toward implementation of a full-fledged MDW.

I concluded with a case study of Wilson & Gunkerk, a midsized pharmaceutical company, and its strategic shift to an MDW.

The coming chapters will delve deeper into the data fabric and data lakehouse architectures, unpacking their benefits and potential use cases in the evolving landscape of data management.

CHAPTER 11

Data Fabric

The *data fabric* architecture is an evolution of the modern data warehouse (MDW) architecture: an advanced layer built onto the MDW to enhance data accessibility, security, discoverability, and availability. Picture the data fabric weaving its way throughout your entire company, accumulating all of the data and providing it to everyone who needs it, within your company or even outside it. It's an architecture that can consume data no matter the size, speed, or type. The most important aspect of the data fabric philosophy is that a data fabric solution can consume any and all data within the organization.

That is *my* definition of a data fabric; others in the industry define it differently. Some even use the term interchangeably with *modern data warehouse*! For instance, the consulting firm Gartner starts with a similar definition (*https://oreil.ly/fan_P*), writing that the data fabric is

> a design concept that serves as an integrated layer (fabric) of data and connecting processes. A data fabric utilizes continuous analytics over existing, discoverable and inferenced metadata assets to support the design, deployment and utilization of integrated and reusable data across all environments, including hybrid and multi-cloud platforms.

Where Gartner's view diverges from mine is in the view that data virtualization (which you learned about in Chapter 6) is a major piece of the data fabric technology that reduces the need to move or copy data from siloed systems. Gartner envisions an "intelligent data fabric" that leverages knowledge graphs and AI and ML for automating data discovery and cataloging, finding data relationships, orchestrating and integrating data, and auto-discovering metadata. However, much of the needed technology does not yet exist, and so far, neither does a data fabric that would satisfy Gartner's definition. I'm hopeful that technology will be available one day, but for now I recommend focusing on data fabric architectures as they exist today.

Data fabric is the most widely used architecture for new solutions being built in the cloud, especially for large amounts of data (over 10 terabytes). A lot of companies are "upgrading" their MDW architecture into a data fabric by adding additional technology, especially real-time processing, data access policies, and a metadata catalog. This chapter outlines eight technology features that take an MDW into data fabric territory. There's some ambiguity here; if you add three of those features, do you have an MDW or a data fabric? There is no bright line between the two. Personally, I call it a data fabric architecture if it uses at least three of those eight technologies. Many people use none of them but nonetheless call their solution a data fabric because they abide by the data fabric philosophy (I think this is perfectly fine).

This chapter gives you an overview of the data fabric architecture and its eight key components: data access policies, a metadata catalog, master data management (MDM), data virtualization, real-time processing, APIs, services, and products.

The Data Fabric Architecture

The data fabric architecture contains all of the components of the MDW but adds several features. Figure 11-1 shows a diagram of this architecture, with the stages of the data's journey labeled by number like they were in Figure 10-2. Data in a data fabric follows the same process as in an MDW; as you may recall from Chapter 10, those stages are (1) ingestion, (2) storage, (3) transformation, (4) modeling, and (5) visualization.

So what does a data fabric offer above and beyond the MDW? This section will take a look at its added features.

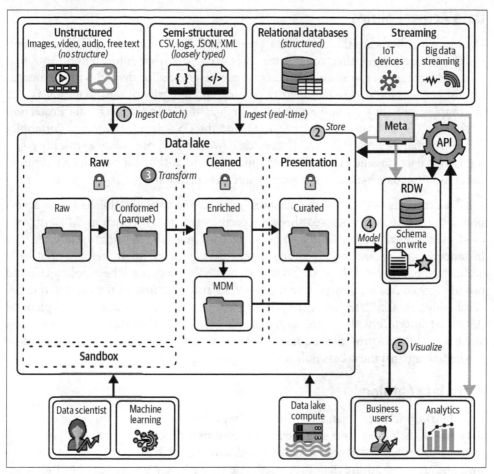

Figure 11-1. An overview of the journey data takes through a data fabric architecture

Data Access Policies

Data access policies are the key to data governance. They comprise a set of guidelines, rules, and procedures that control who has access to what information, how that information may be used, and when access can be granted or denied within an organization. They help ensure the security, privacy, and integrity of sensitive data, as well as compliance with laws and regulations, such as the UK's General Data Protection Regulation (GDPR) (*https://oreil.ly/eYnqO*) and the US's Health Insurance Portability and Accountability Act (HIPAA) (*https://oreil.ly/qI9Yl*). These policies typically cover topics like data classification, user authentication and authorization, data encryption, data retention, data backup and recovery, and data disposal.

All data requests within an organization must adhere to its established data access policies and must be processed through specific mechanisms, such as APIs, drivers, or data virtualization, ensuring compliance with regulations such as HIPAA. For instance, a healthcare organization's data access policies might require that only authorized medical staff have access to patient medical records. These policies should outline procedures for verifying staff credentials and what uses of the information are acceptable. To facilitate this controlled access, the organization might implement APIs that interface with secure authentication systems. With this security in place, when a health care provider requests a patient's record, the API checks the provider's credentials against the access policies before granting access.

Metadata Catalog

Data fabrics include a *metadata catalog*: a repository that stores information about data assets, including their structure, relationships, and characteristics. It provides a centralized, organized way to manage and discover data, making it easier for users to find and understand the data they need. For example, say a user searches the metadata catalog for "customer." The results will include any files, database tables, reports, or dashboards that contain customer data. Making it possible to see what ingestion and reporting has already been done helps everyone avoid duplicate efforts.

An important part of the catalog is *data lineage*, a record of the history of any given piece of data, including where it came from, how it was transformed, and where it is stored. Data lineage is used to comply with regulations such as data privacy laws. It's also where you can trace the origin of data and the transformations it has undergone, which is an important part of understanding how it was created and how reliable it is. You wouldn't want to base important decisions on data unless you knew you could trust it! For example, if a user asks about a particular value in a report, you can look up its lineage in the metadata catalog to show how that value came about.

Master Data Management

As you learned in Chapter 6, MDM is the process of collecting, consolidating, and maintaining consistent and accurate data from various sources within a company to create a single authoritative source for master data. This data is typically nontransactional and describes the key entities of a company, such as customers, products, suppliers, and employees.

MDM helps companies make informed decisions and avoid data-related problems such as duplicate records, inconsistencies, and incorrect information.

Data Virtualization

You also encountered data virtualization in Chapter 6. To refresh your memory, data virtualization is a software architecture that allows applications and end users to access data from multiple sources as if it were stored in a single location. The virtualized data is stored in a logical layer that acts as an intermediary between the end users and the data sources. That virtual layer is a single point of access that abstracts the complexity of the underlying data sources, making it easy for end users to access and combine data from multiple sources in real time without needing to copy or physically integrate it.

Using data virtualization does not mean you need to connect *all* data sources. In most cases, it's used only for a small number of situations, with most data still being centralized. Some in the industry see data virtualization as a definitive feature of a data fabric, arguing that an architecture is not a data fabric without virtualization; I disagree. In my definition of data fabric, virtualization is optional.

Real-Time Processing

As you saw in Chapter 9, *real-time processing* refers to processing data and producing immediate results as soon as that data becomes available, without any noticeable delay. This allows you to make decisions based on up-to-date information (for example, traffic information while driving).

APIs

Instead of relying on connection strings, APIs provide data in a standardized way from a variety of sources—such as a data lake or the RDW—without sharing the particulars of where the data is located. If the data is moved, you only need to update the API's internal code; none of the applications calling the API are affected. This makes it easier to take advantage of new technologies.

APIs can also incorporate multiple types of security measures. They can also provide flexibility with security filtering, providing fine-grained control over which users can access which data.

Services

The data fabric can be built in "blocks," which make it easier to reuse code. For example, there may be others within your company who do not have a use for the full data fabric, but who do need the code you created to clean the data or to ingest it. You can make that code generic and encapsulate it in a service that anyone can use.

Products

An entire data fabric can be bundled as a product and sold. This would be particularly attractive if made specifically for an industry, such as healthcare.

Why Transition from an MDW to a Data Fabric Architecture?

There are several reasons organizations decide to transition from an MDW to a data fabric. While MDWs have traditionally been the foundation for many businesses' data infrastructures, they can be rigid and are sometimes hard to scale as data types continue to evolve rapidly. In contrast, a data fabric is designed with scalability in mind. Its inherent flexibility allows it to adapt readily to various data types and sources, making it resilient to current data demands and, to some extent, future-proof.

In addition, the sheer variety of data sources can be overwhelming. A data fabric can weave varied sources together seamlessly, offering a singular, unified view of the data that makes it much easier and more efficient to handle multifaceted data streams.

In a swiftly changing business environment, the ability to process data in real time and derive immediate insights is crucial. A data fabric meets this need by supporting real-time data processing, granting businesses instant access to the latest data.

Furthermore, as concerns about data breaches increase and the emphasis on adhering to data protection regulations intensifies, data security and governance become even more critical. A data fabric addresses these issues with advanced access policies, providing a more secure data environment. It also enhances data governance by restricting access to properly authorized users, protecting sensitive information from potential threats. And for multinational companies that operate across different jurisdictions, each with distinct data protection regulations, a data fabric's advanced governance capabilities can help maintain compliance no matter where the data is.

Lastly, certain industries—like stock trading and ecommerce—are characterized by rapidly shifting market conditions. In these volatile worlds, staying updated in real time is not just an advantage but a necessity. This immediacy is where a data fabric proves invaluable; its support for real-time data processing keeps such businesses agile, informed, and ready to adapt at a moment's notice.

Potential Drawbacks

While a data fabric architecture has numerous advantages, it isn't devoid of challenges. Transitioning from an MDW to a data fabric can be resource intensive, with initial hiccups related to cost, training, and integration. Also, not all businesses need the advanced capabilities of a data fabric—for small businesses with limited data sources and straightforward processing needs, an MDW might suffice.

Moreover, the inherent complexity of a data fabric can make troubleshooting more challenging. It's crucial to ensure that your organization has the required expertise in-house or accessible through partners before making the shift.

While data fabric offers a cutting-edge solution to modern data management challenges, it's essential for every business to evaluate its unique needs, potential return on investment, and long-term strategic goals before making the transition.

Summary

In this chapter, we delved into the concept of data fabric architecture, an advanced evolution of the MDW designed to enhance data accessibility, security, discoverability, and availability. I defined data fabric and contrasted my definition with industry perspectives, highlighting differences such as the role of data virtualization. The chapter outlined eight key technologies that transition an MDW into data fabric territory, without making a strict demarcation between the two.

I also explained the core components of the data fabric architecture, including data access policies, metadata catalog, master data management, real-time processing, APIs, and optional elements like data virtualization. The chapter emphasizes data fabric's adaptability, especially in handling large data volumes and real-time processing demands.

We looked at reasons for transitioning from an MDW to a data fabric, as well as potential drawbacks such as complexity and resource-intensive transitions. In short, every organization should carefully evaluate its unique needs and capabilities before embracing this cutting-edge solution.

CHAPTER 12

Data Lakehouse

I've touched briefly on the data lakehouse as a harmonization of the concepts of the data lake and data warehouse. The idea behind a *data lakehouse* is to simplify things by using just a data lake to store all your data, instead of also having a separate relational data warehouse. To do this, the data lake needs more functionality to replace the features of an RDW. That's where Databricks' Delta Lake comes into play.

Delta Lake is a transactional storage software layer that runs on top of an existing data lake and adds RDW-like features that improve the lake's reliability, security, and performance. *Delta Lake itself is not storage.* In most cases, it's easy to turn a data lake into a Delta Lake; all you need to do is specify, when you are storing data to your data lake, that you want to save it in Delta Lake format (as opposed to other formats, like CSV or JSON).

Behind the scenes, when you store a file using Delta Lake format, it is stored in its own specialized way, which consists of Parquet files in folders and a transaction log to keep track of all changes made to the data. While the actual data sits in your data lake in a format similar to what you're used to, the added transaction log turns it into a Delta Lake, enhancing its capabilities. But this means that anything that interacts with Delta Lake will need to support Delta Lake format; most products do, since it has become very popular.

Delta Lake is not the only option to provide additional functionality to a data lake; two other popular choices are Apache Iceberg and Apache Hudi, which have very similar features. However, in this chapter I'll focus on Delta Lake.

So far, you've learned about the relational data warehouse (Chapter 4), data lake (Chapter 5), modern data warehouse (Chapter 10), and data fabric (Chapter 11). This chapter adds the data lakehouse. Figure 12-1 shows these architectures on a historical timeline.

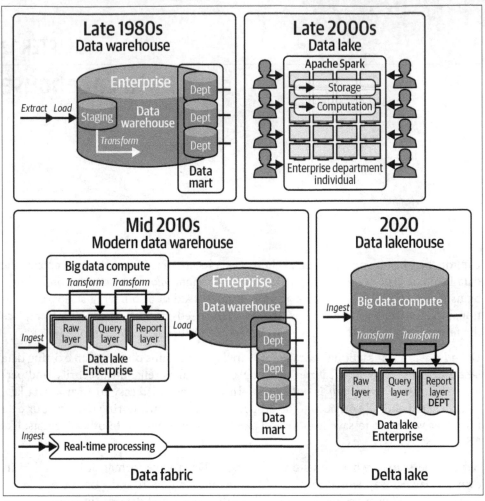

Figure 12-1. Historical timeline of data architectures

Delta Lake Features

Delta Lake adds several RDW-like features to a data lake. This section will walk you through some of them.

Perhaps the biggest reason companies use Delta Lakes is that they support *data manipulation language* (DML) commands, such as INSERT, DELETE, UPDATE, and MERGE. These commands simplify complex data management tasks, making data handling more flexible and reliable within Delta Lake. Data lakes do not provide native support for these operations, because data lakes are optimized for batch processing and storing large amounts of data, not for real-time updates.

Updating data in a data lake typically involves reading the entire file, making the necessary updates, and writing the entire updated file back to the data lake, which can take a long time, especially for large files. In contrast, when Delta Lake initially works with a table—essentially a file that is an organized collection of data in rows and columns—it breaks that table down into several smaller digital files for easier management. The result is a *Delta Table*. Delta Lake then uses a transaction log to track changes, which makes DML commands work much faster due to using optimized storage (columnar storage format), in-memory processing, and optimizations for batch processing. For example, with an UPDATE statement, Delta Lake finds and selects all files containing data that matches the predicate and that therefore need to be updated. It then reads each matching file into memory, updates the relevant rows, and writes out the result into new data files. This updates the data efficiently, without having to rewrite the entire Delta Table. The transaction log maintains a history of changes to the data and ensures that the data is always in a consistent state, even in the case of failures or system crashes.

A common acronym you will hear when dealing with databases is ACID, which stands for *atomicity, consistency, isolation*, and *durability*. These are the four properties that ensure the reliability and integrity of a database transaction. They guarantee that a transaction can be completed as a single, reliable operation, with its data changes either fully committed or fully rolled back. While Delta Lake can be said to support ACID transactions, that statement requires qualifying. Unlike processing ACID transactions in a relational database, such as SQL Server, Delta Lake ACID support is constrained to a single Delta Table. Executing DML over more than one Delta Table in a Delta Lake will not guarantee ACID integrity. With a relational database, ACID integrity works with DML transactions that span multiple tables.

Delta Lake also offers "time travel," a feature that allows you to query data stored in Delta Tables as it existed at a specific point in time. A history of changes to the data is maintained in the Delta transaction log, along with metadata, such as when each change was made and by which user. Users can view and access previous versions of the data, and even revert it to a previous version if necessary. This can be useful for auditing, debugging, or recovering data in the event of unintended data changes or other issues (such as rollbacks).

The "small files" problem, where a large number of small files can slow down read and write operations and increase storage costs, is a common issue in data lakes. Delta Lakes solve this problem by using optimized compaction algorithms to efficiently merge small files into large ones. The compaction process is performed automatically in the background and can be configured to run on a schedule or triggered manually.

With Delta Lake, users can perform both batch processing and real-time streaming on the same data in a Delta Table, eliminating the need to maintain separate data pipelines and systems for batch and streaming processing. This unified solution makes it easier to manage and maintain pipelines and simplifies the data-processing architecture. This also means that Delta Lake supports the Lambda architecture (see Chapter 7).

Schema enforcement is a Delta Table feature that allows you to specify the expected schema for the data in a Delta Table and enforce rules such as nullable constraints, data type constraints, and unique constraints. This ensures that data written to the Delta Table conforms to the specified schema, which helps prevent data corruption. Without schema enforcement, a file with an invalid schema can be added to a folder, which can cause ELT jobs to error out. If incoming data does not match the schema, Delta Lake will reject the write operation and raise an error.

Performance Improvements

Using Delta Lake can improve data lake performance in several ways, including:

Data skipping
> Delta Lake can skip over irrelevant data when reading from a Delta Table, which can greatly improve query performance.

Caching
> Delta Lake supports data caching in Spark, which can significantly improve the performance of repeated queries.

Fast indexing
> Delta Lake uses an optimized indexing structure to quickly locate data, reducing the time required to execute queries.

Query optimization
> Delta Lake integrates with Spark SQL and can take advantage of Spark's query optimization capabilities, resulting in faster and more efficient queries.

Predicate pushdown
> Delta Lake supports *predicate pushdown*, which means that filter conditions are pushed down to the storage layer, reducing the amount of data that needs to be processed.

Column pruning
> With *column pruning*, only the columns required for a specific query are read, reducing the amount of data that needs to be processed.

Vectorized execution
> In *vectorized execution*, multiple data points are processed in a single CPU instruction, leading to improved performance.

Parallel processing

> Delta Lake supports parallel processing, which means that multiple tasks can be executed in parallel, leading to improved performance.

Z-order

> *Z-order*, also known as Morton order, is a data-indexing technique used in Delta Lake architectures to organize data for fast, efficient access and querying.

The Data Lakehouse Architecture

In a data lakehouse, data moves through the same five stages you saw with the MDW and data fabric architectures, as Figure 12-2 shows. These are (1) ingestion, (2) storage, (3) transformation, (4) modeling, and (5) visualization.

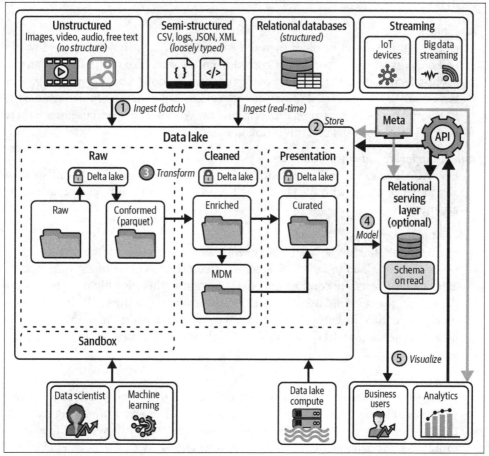

Figure 12-2. Data lakehouse architecture

As you can see in Figure 12-2, with a data lakehouse architecture, there's only one repository for your data (the data lake that is using Delta Lake), rather than two (a data lake and a RDW). The RDW is replaced with an optional relational serving layer, described later in this chapter. This solves six problems commonly seen in the MDW and data fabric architectures:

Reliability

Keeping a data lake and an RDW consistent can be a problem, especially if large amounts of data frequently need to be copied from the data lake to the RDW. If the jobs to copy the data fail, do not copy the data accurately, or put the data in the wrong spot in the data lake, this can cause reliability issues. For instance, running reports against the RDW could return different results than running reports against the same data in the data lake. With a data lakehouse, since there is no RDW to copy data to, this is not an issue.

Data staleness

Data in an RDW will be older than the equivalent data in the data lake. How old will depend on how often data is copied from the data lake to the RDW—and to avoid affecting query and report performance, you don't want to run those jobs too often. As with the reliability issues above, this can result in reports against the RDW and data lake returning different results. With a data lakehouse, since there is no RDW to copy data to, this is not an issue.

Limited support for advanced analytics

Few AI/ML systems and tools work well on RDWs, because data scientists usually prefer working with files in a data lake. They get this with a data lakehouse architecture.

Total cost of ownership

Even though storage is relatively cheap, there are extra costs for the compute needed to copy data to an RDW. Also, the result is two copies of the data, adding extra storage costs. By contrast, in a data lakehouse, there is only one copy of the data. Also, the compute used for queries and reporting in the RDW usually costs much more than the compute used with a data lake. In addition, managing a data lake and managing a RDW are different skill sets, and hiring for both can mean extra costs as well.

Data governance

Having two copies of the data in two different storage environments, possibly with two different types of security, increases the risk of someone seeing data that they should not see. It's also challenging to ensure that both systems follow the same rules for data quality and data transformations. With a data lakehouse and its one copy of data, these problems do not exist.

Complexity

Managing both a data lake and an RDW can be complex, requiring specialized skills and resources. Since a data lakehouse doesn't have a RDW, fewer specialized skills are required.

What If You Skip the Relational Data Warehouse?

Here is where we open a can of worms. Not long ago, I would have told you that skipping an RDW in your architecture was a very bad idea. Now, as Delta Lake continues adding RDW-like features to the data lake, I am starting to see more and more use cases where a data lakehouse is the best architecture. The case for using a data lakehouse is especially compelling with smaller datasets. Because most cloud vendors have serverless compute that you can use against a Delta Lake, you can save costs by paying per query. You also save costs by not having to copy data into relational storage, which is more expensive and uses more expensive relational compute. And if you use dedicated compute for an RDW instead of going serverless, you are paying even if you aren't using that compute. As with any architecture, there are trade-offs and concerns, and it's very important to be aware of them if you choose not to have an RDW in your architecture.

The first trade-off is that relational database queries are faster than queries against a Delta Lake, especially when your RDW uses MPP technology (see Chapter 7). RDWs have features to improve query performance that aren't available in a Delta Lake, including:

- Advanced indexing (such as clustered columnstore indexes and full-text indexes)
- Advanced statistics
- Caching (unless you're using Spark)
- Advanced query plan optimization
- Materialized views
- Advanced join optimization

Some Delta Lake performance features, such as Z-order, can alleviate some of these missing features.

Delta Lake also lacks some of the common staples of RDW security, such as row-level security, column-level security, data-at-rest encryption, column-level encryption, transparent data encryption (TDE), and dynamic data masking (which automatically replaces or obscures portions of the data so that unauthorized users see a masked version of the data instead of the actual sensitive information). Nor does it provide SQL views; referential integrity; workload management; or advanced auditing and compliance features, such as auditing trails, data retention policies, and compliance certifications. RDWs also support higher concurrency than Delta Lake, because they provide advanced features such as advanced locking, isolation levels, and transaction management.

Complexity is also an issue. With an RDW, you have a *forced metadata layer*—you must create a database, schema, and a table with fields that describe the data type and then load the data (schema-on-write). This means you always have the metadata sitting on top of the actual data. This requires up-front work, but the big benefit is that the metadata and data are always locked together, so it's easy to use the metadata to find the data. You will never "lose" the metadata, and it will always accurately describe the data. This is hugely different from Delta Lake, which is a folder- and file-based world. That's the main reason end users who are used to an RDW often struggle with Delta Lake.

In Delta Lake, metadata isn't required to exist with the data. You might find it in one or more separate files, within the file that contains the data, within the same folder, in a separate folder, or not at all. To top it off, the metadata might be wildly inaccurate, since it doesn't have the one-to-one relationship with the data that it has in an RDW. You can see how confusing this can be to end users, who might struggle to find the metadata, wrongly decide that there is no metadata, or even use the wrong metadata. Finally, the metadata can fall out of sync with the data when changes are made outside Delta Lake.

Using certain features of Delta Lake architectures could lock you into having to use Spark. Also, if you migrate from a product that uses a SQL version other than Spark SQL, prepare to rewrite your stored procedures, views, report, dashboards, and so on.

If you do need to use Spark SQL, that might mean retraining end users who are already used to interacting with RDWs and familiar with tools for doing so. They may be using ANSI-compliant SQL or an RDW product like T-SQL (which is used with Microsoft products). They are also used to the relational model and know how to quickly query and report off of it. Switching to a folder-file world would likely force them to learn to use new tools; get used to schema-on-read; and learn to handle the issues with the speed, security, missing features, complexity, and SQL changes described earlier. That's a lot of training.

Existing technology can alleviate some of these concerns and could eventually render them irrelevant. But until that happens, consider them carefully in relation to your needs as you determine whether to use the data lakehouse architecture. For example, if queries to the data lake take an average of five seconds in the data lakehouse architecture, is that a problem? If end users are OK with that, you can ignore this concern, but if they're using dashboards and need millisecond query response times, you would need to copy the data used for the dashboards into an RDW (meaning you'd end up using an MDW architecture). You could instead use a reporting product that allows you to import data into its memory for millisecond query response times, but the data would not be as updated as it is in Delta Lake, and you would need to refresh the data in the reporting tool's memory at certain intervals.

Once again, we are talking about trade-offs. If you are an architect, a major part of your role will be identifying products that could be used in each architecture and determining and analyzing their trade-offs to choose the best architecture and products for your particular use case.

None of the above concerns is necessarily a showstopper in itself, but taken in combination, they could provide enough of a reason to use an RDW. A lot of companies start with some proofs of concept to determine whether any of the trade-offs of skipping the RDW will cause an issue. If not, they proceed with a data lakehouse.

Relational Serving Layer

Because Delta Lake is schema-on-read (see Chapter 2), the schema is applied to the data when it is read, not beforehand. Delta Lake is a file-folder system, so it doesn't provide context for what the data is. (Contrast that with the RDW's metadata presentation layer, which is on top of and tied directly to the data.) Defined relationships don't exist within Delta Lake. Each file is in its own isolated island, so you need to create a "serving layer" on top of the data in Delta Lake to tie the metadata directly to the data. To help end users understand the data, you will likely want to present it in a relational data model, so that makes what you're building a "relational serving layer." With this layer on top of the data, if you need to join more than one file together, you can define the relationships between them. The relational serving layer can take many forms: a SQL view, a dataset in a reporting tool, an Apache Hive table, or in an ad hoc SQL query. If done correctly, the end user will have no idea they are actually pulling data from a Delta Lake—they will think it is from the RDW.

Many companies create SQL views on top of files in Delta Lake, then use a reporting tool to call those views. This makes it easy for end users to create reports and dashboards.

Even with a relational serving layer, Delta Lake still presents some challenges. The relational serving layer could portray the data incorrectly, for instance, or you could end up with two layers that point to the same data but have different metadata. Metadata not being tied to the data is an inherent problem with Delta Lake. RDWs avoid this problem by having a universal data model that everyone can use.

Summary

This chapter explored the concept of the data lakehouse, focusing on the role of Delta Lake as a transactional storage layer that significantly enhances existing data lakes' reliability, security, and performance.

You learned about the potential drawbacks associated with bypassing a traditional RDW, with emphasis on challenges related to speed, security, and concurrency. Just be aware of the trade-offs, and if there are no immediate big concerns, then use a data lakehouse until you can't. If one of those trade-offs becomes too much to overcome for a particular dataset, you can copy that data to an RDW (no need to copy *all* the data). As technology for Delta Lake, for similar technologies like Apache Iceberg and Apache Hudi, and for storage and compute continues to improve, there will be fewer and fewer reasons to maintain an RDW. Most new data architectures will be data lakehouses.

You saw the unique schema-on-read approach of Delta Lake, where data interpretation occurs at the point of reading, not in advance. You also learned about its file-folder structure, which is devoid of context and thus significantly deviates from the structured metadata presentation layer of an RDW. This necessitates a "relational server layer" for establishing a direct context-based link to the data in Delta Lake.

Rapid technological advancements continue to influence data architecture strategies. A few years ago, omitting an RDW from your architecture would have been considered a significant misstep, but current trends indicate an increasing number of use cases where data lakehouse emerges as the optimal architecture.

All of the architectures I've discussed so far are centralized solutions, meaning that source data is copied to a central location owned by IT. You'll see a major difference in the next chapter, as we discuss the decentralized solution of the data mesh.

CHAPTER 13

Data Mesh Foundation

A *data mesh* is a decentralized data architecture with four specific characteristics. First, it requires independent teams within desginated domains to own their analytical data. Second, in a data mesh, data is treated and served as a product to help the data consumer to discover, trust, and utilize it for whatever purpose they like. Third, it relies on automated infrastructure provisioning. And fourth, it uses governance to ensure that all the independent data products are secure and follow global rules.

Although the concepts that make up a data mesh are not new, Zhamak Dehghani, CEO and founder of Nextdata (*https://nextdata.com*), deserves credit for coining the term *data mesh* and combining those concepts.[1] Although others have formed various opinions about what a data mesh is, this book bases its definition on Dehghani's work, in particular her four data mesh principles, which I discuss in this chapter. It is very important to understand that data mesh is a concept, not a technology. It is all about an organizational and cultural shift within companies. The technology used to build a data mesh could follow the modern data warehouse, data fabric, or data lakehouse architecture—or domains could even follow different architectures.

As we delve into the nuanced world of data mesh architectures in this chapter and the next, I offer a road map to navigate the complex data mesh landscape grounded in the principle of decentralization. In this chapter, I dissect the decentralized data architecture, clarifying the buzz surrounding data mesh and explicating its four foundational principles. We'll dive deep into the essence of the pure data mesh and journey through the intricacies of data domains, then discover the logical architecture and

---

1 See Zhamak Dehghani, "How to Move Beyond a Monolithic Data Lake to a Distributed Data Mesh," (*https://oreil.ly/cv2sX*) MartinFowler.com, May 20, 2019; "Data Mesh Principles and Logical Architecture," (*https://oreil.ly/NTOLG*) MartinFowler.com, December 3, 2020, and *Data Mesh: Delivering Data-Driven Value at Scale* (O'Reilly, 2022).

varied topologies that support the infrastructure and draw contrasts between data mesh and data fabric. Finally, I'll discuss the proper use cases for data mesh.

Shifting focus in Chapter 14, I address potential challenges in implementing a data mesh, debunking common myths to assist organizations in informed decision making regarding its adoption. Next I'll discuss conducting an organizational assessment to determine if adopting a data mesh aligns with your organization's needs. From there, I'll delve into recommendations for implementing a successful data mesh, ensuring a seamless transition and maximum benefits. Then I'll gaze ahead at the anticipated trajectory of data mesh in the ever-evolving data landscape and conclude with a discussion of when to use each of the four architectures: modern data warehouse, data fabric, data lakehouse, and data mesh.

Join me as I unravel the intricacies of data mesh architectures, providing you with a deep yet concise insight into its decentralized framework.

A Decentralized Data Architecture

The data architectures I have talked about in this book so far—modern data warehouse, data fabric, and data lakehouse—are all centralized architectures where all analytical data is created and owned by the IT team. A big difference between data mesh and those other data architectures is that data mesh is decentralized. That means the data, along with everything used to manage it, is owned and managed by individual teams or "domains" within an organization and grouped by business domain, as opposed to a central authority or single team in IT. These domain teams are responsible for collecting, processing, and managing their own data, and they have the autonomy to make decisions about how their data is used and shared. The data is kept within the domain; end users can access and query the data where it lives, without copying it to a central location. This leads to greater accountability and ensures that data is managed and maintained by those with the greatest expertise about it.

This solves the main problem with centralized architectures, which is organizational and technical scaling. As a company grows and more data has to be centralized quickly, IT often gets overloaded and becomes a bottleneck.

When I talk about all the other data architectures in this book being centralized, I'm referring to a wide variety of aspects of these architectures. Not only does a central IT team own and control data, that team is also responsible for:

- Integrating data from different sources
- Storing data in a centralized location that it owns
- Building data models and housing them in a central repository

---

- Governance and compliance, including defining and enforcing data quality, security, and privacy standards
- Creating and maintaining data pipelines and transformation logic
- Enforcing data quality via profiling, validation, cleansing, and other processes
- Optimizing performance
- Managing all compute technology
- Managing analytics and reporting tools
- Storing and managing metadata
- Disaster recovery and backup

In addition, in a centralized architecture, the hardware and processing power are designed to scale vertically.

Data Mesh Hype

Data mesh has drawn a lot of attention since it was first introduced in 2019. Gartner has a well-known "hype cycle" for data management, which measures the maturity of technologies based on the current level of adoption and the number of years to mainstream adoption. In its Hype Cycle for Data Management 2023 (*https://oreil.ly/ xgsrW*), it placed data mesh near the top of the hype cycle (approaching the "peak of inflated expectations") and "moderate" on the benefit rating. Data mesh has a market penetration of 5% to 20%, and interestingly enough, Gartner predicts that "Data mesh will be obsolete before the plateau. The practice and supporting technology will evolve toward data fabric as organizations start collecting passive metadata."

Many who hype the data mesh will claim that data warehousing projects fail at a very high rate, are unsustainable, and can no longer handle big data because they can't scale. With all the hype, you would think building a data mesh is the answer to all of these "problems" with data warehousing. The truth is that while data warehouse projects do fail, it is rarely because they can't scale enough to handle big data or because the architecture or the technology isn't capable. Failure is almost always because of problems with the people and/or the process, or that the organization chose the completely wrong technology. Sometimes I feel as if data mesh is a solution looking for a problem, and the people hyping data mesh are oversimplifying the whole challenge of managing and integrating data.

I have seen big data solutions work very well for many years without data mesh, from the late 1980s (when a terabyte was considered "big data") to today's petabytes of data. The technology hasn't stood still. Centralized data architectures and cloud products are quite capable of handling just about any amount of batch and streaming data.

These solutions have worked for big data for decades. Why should we assume they won't work in the future?

Of course, this is all guesswork. Data mesh is still new, but clearly not everyone believes the hype. I fall into the skeptics' camp. I have been working with databases for over 35 years and data warehousing for 15, and I've seen plenty of much-hyped technologies come and go. While I don't believe data mesh will become obsolete, I don't believe any companies will build a "pure" data mesh. A small number of companies will build a modified data mesh, and the rest will use another architecture.

I have seen very few companies put a modified data mesh into production. Many claim they have, wanting to seem cutting-edge, but most of the time it's really a data fabric or data lakehouse. But even with a very loose interpretation of "data mesh," the percentage of companies building one is very small. When I speak on data architecture, I always ask the crowd, "How many have heard of data mesh?" Usually, at least 75% raise their hands. I then follow up with, "How many are building a data mesh?" Maybe one or two hands will be raised, in a crowd of a hundred. Then I ask, "How many have a data mesh in production?" I have yet to see a single hand raised. Other colleagues report similar experiences. While this is anecdotal, it appears to indicate that data mesh is not living up to the hype. Nevertheless, data mesh architectures have a lot of positive aspects that can improve any of the other data architectures. This chapter and the next will explain in more detail.

Dehghani's Four Principles of Data Mesh

The data mesh tries to solve the four biggest challenges of centralized data architectures: lack of ownership, low data quality, technical scaling, and organizational scaling. The four principles that Dehghani lays out address these challenges.[2] Let's look at each in turn.

Principle #1: Domain Ownership

Principle #1 recommends that you decentralize and distribute responsibility to people who are closest to the data in order to support continuous change and scalability (for example, manufacturing, sales, supplier).

In a centralized architecture, there is usually confusion (or, in some meetings, loud arguments) about who "owns" the analytical data.

Most source data is generated by homegrown operational systems, CRM tools such as Salesforce and Microsoft Dynamics, and enterprise resource planning (ERP) tools

---

2 See Zhamak Dehghani, *Data Mesh: Delivering Data-Driven Value at Scale* (O'Reilly, 2022), page 15 for principle #1, page 29 for principle #2, page 47 for principle #3, and page 67 for principle #4.

such as SAP and Microsoft Dynamics. Each of these domain-specific systems and applications is run by dedicated operational people who usually have little to no communication with the central IT data platform team. Often, the operational people are unaware that "their" data is being sent to a data platform.

When data is in an operational database, it belongs to the operational domain that owns the database. When it's copied to the centralized data store (usually a data lake), IT usually owns it—but some argue that it should still belong to the domain.

For its part, the central IT data platform team rarely has a solid understanding of how the operational systems or business applications operate. They simply don't understand the data well and have no context for how the data was generated or what it actually means. They just see table and field names or files. As a result, they struggle to produce quality data and usable analytics.

This challenge is cleared up by the first principle of the data mesh—domain ownership. The people in charge of the operational databases are *always* the owners of the analytical data, and they are responsible for managing and maintaining the data. Responsibility and ownership are decentralized and distributed to the people who are closest to the data, to support continuous change and scalability. These people are grouped according to business domain, such as manufacturing, sales, or supplier; defining a company's domains can be challenging. Each domain owns its operational and analytical data.

Principle #2: Data as a Product

Principle #2 suggests treating analytical data provided by the domains as a product, and the consumers of that data as customers. Each domain has domain teams, API code, data and metadata, and infrastructure.

In a centralized architecture, the IT team owns the analytical data and therefore is responsible for data quality—but they usually don't know the data well and may make mistakes transforming it. The domain team, on the other hand, has a deep understanding of the data and its context within their business domains. This knowledge allows them to identify and address data quality issues that may be missed by central IT teams, who have less context to aid in understanding the business needs.

The second principle of data mesh is that instead of thinking of analytical data as an input, an asset, or a byproduct of a process that others manage, data owners treat data as a *fully contained product* that they are responsible for. They treat the consumers of that data (data users, data analysts, data scientists) as customers. This means that domain teams apply product thinking to their data to make sure it can be easily discovered and that it's trustworthy, accessible, secure, and understandable.

Your first step in treating data like a product is to identify exactly what a data product is in your organization. A *data product* is a self-contained, independently deployable unit of data that delivers business value. It contains analytical data sourced from operational or transactional applications. It is designed, built, and managed by a single product team. Each data product is autonomous and managed completely independently of the other data products. It solves a particular business problem and should be designed with a clear understanding of the needs of its target users. A data product is associated with a particular data domain, so it serves a specific area of the business and should be aligned to that area's business goals. There are usually many products under each domain.

Be aware that *data product* is not the same thing as *data as a product*. *Data as a product* describes the idea that data owners treat data as a fully contained product that they are responsible for, rather than a byproduct of a process that others manage, and should make the data available to other domains and consumers. *Data product* refers to the architecture of implementing data as a product. Some within the IT industry view datasets, analytical models, and dashboard reports as data products, focusing on the physical representation of data, and do not consider any metadata, code, or infrastructure to be data products.

Note that a data product can be composed of subproducts, each responsible for providing a specific subset of data or functionality that is organized around a subject area. For example, a data product for customer data could have subproducts for transactional, demographic, and behavioral data, each managed by a separate team.

Data products are consumed through *data contracts*, which are agreements between data domains or data products that define the format and structure of the data exchange between a producer and a consumer. The data contract is a very rich document that typically contains metadata, data schemas, data transformation info, and data access rules. It also contains information on how other domains, products, or consumers will access the data product, typically through APIs, a database, a standard file format, an event stream, or a graph.

Since domain teams are directly responsible for the data, they can quickly identify and address any quality issues. This leads to faster resolution times, reducing the risk of inaccurate data being used in business decisions. Finally, domain teams are embedded within the business, so they have a better understanding of the specific data needs for their domains. This ensures that data is managed and maintained in a way that aligns with the business's needs, resulting in higher-quality and more relevant analytical data.

One more item about principle #2: each domain team is responsible for acquiring and managing its own infrastructure and resource allocations, as well as hiring people to build the architecture and manage the data. This is a big change; instead of IT cleaning and processing data for consumption (by copying operational data into analytical data), these responsibilities now fall on the domain team. The domain teams must also determine the business needs for their data. This means that each team can determine its own resource needs based on the domain's requirements and data volume. Each team can also independently provision and scale resources as needed to handle fluctuations in demand, so multiple domain teams aren't competing for infrastructure resources from a central IT team.

Principle #3: Self-Serve Data Infrastructure as a Platform

Principle #3 recommends that you simplify data product creation and management by automating infrastructure provisioning (for example, storage, compute, data pipeline, and access control).

As I noted in the beginning of this chapter, in centralized architectures, the central IT team can become a bottleneck, making it difficult to scale effectively. This team stands up and monitors all of the architecture, including storage, compute, data pipelines, and data access policies. Often, they just don't have enough people to make data available in a timely manner.

In a data mesh, because each domain team owns its domain data and treats its data as a product, it needs its own engineering teams and infrastructure to build, deploy, monitor, and provide access to its data product. This extends domain teams' responsibility from building operational applications to include building analytics and creating a solution to share the data. In short, the first two data mesh principles impose additional effort on the domain engineering teams. This principle is about reducing that.

Domain teams might be dismayed at the thought of managing, staffing, overseeing, and paying to develop and manage their data product. To avoid frustration and pushback, you need to give them a "shortcut" to overcome some of this extra work. You don't want each domain going off and building its own infrastructure from scratch, either; "reinventing the wheel" by duplicating efforts in each domain would significantly delay putting the data mesh into production, increase costs, and risk large-scale inconsistencies and incompatibilities across domains.

To prevent these problems, a data mesh platform should be built by a dedicated, central platform team. Not everything in a data mesh is decentralized. The platform must implement all the tools and interfaces a domain-engineering team needs to simplify the lifecycle of building, testing, deploying, securing, maintaining, and sharing a data product with a consumer or with other data domains. The domain teams shouldn't need to worry about the underlying infrastructure resource provisioning. You can do this by exposing a set of standardized platform APIs or scripts that the data product developer can use to state their infrastructure needs. Then you can let the platform handle the creation and management of storage, compute, data pipelines, and access control. This will result in a standardized way of creating data products, securing them, finding them, connecting to them, and reading data from them. In a data mesh, the domain-engineering teams are made up of generalist technologists instead of specialists, so reducing complexity through a data mesh platform can free them up to innovate with their data.

The aim of this principle is to save costs, reduce complexity, lighten the load on domain teams, reduce the need for technical specialization, and automate governance policies.

Principle #4: Federated Computational Governance

Principle #4 states that a collaborative data governance between domains and a central data team exists to define, implement, and monitor global rules (for example, interoperability, data quality, data security, regulations, and data modeling).

Data governance in a centralized architecture is much easier than in a data mesh, because with a centralized architecture approach, just one central data team owns all the data and defines, implements, and monitors all the data governance. However, this centralized approach often results in a bottleneck, slowing down the decision-making process and limiting the ability of individual domains to respond swiftly to the changing conditions and specific situations they face. It can also lead to a lack of localized expertise and contextual understanding, as the central team has to govern a vast variety of data without in-depth knowledge of each domain's nuances.

In a data mesh, a central data team defines and oversees all the data governance standards and policies, including such things as data quality, data security, regulations, and data modeling. The central data team is composed of domain representatives and subject matter experts (on compliance, legal, security, and so forth). However, implementing and monitoring data governance is left to the domains, since they own the data and know it best.

The challenge with distributing responsibilities across multiple domain teams is the potential for inconsistencies and conflicting practices, leading to operational inefficiencies and increased complexity. Domains might implement different standards for data quality (for instance, using full names of US states versus two-letter postal abbreviations). They might use different security systems or data-modeling techniques. But not all governance rules can be set globally; some are context specific and really should be set by the domain. For example, the central data team can specify that users must be authenticated, while the domain teams define what data products each user has access to.

This kind of inconsistency can lead to bad data, people seeing data they should not see, and other issues. Centralized systems often struggle with these nuances as they try to impose a one-size-fits-all policy, which can lead to misalignments and a failure to meet specific needs and demands of different departments or divisions.

That's why the concept of federated data governance, which combines centralized oversight with domain-specific autonomy, is crucial for maintaining consistency and security across the organization. The hope is to strike a balance between domain independence and central data team oversight. Whenever possible, it helps to automate implementing and monitoring policies and to tag data for easier identification.

The "Pure" Data Mesh

Now that you understand the four principles, take a look at Figure 13-1. It shows a high-level data mesh architecture that uses the four principles. The first two principles are decentralized, with each domain creating analytical data using its own IT team and infrastructure. But the other two principles require centralized teams—one to implement a data infrastructure platform and one to implement a shared governance for all the domains to use.

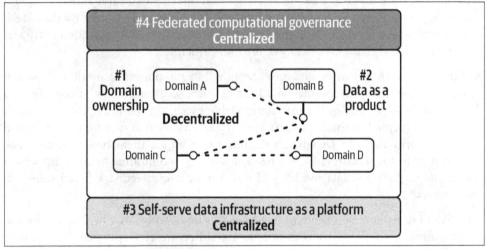

Figure 13-1. Data mesh architecture

So what makes a *true* data mesh? This is where the confusion starts. There are no universal rules on when a solution can be called a data mesh.

If a company builds a data mesh that completely follows all four principles, we would all feel confident calling that solution a "pure" data mesh. But what if the solution uses only three of the principles? Can we still call it a data mesh? What about two?

What if the solution uses all four principles, but in a way that doesn't fulfill all the requirements of the principle? For example, you could follow principle #2, but have the domains share the same infrastructure by having one physical data lake that is logically separated into domain-specific folders that are accessible only by their respective domains, or perhaps by assigning multiple domains to one of a handful of compute clusters. As another example, using principle #3, central IT might offer scripts that help build domain storage and management, but leave the domains to build out the rest of the infrastructure themselves. And consider one more: for principle #4, central IT could establish standards for data security and regulation, but have domains self-monitor for compliance and leave them free to do data quality and modeling as they see fit.

Some companies build a solution with two or three partially implemented principles and call it a data mesh. Others create separate data lakes for each domain and say they've built a data mesh. However, simply grouping data by business departments or organizing data into domains is not a data mesh. Even assuming they've properly designed their domains (the subject of the next section), that approach applies principle #1 but none of the others.

Some vendors will tell you that if you use their product, you will have a data mesh, even though data mesh is all about an organizational and cultural shift, not about technology. I have even heard people say that all you need to do to create a data mesh is to connect all your data lakes and data warehouses using virtualization software! Never mind that this doesn't use *any* of the four principles.

As you can see, there can be lots of "exceptions" to the pure data mesh within each principle. How many exceptions would it take for a solution not to be considered a data mesh (think of this as the minimum viable mesh)? If the four principles aren't universally accepted in total, we can't even try to answer that question. And should we all conform 100% to Dehghani's definitions or adjust them based on feedback from others in the industry? Do we need an industry committee to come up with a revised definition of a data mesh? And how do we avoid feedback based solely on self-interest?

I'm afraid I don't have all the answers. I hope this book will start a healthy discussion by providing some clarity on common data architecture concepts and the architectures that have preceded data mesh.

Data Domains

The process of designing a domain-oriented architecture, called *domain-driven design* (DDD), is very difficult and time-consuming. DDD comes from software design, but it gets much more challenging when dealing with data. The first step is to define what *domain* means in the context of your company.

According to Dehghani's first principle, analytical data should be owned by the business domains that are closest to it—either the source of the data or its main consumers. She defines three types of domain-oriented analytical data:

Source-aligned domain data
> Source-aligned domain data is analytical data that corresponds closely to the operational sources where the data originates. Data is copied from the source

application's operational databases to the domain and transformed to become collaborating analytical data. This data is not fitted or modeled for a particular consumer. Source-aligned domains can have one or more sources: the data usually come from that domain's operational systems but could be operational or analytical data from other domains. For example, a company that sells books online could divide its data into domains based on the customer's purchasing journey: product search, browsing, checkout, and payment. The challenge of creating domains is ownership; for example, if a business is currently divided into application domains (domains based solely on supporting a particular application) but instead needs to be divided into business domains (based on business capabilities), a business domain could own more than one application.

Aggregated domain data
Aggregated domain data is analytical data that combines and/or aggregates data from other domains, generally to help with query performance. For example, you could combine data from the manufacturing domain and the sales domain to more easily and quickly create a profit and loss report or to create a data model that is much easier for consumers to use.

Consumer-aligned domain data
Consumer-aligned domain data is analytical data that has been transformed to fit the needs of one or more specific departments or use cases. Consumer-aligned domains almost always receive their data from source-aligned domains. For example, the domain data for a manufacturing domain can be modeled and described in two different ways: one for those who know manufacturing (source aligned) and one for those outside manufacturing (consumer aligned). Another example is transforming source-aligned data into consumer-aligned data as a way to make it easier to train machine learning models.

For more details on data domains and domain-driven design, I highly recommend Piethein Strengholt's *Data Management at Scale*, second edition (O'Reilly, 2023).

Data Mesh Logical Architecture

Figure 13-2 shows how a data mesh logical architecture could look for a company with a handful of domains. Each of these domains would have one or more products.

In Figure 13-2, manufacturing, sales, and supplier are all source-aligned domains. Each domain has its own operational and analytical data. For example, the sales domain could use Salesforce to track all the information about its customers (operational data). Sales could then put its data in a data lakehouse architecture (see Chapter 12) and combine it with other data sources that contain operational data and with analytical data from the supplier domain. This would create sales analytical data that could then land in the data lakehouse. Sales also creates APIs to share that analytical data and its associated metadata with other domains and consumers.

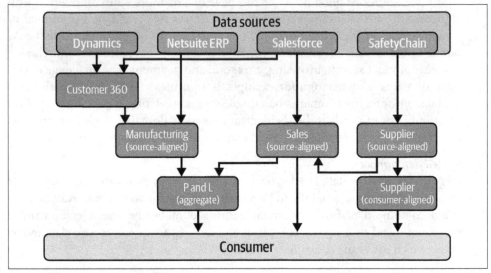

Figure 13-2. Data mesh logical architecture

Note the consumer-aligned domain for supplier. This was created because the analytical data in the supplier source-aligned domain was too complex for people outside the supplier domain to understand. In the supplier consumer-aligned domain, the data model is simplified and the supplier jargon made easier to understand.

There is also a profit and loss (P&L) aggregate domain that is built using data from the manufacturing source-aligned domain and the sales source-aligned domain. In large part, this is done for performance reasons. Executing a query or report that combines data from multiple domains can be too slow if those domains have separate data lakes that are very far apart geographically.

Finally, there is a customer 360 domain. This takes customer data (such as demographic, behavioral, transactional, and customer feedback data) from various sources, cleans and masters it (see Chapter 6), and combines it to get a full picture of the customer. All domains that need customer data pull from this customer 360 domain. This is a much better solution than having each domain pull, clean, and master customer data themselves.

As you've seen, having many domains can lead to a complicated mess. Imagine what the diagram in Figure 13-2 could look like with dozens or even hundreds of domains. This is why domain design is so important. I covered it earlier in this chapter, but I encourage you to look at other resources that go into depth on this topic. You will need to spend a lot of time up front designing domains and products before you begin building your data mesh to ensure you won't have to go back and redesign it months in.

Different Topologies

There are many possible variations or topologies of a data mesh architecture. Figure 13-3 shows three types that I will discuss:

Mesh Type 1

In this architecture, all domains use the same technology. For example, they might all use the same cloud provider and be limited to that provider's products, so each domain would be using the same products for storage, data pipelines, security, relational data warehouses, reporting, metadata catalog, MDM, data virtualization, APIs, ML tools, and so on. There may be a few options within some products, but these choices would be minimal. Each domain would have its own infrastructure, so everything would be decentralized—except storage. Instead of each domain having its own data lake, there would be one enterprise data lake, with each domain getting its own container or folder in the lake that only it can access.

Logically, then, the domains each have their own data lakes, but physically, the data for all the domains is in one data lake. Many customers use Mesh Type 1 because of performance problems with combining data when you have multiple physical data lakes, which could be located many miles apart. In addition, having one physical data lake greatly simplifies securing and monitoring the data, as well as doing disaster recovery backups.

Mesh Type 2

In this architecture, domains use the same technology as in Mesh Type 1. Instead of one enterprise data lake for all the domain data, each domain has its own data lake. All the data lakes use the same technology. This makes the infrastructure truly decentralized, but at a cost: the technical challenge of linking all the data lakes together and getting acceptable performance when combining data from multiple domains. This is why I see more companies using Mesh Type 1.

Mesh Type 3

In this architecture, each domain can use whatever technologies and whichever cloud provider it wants and have its own data lake (which can also use any technology). You might have DomainA and DomainD using Azure, DomainB using AWS, and DomainC using GCP, while DomainA chooses Azure Synapse for its relational data warehouse and DomainD chooses SQL Server in a VM for its data warehouse. The challenges would include dealing with different types of security for each domain, finding and supporting experts for dozens of products, creating governance standards for many products in different clouds (principle #4), creating automated infrastructure that can allow for all this variety (principle #3), *and* trying to combine data from multiple products in different clouds. This fits into the category of the pure data mesh discussed earlier. This formidable list is why I feel Mesh Type 3 will never be adopted.

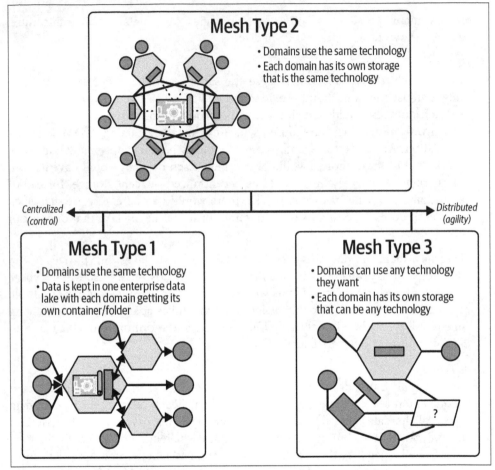

Figure 13-3. Three data mesh topologies on a spectrum from control to agility

On the left of Figure 13-3, the architectures have the most centralization, and the architectures become more distributed as you move to the right.

Data Mesh Versus Data Fabric

Data fabric and data mesh are both instrumental concepts in today's data landscape, but they serve distinct roles and should not be confused. At its core, a data fabric is an *architectural framework*, designed to be employed within one or more domains inside a data mesh. The data mesh, however, is a *holistic concept*, encompassing technology, strategies, and methodologies. In fact, its definition is so encompassing that I hesitate to even label it an architecture.

On the other side of the spectrum, a data fabric's technological and architectural underpinnings can be tailored to support the various intricacies and components within a data mesh. Their relationship is not one of competition or interchangeability but rather of synergy. A single data mesh might incorporate multiple data fabrics, each tailored to the unique needs of its respective domain.

In this context, you can think of each domain in the data mesh as its own ecosystem. Within this ecosystem, the domain can build, refine, and operate its own data fabric, ensuring that it aligns with specific requirements and goals. To put it another way, while the data mesh provides a blueprint for a decentralized and domain-oriented approach to data, data fabrics furnish the architectural and technological infrastructure that powers these domains. Utilizing them in tandem can lead to a more integrated and efficient data infrastructure. This also applies to combining data mesh with a modern data warehouse or data lakehouse architecture.

Use Cases

Hopefully by now you have a good understanding of data mesh as described by Dehghani, which I will call the "pure" data mesh. While the pure data mesh sounds great in theory, it is very hypothetical and has limited technology to support it. Therefore, practical data mesh solutions will include many exceptions to Dehghani's vision. With most of the built solutions, there are so many exceptions to the pure data mesh that these "data mesh" implementations should not even be called a data mesh.

The main question to ask is this: are you trying to accomplish just data federation—integrating data from multiple, disparate sources without physically consolidating or storing the data in a single repository owned and managed by IT—or are you really trying to build a data mesh? You can accomplish data federation without building a data mesh; basic data federation can be thought of as satisfying principle #1 of data mesh and not the other three principles. If you go this route, should your solution should still be called a data mesh? I think you can call it whatever you like, but it may be more accurate to call it an enterprise data lakehouse or data fabric architecture, especially when each domain has its own workspace; the most accurate description of what you have built is that it is an enterprise data lakehouse or data fabric architecture with multiple workspaces (one workspace for each domain). Remember that you can satisfy principle #1 of a data mesh if each domain owns the analytical data derived from their operational data, even if IT creates the analytical data. However, you can't satisfy principle #2 unless each domain creates their own analytic data *and* creates the interface to share that data.

Also keep in mind that to satisfy principle #1, your organization has to have gone through the process of reorganizing your company by business domains. I question whether doing the work of creating domains is worth it if you are not also satisfying principle #2 (data as a product); if IT, not the domains, will be the cleaning that data, then you will be missing a big point of having a data mesh.

As an example, say your company acquires a lot of other companies. You have each of those acquisitions own their data, and IT use virtualization software to access it. In this scenario, you have accomplished data federation, but you certainly do not have a data mesh; you are not splitting your organization out by data domains (unless you define domains by business function and decide that acquired businesses are their own domains, which doesn't make sense because you would then, for example, have multiple HR domains with duplicate HR products). Even so, again, organizing domains based on acquisitions is only satisfying principle #1. I would argue that principle #2 needs to be satisfied to call the architecture a data mesh, as it realizes the two biggest benefits of a data mesh: organizational and technical scaling.

One last point: in the quest to strike a balance between centralization and decentralization within a data mesh, understanding the distribution of responsibilities is crucial. Figure 13-4 is a scale that shows where each responsibility area might fit for a fictional use case.

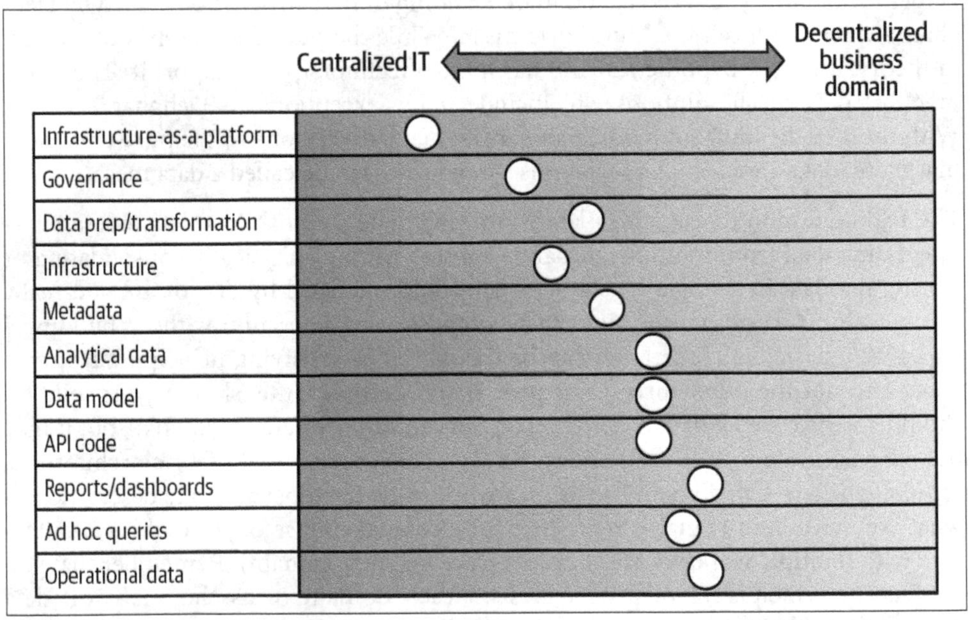

Figure 13-4. Division of responsibilities and ownership between a centralized IT department and decentralized business domains (fictional example)

On the left of Figure 13-4 is centralized IT, and on the right are the decentralized business domains. A dot in the far-left means centralized IT does all of the particular item, and a dot in the far-right means each decentralized business domain does all of the particular item. Dots in between show where each responsibility area falls on this spectrum.

If most of your dots are on the far left, there is so much centralization in your solution that calling it a data mesh might not be appropriate. It might be better classified as an enterprise data fabric or data lakehouse.

Summary

This chapter provided a comprehensive overview of the data mesh concept and its fundamental principles. It began with a comparative analysis of centralization and decentralization, emphasizing the shift from a monolithic architecture to a decentralized data landscape where data is treated as a valuable product owned by cross-functional teams. I then explained Zhamak Dehghani's four principles of the data mesh: domain-oriented decentralized data ownership, data as a product, self-serve data infrastructure as a platform, and federated computational governance. These concepts highlight the importance of understanding data as a holistic entity that is owned, maintained, and utilized by specific domain teams. The idea is to treat each data unit as an individual product with its own lifecycle, governed by the team that best understands its value and use.

After detailing foundational principles, the chapter dove into the pure data mesh, emphasizing its unadulterated form. We then explored data domains, highlighting their role in structuring the decentralized environment. The data mesh logical architecture and the various topologies supporting the data mesh were discussed, showcasing their influence on data flow and interaction. A comparison between the data mesh and data fabric clarified their distinct characteristics and applications. Finally, use cases for the data mesh were discussed.

Even though the data mesh approach can be a game changer in how we handle data, it's not without hurdles and difficulties, which I'll delve into in the next chapter. I'll also address some of the common misconceptions about the data mesh and help you figure out if adopting a data mesh is the right move for your organization.

CHAPTER 14

Should You Adopt Data Mesh? Myths, Concerns, and the Future

I'll be up-front—this chapter about the challenges of data mesh is one of the book's longest chapters. That's not because I think a data mesh is a bad idea or that the other architectures I've discussed are better; it's that there are a lot of myths, concerns, and challenges you need to be aware of. If you decide to pursue building a data mesh, I want you to make an educated choice and not be swayed too much by the hype.

In the pages that follow, I'll dissect the misconceptions surrounding the data mesh, address the genuine concerns that often go unspoken, help you assess its fit within your organizational structure, and provide actionable recommendations for successfully implementing it. Finally, I'll glance toward the potential horizon of data mesh's journey and end with a discussion of the best use case for each of the four data architectures.

Myths

As the concept of data mesh gains traction in the tech community, a variety of misconceptions have emerged, often clouding the understanding of data mesh's actual scope, benefits, and challenges. In this section, I aim to demystify these myths, providing a nuanced perspective on what data mesh truly entails and how it fits into the broader data architecture landscape.

Myth: Using Data Mesh Is a Silver Bullet That Solves All Data Challenges Quickly

In fact, the reality is the exact opposite. Building a data mesh takes much longer than building the other architectures mentioned in this book. Dehghani doesn't claim that a data mesh is a silver bullet, but in the media hype, her ideas often come across as such. That's why it's important to discuss the complexity and challenges of using data mesh.

Myth: A Data Mesh Will Replace Your Data Lake and Data Warehouse

As you learned in Chapter 13, each domain in a data mesh still needs a data lake and possibly also a relational data warehouse. What changes is that you no longer have a "central" data lake and RDW owned by a central IT team. Instead of having all data for all domains land in one data lake and one RDW, each domain keeps its own data. Thus, with a data mesh, you in fact have *more* data lakes and data warehouses, with which the domains must work in collaboration.

Myth: Data Warehouse Projects Are All Failing, and a Data Mesh Will Solve That Problem

I often hear people claim that current big data solutions don't scale and propose a data mesh as the solution. I have to take issue with that argument. While hundreds of thousands of organizations have implemented successful big data solutions, there are very few data meshes in production (none of which are "pure" data meshes).

In my 15 years working in data warehousing, I've seen many "monolithic" architectures scale their technology and IT people very well, even supporting petabytes of data.

Sure, many big data projects fail. However, most fail for reasons (usually related to people and processes) that would also make a data mesh fail. The available technology for centralizing data has improved greatly and will continue to improve. Serverless options now meet the big data needs of most organizations, allowing solutions to scale along with saving costs.

Myth: Building a Data Mesh Means Decentralizing Absolutely Everything

This is perhaps the most common myth. The reality is that even with a pure data mesh, a central IT team is still responsible for creating infrastructure as a service (principle #3) to jumpstart each domain's infrastructure. A central IT team is also responsible for creating and monitoring the data governance policies that each domain follows (principle #4). It wouldn't make sense for each domain to build its own infrastructure from scratch. Nor would it make sense for each domain to create its own data governance policies—you'd end up with as many types of security and interpretations of standards and regulations as there are domains.

Myth: You Can Use Data Virtualization to Create a Data Mesh

I've heard many data virtualization advocates say that if you use data virtualization to connect all your data lakes and data warehouses, you will have a data mesh! But that approach completely ignores the four principles of the data mesh (see Chapter 13).

It is a myth that you can take a single-enterprise data fabric (Chapter 11), apply data virtualization to it, and turn it into a data mesh. You can try to do that, but the result is far from a data mesh—it's *data federation*, which means integrating data from multiple, disparate sources without physically consolidating or storing it in a single central repository. Decentralization is one small piece of what makes up a data mesh—just adding virtualization won't satisfy any of the four data mesh principles!

For example, say a company has an enterprise data fabric that uses data virtualization. Each domain generates its own analytical data, and the data fabric connects to that data via data virtualization software. Is this a data mesh? Let's apply the four principles to find out:

- Principle #1 is about domain ownership. Are these true data domains or simply separate organizations within the company?

- Principle #2 is about treating data as a product. Does each domain have its own team building the analytical solution, using that domain's own infrastructure? Are those teams following a data contract that governs how they make data and metadata available to everyone else? And is this organization using data virtualization to connect to all of its domains, or only some?

  Importantly, if each domain doesn't have its own domain team and infrastructure, then a siloed data engineering team is still acting as an IT bottleneck. Likewise, if any domains aren't using data virtualization, their data needs to be collected and centralized. Helping to scale infrastructure and the organization are the two main benefits of a data mesh, and if the domains aren't following principle #2, they're not realizing those benefits.

- For principle #3, we can ask: Is a separate team creating self-serve data infrastructure as a platform?

- And for Principle 4: Is there a separate team creating federated computational governance?

As you can see, there is a big difference between a true data mesh solution and a data fabric solution that uses data virtualization.

Concerns

There's plenty of data mesh hype, but so far very little has been published about its downsides and challenges. This section attempts to cover those challenges comprehensively, grouping them by subject area and offering solutions to help overcome the concerns when possible. If, after reading all these concerns, you're sure you can overcome any that pose a problem, great! A data mesh may be for you. And when you run into any of these concerns down the road, you won't be surprised—you'll be prepared. My hope is that by knowing about these issues, you can address them before you get started, greatly increasing your odds of success.

While this list focuses on data mesh, many of these concerns apply to other architectures, so it's good to review them all. Even if you are using one of the other data architectures, I've seen firsthand that learning about data mesh can start lively conversations that can help you improve whatever architecture you use.

Philosophical and Conceptual Matters

Zhamak Dehghani's original blogs and book on data mesh set the standard, but people have interpreted her writings in many different ways. Some have come up with "exceptions" to the pure data mesh and other ideas about what a data mesh should be. So, if you want to build a data mesh, what definition are you going to use? Just getting everyone involved in building the data mesh to come to a consensus can take months. It's especially challenging when the makers of the many products used to build a data mesh all have different ideas of what a data mesh is.

To align your team on a shared understanding of data mesh, consider forming a cross-functional governance committee to set foundational definitions and standards. Utilize stakeholder workshops and documented definitions to ensure everyone is on the same page. Pilot projects can serve as practical tests for these definitions, allowing you to adapt as needed. Open communication and periodic reviews will help maintain this alignment as you implement your data mesh.

Having a single source of truth helps ensure that the organization bases its decisions on reliable data, with no ambiguity or disagreement about which data is correct. Everyone working from the same set of information makes operations more efficient and effective.

In a data mesh, data can be read from one domain and transformed and stored by another domain. This dynamic topology can make it very difficult to maintain a single source of truth. In fact, Dehghani has called the idea of a single source of truth a "myth."[1] I strongly disagree; I personally have seen dozens of companies implement a

---

1 Zhamak Dehghani, *Data Mesh: Delivering Data-Driven Value at Scale* (O'Reilly, 2022), p. 26.

single source of truth in various data architectures and have read about hundreds more. It can be done with a data mesh if the organization establishes rigorous data governance and utilizes a centralized data catalog (see Chapter 6). Coupled with cross-domain data quality metrics and strong collaboration among data domains, not only is a single source of truth feasible, but it can also enhance the mesh's flexibility and scalability.

There are huge risks in implementing a data mesh, especially compared to the proven success of the data warehouse. It requires drastic organizational change and a whole new architecture. Plus, the data mesh assumes that each source system can dynamically scale to meet consumer demand. That can get particularly challenging when certain data assets become "hot spots" within the ecosystem, seeing a surge in queries or usage.

Combining Data in a Decentralized Environment

You will always need to combine data from multiple domains for queries or reports. Sometimes you might need to combine data from dozens of domains, which could be in many separate data lakes that are geographically far apart. You'll need to think carefully about how to overcome performance issues because solutions like data virtualization (see Chapter 6) and aggregate domains have their own trade-offs.

Another trade-off of having autonomous domains is that each domain tends to focus only on data products for its own analytical needs. Often, the owners forget to think about how their data might be combined with data from other domains and do little to make it easier to combine their data model with others. When someone needs to combine data from multiple domains, they could face a lot of difficulty.

Principle #4 can help you define a set of data modeling rules for all domains to follow, but that requires someone to understand *all* of the domains—a feature of centralized architectures that the data mesh tries to get away from. With the internal focus of domains in a data mesh, the company might not have someone who investigates ways to get value out of combined data. Thus, it's important to ensure that such a person exists.

If you are using a Common Data Model (CDM; see Chapter 8), then every domain needs to use it. You will have to coordinate to make sure each domain has its own set of unique IDs for records with the same types of data as other domains (such as customers or products). Otherwise, when you combine data from multiple domains, you could end up with duplicate IDs. That could introduce counting errors, aggregation errors, and data inconsistencies into queries and reports. To prevent duplicate IDs in a CDM across multiple domains, you can use a globally unique identifier (GUID) or establish a centralized ID management system to allocate unique IDs. Alternatively, you can apply namespacing, where each ID is prefixed or suffixed with a domain-specific code.

Additionally, as domains build their products and data models, other domains and consumers will consume their data and combine data from multiple domains based on those data models. When a domain changes its data model or interface, dependencies can cause problems for the other domains and consumers using it with core data models or queries that join domain data models. You'll need to arrange for all domains to coordinate when any domain changes its data model.

Finally, the domain teams may have different ideas about what counts as "clean" or "standardized" data. If domains disagree on questions like whether to define states with abbreviations or full state name, combining data from multiple domains can cause havoc. And what if the domains don't have the time to build the code to clean the data properly? To tackle inconsistencies in data cleanliness across domains, establish a centralized governance framework that sets standard definitions for clean or standardized data. Offer data-cleaning templates or shared libraries to save time and ensure uniformity. A governance committee or data steward can help enforce these standards, making it easier to combine data from multiple domains without issues.

Other Issues of Decentralization

Aggregate and consumer-aligned domains (see Chapter 13) aren't decentralized. To create an aggregate domain, you are taking data from multiple domains and centralizing that data. With aggregate and consumer-aligned domains, you must decide who owns, builds, and maintains them—the problem that principle #1 is intended to prevent. Building such domains also results in duplicating data. All of this seems to run counter to the spirit of a data mesh.

To reconcile aggregate and consumer-aligned domains with the principles of a data mesh, consider shared governance and designated data stewards to manage these domains. Utilize data virtualization to minimize duplication and implement an API layer for abstraction. Maintain transparency through robust metadata and audit trails.

Security is also an issue. In a centralized architecture, one team is responsible for securing all data. In a data mesh, that responsibility is farmed out to dozens or even hundreds of domains, creating many more doors a hacker can break through. This greatly increases the risk of security infringement.

You'll need to assign someone to scan for personally identifiable information (PII) and see who is accessing it, as well as someone to fix the issue if anyone is seeing PII that they should not be allowed to see. Someone should be responsible for making sure all domains have sufficient security.

It's also hard to choose and implement technology consistently across domains. Although principle #3 (infrastructure as a service) is supposed to prevent this, if you have dozens of domains whose people have different levels of skills and experience, they'll likely choose different technologies, set up their infrastructure differently, and configure their cloud-product settings differently. This can lead to major issues with consuming data.

You could limit what technologies you automatically provision for each domain, but that violates principle #1 by limiting each domain's freedom to choose technology for their own use case. Supporting many different technologies may be challenging, as will creating a common interface across all domains. As a compromise, you could create a large catalog of approved, vetted technologies—offering domains a choice, but within a framework that ensures easier integration.

Furthermore, although principle #4 (federated governance) creates data mesh policies, each domain is left to implement them. This could lead to inconsistent implementations, potentially resulting in performance degradations and differing cost profiles.

Complexity

The ideas behind data mesh are complicated. I'll freely admit that I had to read Dehghani's blogs dozens of times to fully understand this architecture. Even years later, I sometimes still realize that I did not understand a part of it correctly. I'm not the only one; nearly everyone I talk to is confused about data mesh. This complexity, combined with the lack of a standard definition of a data mesh, means that most teams that plan to build a data mesh will have to invest a lot of time up front in making sure everyone understands it (and understands it *correctly*). If it's going to take a long time to get started and ramp up, be sure that the data mesh will bring you enough benefits to make it worth the time and effort.

This complicated nature extends to organizational complexity, though data mesh proponents claim the opposite. Distributed teams involve many more people, and they may not always communicate effectively.

Duplication

Dehghani argues that duplicating source data isn't a problem in data mesh, writing that for each domain, "it's very likely that we won't need a data lake, because the distributed logs and storage that hold the original data are available for exploration from different addressable immutable datasets as products."[2] But you can't always directly access the original data from those immutable datasets, as there are often problems with security or immediate retrieval. (I still have many customers using mainframes that are impossible to connect to.) So, to do anything with that source data, you'll still

---

2 Dehghani, "How to Move Beyond a Monolithic Data Lake to a Distributed Data Mesh," (*https://oreil.ly/cv2sX*) MartinFowler.com, May 20, 2019.

have to make a copy and store it in a data lake. In fact, a data mesh may result in *more* copies of data than in other architectures, since domains may need to copy data from other domains to complete their data products or to create aggregate or customer-oriented domains. Keeping all the copies in sync can incur extra cost and effort.

Similarly, a *conformed dimension*, used in a star schema (see Chapter 8), has the same meaning to every fact with which it relates. Conformed dimensions allow you to categorize and describe facts and measures (like a date or customer dimension) in the same way, ensuring consistent reporting across the enterprise. Conformed dimensions are very popular in a star schema solution. In a data mesh, those conformed dimensions must be duplicated in each domain that has related fact tables. That's a lot of duplicated data that needs to be kept synchronized.

Chances are, your company is purchasing third-party data, such as weather, stock, or competitor data. In a centralized architecture, this is handled by one person or group, so the chances of two teams in the same company purchasing the same data are remote. However, in a data mesh, each domain purchases its own data. How do you prevent two domains from wasting money by purchasing the same datasets? None of the data mesh principles seem to cover this area, but you can enhance principle #4 by setting up a centralized team that handles all requests for third-party data.

Despite principle #3, some domains will likely build similar data ingestion or analytics platforms. With a centralized approach, there is only one team building a platform, but in a data mesh, dozens of domains might do so. It's a good idea to promote sharing these solutions so domains aren't duplicating one another's efforts or missing out on helpful solutions other domains create.

Feasibility

Migrating to a data mesh is a massive undertaking that requires a huge investment in organizational change and technical implementation, far more than with the other data architectures. This will result in a much higher cost and a much longer timeline—many months, possibly even years, before you can put it into production. It takes a lot to get domains using their own created reports and dashboards well enough that central IT can stop supplying them. In the meantime, unless you are a brand-new company, you will have to keep your existing platform running. This can be quite challenging, especially as new domains transition from supplying operational data to central IT to keeping it within their domain.

Again, data mesh is a concept, not a technology. It's all about creating organizational and cultural shifts within a company. Dehghani's book doesn't discuss how to use existing technology to build a data mesh. That's likely because there are major gaps in the available technology in areas such as data quantum, automation, product sharing, domain infrastructure setup, and collaborative data governance.

Principle #2 requires that technology be available to publicize and share domains, but the current technology for this is in its infancy. Principle #3 requires very sophisticated solutions for automating infrastructure provisioning, but current solutions do only a small piece of this at best. And creating and managing principle #4's global rules—at the same time that domains create and manage their own rules—means relying heavily on automation and coding solutions for data product lifecycle management, standards as code, policies as code, automated tests, automated monitoring, and embedding policy execution in each data product. This requires very sophisticated software that, where it exists at all, is so far quite limited. Companies have to build it themselves or just skip this step, thus violating the data mesh principles.

Dehghani describes data products as having output data ports (interfaces) with explicitly defined contracts and APIs. These APIs would serve multimodel access, bitemporal data, and immutable read-only access, and they could transfer huge amounts of data and scale to a huge number of requests. In addition, these APIs would span one or more multiple physical infrastructures, multiple clouds, and on-prem hosting environments. So far, the technology for APIs to support all of that does not exist. It likely never will.

Further, APIs are rarely used with data; interacting with data is usually left to SQL queries. Creating APIs for all interactions with data is a big culture shift that would take way more time than using SQL queries.

In her book, Dehghani introduces a new unit of logical architecture called a *data quantum*, which controls and encapsulates all the structural components needed to share data autonomously as a data product that others can consume. This includes data, metadata, code (compute), policy, and infrastructure dependencies. Data and compute are logically joined as one unit, but the underlying physical infrastructures that host code and data are kept separate. There is currently no technology for this. While Dehghani has started a company to create a data quantum using data product containers, it could be years before her company or any other builds components to tackle the majority of these requirements.

I think that data quantum is a very risky concept. You can certainly build a data mesh without making use of it. Think of data lineage using a data quantum. If each domain's metadata is only available within the data product itself, to see its metadata, lineage, or data quality information, you'd need to perform complex federated queries against *all* the data products. You could replicate all the metadata to a central location, but that would require constant syncing and make the overall architecture much more complicated. Then there is the matter of security; you'd need to update metadata such as sensitivity labels, privacy classifications, and ownership information for data that is physically located in multiple places.

The issues with copying data extend to data products. If they are copied, their metadata is copied too, resulting in multiple copies of the same metadata that need to be kept in sync. Any updates to the metadata would need to be carried out simultaneously over multiple data product containers, requiring these containers to always be available and accessible. You risk ending up with different owners for the same metadata.

Finally, running hundreds or even thousands of small data products side by side dramatically increases complexity, increases utilization of infrastructure resources and networks, complicates configuration management, and introduces challenges with performance and reference data consistency.

Dehghani holds that since no data mesh–native technologies have yet been created, "you can utilize data warehousing technologies as an underlying storage and SQL access mode but allocate a separate schema to each data product,"[3] thus sharing compute. But this results in a centralized infrastructure, violating principle #1 and losing the biggest benefit of using a data mesh: technical scaling.

People

You'll need to find and hire quality engineering people and other skilled workers for each domain. It's hard enough finding good people for a central IT team, but in a data mesh, each domain is tasked not only with learning to build an infrastructure and analytical platform, but also creating and hiring its own mini IT team. If you have a lot of domains, that's *many* more people than you'd need in a centralized architecture—a huge trade-off when you're doing horizontal organizational scaling.

Principle #3 is designed to take away the need for deep technical skills and instead use higher cross-functional skills. This often entices organizations to have people from business domains, instead of experienced people with strong technical skills, do the implementation in each product group, especially since it's hard to find enough people with quality technical skills. Inexperienced people tend to build expensive, complex, badly performing data products.

Data mesh assumes that central IT data engineers don't have business and domain knowledge and thus that it's better to use people familiar with the domains that own the data. It further assumes that each domain team has the necessary skills to build robust data products or can acquire these skills.

That's not always true. Surprisingly, I've seen central IT people with more domain knowledge than the domain experts! The IT people also understand how to combine data from different domains. Sometimes the people running the operational systems have very little understanding of their data, especially from an analytical perspective; they're just focused on keeping the lights on. If central IT data engineers don't have

---

3 Dehghani, *Data Mesh*, p. 300.

the domain knowledge they need, why not have them obtain that knowledge and improve communication between IT and the domains? That could be a better solution than introducing a whole new way of working.

Data mesh proponents boast that instead of having data specialists with deep expertise in only one area, data mesh encourages *generalists*. No one works on one isolated step. Data mesh envisions cross-functional teams of people who have intermediate skills in many areas: for instance, streaming, ETL batch processing, data warehouse design, and data visualization, along with software-engineering practices such as coding, testing, and continuous delivery (DataOps). Think "jack of all trades, master of none." Again, if you have many domains, this means many roles to fill and salaries to pay. It's not easy to find and recruit people with such a wide range of skills, let alone lots of people. It's debatable whether these multiskilled people would be better than individuals with years of deep expertise in one area.

Domain-Level Barriers

Let's say your domain has finally been granted permission to have central IT add desperately needed features to the domain's analytics so that you can get real value out of your data. You've mapped out a plan with central IT to create the analytics in the next few months. Then you learn that your company will be building a data mesh and it's on *you* to hire a whole new team to create those needed features and the APIs to go with them. *Then* you're asked to delay the project for months while the company implements principles #3 and #4, designs the data domains, and writes the contract that will guide each domain's upgrades.

How would you feel? And what if people in dozens of domains feel that way? The company can't have a rogue domain; consumers as well as other domains depend on having data available from each domain, so it's crucial that every domain buys into the data mesh project. You'll need to:

- Provide compelling incentives to make up for the extra work, hassle, and delay. It's not enough incentive to tell them they're doing it "for the greater good."
- Gain buy-in from every domain for implementing a data mesh.
- Secure top-level executive sponsorship.
- Communicate a clear vision that shows benefits for each domain.
- Run pilot programs to demonstrate the efficacy of the new approach.
- Offer incentives, both financial and nonfinancial, to encourage participation.
- Establish transparent channels for ongoing communication.
- Offer support through competency centers or centers of excellence.

Plan for what you'll do if a domain does not want to follow the rules. This could be especially troublesome for data security and data quality standards. If you decide that domains that don't follow the rules can't join the data mesh, you'll have data silos.

There could also be domains that *can't* join the data mesh, even if they want to. Perhaps they don't have the budget to build a team to create an analytics platform, or circumstances force them to keep using older technology that can't handle an analytics platform. To incorporate their data into the data mesh, you might need a centralized architecture alongside the data mesh.

Effective product sharing is crucial to your data mesh's success. Sharing products within and outside each domain in a data mesh is very different from sharing data. You'll need a way for other domains or consumers to keep track of all the domains in your company and their data products. This will require all the domain metadata to be cataloged somewhere with a search mechanism and a way to request access: a sort of data marketplace, as described in Chapter 6.

The major cloud providers offer many software solutions for sharing data, but very few for sharing data products (and these are all recently released as of this writing). You'll need to decide: Will you purchase one or create your own?

A data mesh results in a shift toward a self-serve model for data requests, which presents challenges. Traditionally, domains have relied on central IT departments to handle the entirety of their analytical data needs, which encompassed everything from managing data to addressing specific requests like queries and reports. With data mesh, this responsibility is decentralized, landing squarely on the individual domains to satisfy those data requests. A potential risk is that some domains may lack the expertise to manage these tasks efficiently. Additionally, they can't merely replicate the solutions implemented by central IT, they have to improve them to show the value of a data mesh. As they craft their unique solutions, there's a possibility that these might not even be as effective or robust as the centralized systems they replace.

Organizational Assessment: Should You Adopt a Data Mesh?

By now, you understand what a data mesh is and the potential concerns that come with it. If you still feel like a data mesh is an option, the next step is to do a thorough assessment to find out if your organization is *ready* to build a successful data mesh. You can use the criteria in Table 14-1, which are drawn from Dehghani's book.[4] Dehghani recommends that companies consider building a data mesh only if all criteria are somewhat or highly applicable.

---

4 Dehghani, *Data Mesh*, pp. 271–75.

Table 14-1. Self-assessment of your company's readiness for data mesh

Criterion	Rating (select one)		
We have too much organizational complexity for our current system and our existing data architecture has become a blocker; it can't scale quickly enough to get value from data from many parts of the business.	Not applicable	Somewhat applicable	Highly applicable
Our company has a data-oriented strategy and a strategic vision for using and getting value out of data.	Not applicable	Somewhat applicable	Highly applicable
Our executives support the culture and work changes needed for a data mesh and are committed to motivating the entire organization to change how people work.	Not applicable	Somewhat applicable	Highly applicable
We see data as a valuable asset and regularly collect it, analyze it, and use it to inform business decisions. We have built our operations, decision-making processes, culture, and strategies around data. We invest heavily in a data technology infrastructure, analytics platforms, and machine learning. Our employees are data literate.	Not applicable	Somewhat applicable	Highly applicable
Our company likes to be on the "bleeding edge" and is always one of the first to adopt and implement new technologies and innovations, even when it involves some risk.	Not applicable	Somewhat applicable	Highly applicable
Our company employs modern engineering practices and technologies, including data-driven decision making and user-centered design, that enable many smaller teams instead of one large centralized team.	Not applicable	Somewhat applicable	Highly applicable
Our organization is structured around specific business areas or data domains, each with dedicated technical teams who build and support the products that serve that domain. Every domain has (or will soon have) a budget for creating analytical data from its operational data and for building its own data mesh infrastructure.	Not applicable	Somewhat applicable	Highly applicable
Even if it takes a long time, our company is committed to using machine learning and analytics to gain a competitive advantage over our competitors. We are committed to a process of culture change and to designing and building the technology necessary for data mesh, as well as a network of domain-oriented teams.	Not applicable	Somewhat applicable	Highly applicable

The reality, based on my experience, is that only a tiny percentage of companies—maybe 1%—find *all* of these categories somewhat or highly applicable. High scores on the early adopter, domain-oriented, and modern engineering categories are particularly rare.

Recommendations for Implementing a Successful Data Mesh

If you have a current data solution and decide to build a data mesh, I recommend a hub-and-spoke model, in which you build the data mesh as an extension to a centralized data solution (Figure 14-1). You might start by using new data to create new data mesh domains, but supplement those domains with your current centralized data solution in alignment with business needs. Slowly migrate your centralized data into data mesh domains over time as you continue adding more new domains from new data—don't try to convert all of your centralized data into data mesh domains in one fell swoop.

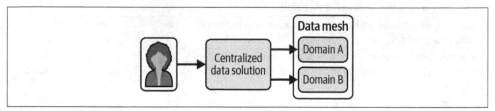

Figure 14-1. A hub-and-spoke model, with a data mesh supplementing and extending a centralized data solution

Implementing the data mesh gradually helps you manage the risks associated with a complete overhaul of your existing data architecture. If there's a failure in one part of the mesh, it's contained and doesn't affect the entire system. You get better control over compliance and security measures and time to establish proper governance and security protocols. This gradual approach also spreads out the cost and the demands on the workforce. Existing business processes that rely on the centralized data can continue to function smoothly during the transition, minimizing disruption to the business.

What I'm suggesting is an iterative approach. Implementing new domains gradually allows you to learn from each phase, make necessary adjustments, and apply those lessons to subsequent domains, creating a more robust system in the long run. Furthermore, it allows you to leverage your existing technology investment while moving toward a more modern architecture.

This approach is also an agile one. It gives you the flexibility to prioritize certain domains that provide more immediate value or align with strategic business initiatives. It allows for alignment with business needs rather than a forced migration all at once. You also get a chance to optimize the performance of each domain's infrastructure and can tailor it to that domain's specific needs and constraints.

Finally, the hub-and-spoke approach paves the way for a cultural shift over time, fostering cross-functional, domain-driven collaboration among data product owners, engineers, and business stakeholders.

This piecemeal data mesh implementation is a strategic approach that allows for careful planning, risk management, and alignment with business goals. It supports a gradual transition from a centralized data architecture to a decentralized one, leveraging both the old and the new systems during the transition period. It's a more adaptable and resilient approach than attempting a complete transition all at once, which is fraught with risk and complexity.

The Future of Data Mesh

I have talked to many people who believe that the idea of a centralized team building the entire data architecture is dying out and that eventually every company will move to a decentralized model. After all, centralized models don't scale well.

This was discussed back in the days of the Kimball versus Inmon debates (see Chapter 8). In the Inmon camp, IT centralized everything; but in the Kimball camp, the methodology was to build loosely centralized subject matter data marts and hold them together using conformed dimensions with a bus architecture. In practice, however, you had many domains building their own data marts in isolation, sometimes with different technologies, resulting in a decentralized architecture. When people needed to join and aggregate data from multiple domains, they created additional data marts and/or OLAP cubes.

Sometimes this strategy worked fine, but often it led to duplicated efforts, using all sorts of different technology and products. It was also difficult and commonly sent costs spiraling out of control. The company would then move back to a centralized model to prevent these problems.

Will the data mesh lead to the same cycle of problems? What makes this time any different? Although technology has come a long way since the data mart days, the problem really isn't one of technology—it's a people and process problem, and we haven't come nearly as far in solving those issues. Come up with all the cool new buzzwords and methods you like, but it's extremely hard to get people to change—and data mesh requires a ton of change.

I predict that very few companies will adopt data mesh architectures, and I don't believe that any of those solutions will be a pure data mesh. For those that do call their solution a data mesh, I estimate that most—perhaps 90%—will adopt domain ownership (principle #1), while fewer—perhaps 70%—will adopt data as a product (principle #2). Perhaps a very small percentage of those will take it to the level of a data quantum. About a third of companies will use some form of automated infrastructure for each domain (principle #3: self-serve data infrastructure as a platform), and maybe half will adopt federated computational governance (principle #4). I expect a very large percentage of solutions to place limits on the technologies that each domain can use.

Instead of trying to implement every element of a data mesh, I recommend focusing on how you can empower your data teams to deliver value faster and more frequently for your customers. From there, you can work backward to identify and adopt specific elements of a data mesh that will help you to achieve this goal.

In the end, a data mesh is a battle between centralization and decentralization. There will always be a mixture of both in any data mesh solution. It's about finding the right balance for your use case.

Zooming Out: Understanding Data Architectures and Their Applications

In the modern world of rapid technological advancement, businesses stand at a crossroads, surrounded by an abundance of data. This data, if harnessed correctly, can unlock unprecedented insights, streamline operations, and provide a competitive edge. The key to unlocking this potential lies in the architecture—the framework that decides how data will be stored, processed, and accessed.

Over the course of this book, I've delved deep into the intricacies of various data architectures, their evolution, and their practical application. Now, as I prepare to close this chapter, it's crucial to take a step back and view the landscape from a higher vantage point.

You have a great many choices. How can you know which one is right for your organization? To address this, let's look at some high-level use cases for each architecture, categorized by cost and complexity:

Modern data warehouse
    MDWs are most suitable for businesses that handle a small amount of data and are already accustomed to relational data warehouses, making for a gentle transition.

Data fabric
    As businesses grow and diversify, they often find themselves grappling with data from myriad sources, each differing in size, speed, and type. Data fabric is the architectural choice for those who need a seamless way to integrate these diverse data streams.

Data lakehouse
    This can be visualized as a middle-ground solution. You should engage with a data lakehouse as your primary solution until you encounter its limitations. When you do, you can transfer specific datasets to an RDW to better cater to your organization's needs.

Data mesh
    Tailored for very large, domain-oriented companies, the data mesh is for organizations that are confronting major scalability challenges and have the resources and time to invest in a robust solution.

These architectures are not mutually exclusive. The real world rarely deals in absolutes. Most organizations will find that their unique needs demand a mosaic of features from multiple architectures. Such a tailored solution can combine aspects of any or all of these architectures, adapted to the organization's specific data use cases and its evolving business capabilities.

Summary

This chapter addressed common myths about data mesh, clarified valid concerns, and assessed its fit within various organizational structures. I provided key recommendations for successful implementation, grounded in real-world practices and case studies. We explored the future of data mesh in the context of evolving technologies and business trends. Finally, I summarized all the data architectures to help guide you in the selection of the most appropriate data architecture for your specific business needs. Hopefully you now have both a theoretical understanding and practical insights that will allow you make informed decisions about data mesh adoption.

The future of business is inextricably linked with the future of data. As we move forward, the architectures we choose will determine not only how we store and access our data but also how our businesses grow, innovate, and compete. It's essential to approach this choice with deep understanding, adaptability, and a vision for the future. Remember, the architecture you choose today will pave the path for your business tomorrow. Choose wisely, and let your data lead the way.

The previous chapters of this book delved into technological aspects of data architectures. In Chapters 15 and 16, we'll explore the crucial topics of people and processes, examining team organization, the causes of project failures, and the keys to project success.

PART IV

People, Processes, and Technology

Congratulations! You have gotten through the foundational sections, the common data architecture concepts, and the four data architectures. But you're not done yet. Chapter 15 covers the biggest determining factors in the success of whatever solution you build: people and processes. Chapter 16 covers data architecture technologies. To ensure that it stays relevant for many years to come, this discussion takes a vendor-neutral, historical, and high-level perspective.

CHAPTER 15

People and Processes

In the complicated world of data architectures, while technology and tools might command the spotlight, people and processes form its heart and soul. As organizations transition from traditional data models to innovative structures like MDW, data fabric, or data lakehouse, and even further into decentralized paradigms like data mesh, the human element remains central. But why?

In my many years building data warehouses, applications, and reporting projects, I have seen what helps projects succeed and what makes them fail. Imagine constructing an architectural marvel—a skyscraper with state-of-the-art amenities. The blueprint is flawless, the materials top-notch. Yet if the builders, engineers, and managers aren't aligned in their vision, or if processes aren't in place to ensure cohesive action, the project can crumble before it even begins.

In much the same way, the transformation of a data architecture demands not just technological reshuffling but profound shifts in organizational culture. Changing how data is managed, processed, and valued means realigning how teams think about and interact with data. It means challenging established norms and embracing new methodologies. Such transitions are never merely technical; they are deeply human.

Central to this human element is delineating roles. Who does what? Who shoulders the responsibility for ensuring that data flows smoothly, that it is processed correctly, and that it is used ethically and effectively? Misunderstand or underestimate these roles, and you teeter on the precipice of inefficiency or, worse, project failure. Conversely, getting the roles right—ensuring that each team member understands their responsibilities and has the resources to fulfill them—is akin to setting solid foundational stones for your architectural wonder.

Yet, like any major endeavor, data projects come with their success stories and cautionary tales. The line between a triumphant data transition and a failed solution can often be traced back to how people were managed and how processes were designed. Learning from both the victories and the pitfalls offers invaluable insights into navigating the challenges and complexities of data architecture transformations.

As we delve into this chapter, we'll explore the intricacies of team organization, the nuances of roles in various data frameworks, and the critical factors that spell the difference between the success and failure of data projects. By the end of this journey, you'll appreciate that while tools and technologies evolve, it's the people and processes that determine whether they're wielded for success or relegated to the annals of missed opportunities.

Team Organization: Roles and Responsibilities

Building a data architecture requires a team (or many teams) with a diverse set of skills and roles. This section outlines some key roles, their responsibilities, and how they can collaborate to build a modern data warehouse, data fabric, or data lakehouse. (For a data mesh, you'll need additional roles; I'll talk about those next.) In smaller companies, one person might take on multiple roles; for example, the same person might serve as both data governance manager and data quality manager. In larger companies, several people may fill the same role—for example, you might have a dozen data engineers.

Roles for MDW, Data Fabric, or Data Lakehouse

Let's look first at the general roles:

Data architect
> Designs the high-level structure of the data architecture (MDW, data fabric, or data lakehouse) and decides what technologies and data governance policies the project should use.

Data engineer
> Responsible for building, testing, and maintaining the data architecture. They write scripts to extract, load, and transform data (ELT) from various sources into the data solution and work closely with the data architect to implement the designed architecture.

Data steward
> In charge of data quality and governance. They define and implement rules for data usage and standards, oversee data cleansing, manage data access rights, and work with users to resolve any data quality or access issues.

Database administrator (DBA)

Responsible for the operation, maintenance, and performance of the data system. They implement backup and recovery plans, optimize queries for performance, and keep the system running smoothly.

Data analyst

Collects, processes, and performs statistical descriptive and diagnostic analyses on large datasets, identifying patterns and trends, transforming these complex findings into understandable insights, and communicating them to stakeholders. They create comprehensive reports and dashboards to track business metrics.

Data scientist

Uses advanced statistical techniques, predictive modeling, and machine learning to extract valuable insights from data and solve complex problems. They design and implement ML models, perform predictive and prescriptive analysis, conduct A/B tests, and mine the data. They also contribute data-driven insights and recommendations to influence strategy and operations decisions.

Business analyst

Communicates between the data team and business users and helps define the business requirements for the data architecture, then translates those into technical requirements. They also validate data analysts' and scientists' insights and communicate them to business users.

Project manager/scrum master

Coordinates the team's work, ensures they are on track to meet their goals, and resolves any blockers. They also communicate the project's status to stakeholders and manage any risks.

Data privacy officer

Ensures compliance with data privacy regulations, works with the data steward to set usage policies, and responds to any data privacy incidents. In some sectors or regions, regulations mandate this role.

Data governance manager

Ensures the availability, usability, integrity, and security of the organization's data and creates and enforces data management policies and procedures for to ensure best practices across all business units.

Data quality manager

Oversees the completeness, consistency, and accuracy of data, including implementing data quality rules, monitoring data quality metrics, and coordinating with other teams to fix any data quality issues.

Roles for Data Mesh

As you learned in Chapters 13 and 14, the data mesh approach views data as a shared asset across different domains within an organization. Instead of having a central data team handle all aspects of data, the data mesh approach distributes responsibilities to cross-functional domain teams. Each team is responsible for the data it produces, which includes providing data as a product, ensuring its quality, and making it accessible to others. This changes the required teams, roles, and responsibilities quite a bit. Let's break it down team by team.

Domain teams

Each domain has one domain team. Its members are responsible for building their domain's analytical solution and implementing governance policies and the data mesh principles (outlined in Chapter 13). Most of the roles in the domain team, such as domain data engineers, data analysts, and domain data stewards, mirror the roles listed above for an MDW, data fabric, or data lakehouse, except their scope is a specific domain instead of the entire organization. Since each domain has its own solution, most, if not all, of these roles exist within each domain. One additional role specific to data mesh is the data product owner.

A domain data product owner takes responsibility for the data that their domain produces. This includes managing its lifecycle, ensuring its quality, making it accessible, and aligning it to business needs. The product owner should understand both the technical and business aspects of the data.

Self-service data infrastructure platform team

A platform team focused on self-service data infrastructure, in alignment with data mesh principle #3, can provide domain teams with the technology infrastructure, tools, and guidelines to build and manage their data products. Roles on this team include:

Data mesh architect
> Designs the general architecture and guidelines, coordinates the efforts of the domain teams, and facilitates communication and learning. While each domain team manages its data, this architect role ensures the data mesh's overall coherence.

Platform architect
> Designs the overall architecture of the data platform to supports the needs of the domains and accommodate a variety of data types, workloads, and analytical tools.

Platform engineers/developers
> Builds and maintains the platform infrastructure, including databases, APIs, container orchestration, and other aspects.

Data engineer
> Works on the pipelines that move and transform data within the platform, ensuring that the data is clean, consistent, and available to all who need it.

DevOps engineer
> Automates platform deployment, scaling, and management, ensuring that the platform is stable and reliable and can handle the data teams' needs.

DataOps engineer
> Manages and optimizes the lifecycle of data and data science models from end to end, including by monitoring data quality and ensuring that data privacy and compliance requirements are met.

Security and compliance officer
> Ensures that the platform follows all necessary regulations and best practices for data security and privacy.

Product owner/manager
> Acts as the link between the technical team and the business stakeholders, prioritizing and managing platform features and enhancements to align with users' needs and the business's objectives.

User experience (UX) designer
> Designs the interfaces that domain teams use to interact with the platform, aiming for ease of use and effectiveness.

Support and training staff
> Assists domain teams in using the platform, troubleshoots issues, and trains new users.

Federated computational governance platform team

In accordance with data mesh principle #4, another platform team is focused specifically on federated computational governance, providing each domain with the blueprints to help it comply with security and privacy regulations. Most domain teams implement these blueprints themselves, but this platform team may sometimes implement global polices. It provides the necessary guidance to help each domain team manage its data in alignment with the organization's policies and standards. This team must have a deep understanding of each domain's specific data needs and work to balance those needs with the organization's overall data governance requirements. Roles in this team include:

Data governance lead
> Guides the overall governance strategy and ensures that the team's initiatives align with the organization's strategic goals. They coordinate with various domain representatives and subject matter experts to define governance standards and policies.

Data governance specialist
> Establishes and oversees data standards and policies, working closely with domain teams to ensure they apply the guidelines correctly.

Data privacy and compliance officer
> Ensures that domain teams adhere to data privacy regulations and internal compliance policies, guiding them on legal and regulatory considerations in collaboration with external legal and compliance experts.

Data security analyst
> Defines the security standards and procedures that domain teams must follow, provides them with guidance, and ensures that they follow the security aspects of the governance policies.

Data quality specialist
> Defines quality standards and procedures to ensure the quality of the data being generated across the organization. They work with domain teams to set up data quality metrics and monitoring systems.

Domain representative
> Serves as a representative from their domain teams, bringing domain-specific data knowledge to the governance platform team and ensuring that governance policies align with their domain's needs.

Data architect
> Defines data-modeling standards, including designing and managing logical and physical data models.

DataOps engineer
> Automates the implementation and monitoring of data governance policies. May also maintain the systems and tools that enable data tagging and other data identification and management mechanisms.

The exact roles and responsibilities of each team will vary, depending on the specifics of the organization and its data mesh. What's most important is that each domain team takes responsibility for that domain's data as a product.

These roles need to collaborate closely to make sure that the data architecture meets the needs of the business and users. The architecture should be flexible to handle changes in the business and technology landscape and robust enough to ensure data quality and availability.

As we delve deeper into understanding the intricacies of team dynamics, it's imperative to recognize that even the best-organized teams can face unforeseen challenges. Let's shift our focus from the roles that drive success to the common pitfalls that can hinder a project—and how you can take preventative measures.

Why Projects Fail: Pitfalls and Prevention

Now let's talk about the common reasons big data projects fail. Some studies (*https://oreil.ly/ZwGQY*) show high failure rates; for instance, in 2019, *VentureBeat* reported (*https://oreil.ly/JmAw5*) that "87% of data science projects never make it into production." This section outlines some of the most common reasons I have seen them fail, along with ways to avoid these pitfalls.

Pitfall: Allowing Executives to Think That BI Is "Easy"

I've met a number of executives with very unrealistic ideas about how long it takes to build a data architecture. They often pressure project managers into adopting unrealistic timelines and milestones, thus setting the project up to fail.

To prevent succumbing to this pitfall, you must educate the executives. Help them understand the process and the time it takes to properly build and test a solution. I've even had executives attend a one-day coding session so they can see firsthand how hard it is to build a data solution.

Pitfall: Using the Wrong Technologies

When companies fail to educate themselves about all of the available data solution products and their use cases, they can end up using the wrong product for the job. (For example, I've seen a company use SQL Server as a data lake!) People don't know what they don't know, so they only use products they've heard of. As the saying goes, when you have a hammer, everything is a nail.

Decision makers must invest time in understanding all the possible tools, then choosing the right tool for the job to prevent this. I recommend forming several committees, each one focused on researching a specific group of products, such as ETL, analytical, or reporting tools.

Pitfall: Gathering Too Many Business Requirements

When I was a developer, I worked for a company that spent over a year gathering business requirements for a data solution while we sat around waiting for them to finish. They wound up producing hundreds of pages of requirements, putting everything behind schedule. No one read the whole document; the requirements phase had taken so long that we read just a few sections before starting development.

To avoid this pitfall, spend just a few weeks on requirements, gathering enough to allow the developers to start coding, then continue gathering requirements *in parallel* with coding.

Pitfall: Gathering Too Few Business Requirements

Some project teams spend barely any time with end users gathering requirements; some leave it up to the developers to guess what the end users want. They often end up developing the wrong features, not at all giving users what they need or want.

If you adopt an iterative method for project development, you can avoid this issue. This approach involves constructing parts of the solution, then revisiting design and planning phases, allowing for adjustments based on feedback and evolving requirements in a continuous cycle.

Pitfall: Presenting Reports Without Validating Their Contents First

If you present an end user with a report from the new solution you're building and it contains an incorrect number, their first impression will be a bad one. When users lose confidence in reports, it's very hard to win back their trust. Companies don't always take the time to make sure everything in the report is correct, and the result can be a major setback.

Have a rigorous QA process that includes comparing the report totals in the new solution with those in a production report that is known to be valid. Ask end users for help, if possible; not only will they be able to confirm the reports are correct, but they'll also feel some ownership from being part of building the new solution.

Pitfall: Hiring an Inexperienced Consulting Company

Most companies don't have the time or expertise to build a data warehouse solution on their own, so they hire consultants to build it. That's a great idea, as long as you pick the right consulting company. They could be experts—but in a completely different type of project. Consulting companies sometimes involve experts with relevant experience when they are trying to win your business, but then substitute less experienced people once the project starts.

To prevent falling prey to this pitfall, ask questions. Do the consultants have experience building the particular solution you want? If so, will those people be working on your project?

Pitfall: Hiring a Consulting Company That Outsources Development to Offshore Workers

Consulting companies use offshore developers to save costs, but that can lead to problems. Time zone differences can make it difficult to meet, language barriers can make it hard to communicate the requirements properly, and the quality of work may be lower.

Ask questions to ensure that the consulting company isn't passing your project off to an offshore team to avoid this issue.

Pitfall: Passing Project Ownership Off to Consultants

It can be tempting to "hand over the keys" of the project to the consulting company, having them not only develop the project but manage it entirely. This can result in a lack of transparency; the project can become a "black box," where you have no idea what the consultants are working on or how well they're doing the job.

Make sure you're getting the full, true story of the project's progress. Status reports won't cut it; put project managers in place to keep a close eye on things.

Pitfall: Neglecting the Need to Transfer Knowledge Back into the Organization

If you use a consulting company, you don't want them to come in, do the project, and leave without educating you on what they've built. You need to be able to fix bugs and add features without having to hire the consulting company again.

Have some of your people work alongside the consultants as they build the solution, even if just for a few weeks, to become familiar with it. Set aside time for knowledge transfer near the end of the project and have the consulting company hold training and review sessions to educate your organization about the new solution.

Pitfall: Slashing the Budget Midway Through the Project

Poorly planned projects sometimes max out their budgets, running out of money just as they near the finish line. If you want to ensure failure, start making cuts. This includes actions like laying off developers, testers, program managers, or DBAs; cutting back on the solution's hardware; or reducing end-user training on the new system. Don't make cuts in those areas.

Either increase the budget or make cuts in less critical areas to avoid this pitfall. For instance, you might reduce the number of data sources to ingest initially, leaving them for the next phase of the project.

Pitfall: Starting with an End Date and Working Backward

Focusing on a strict deadline can compromise the project's quality. First, rushing the intricate stages of data sourcing, integration, establishing quality standards, building ETL processes, designing data models, and creating user interfaces can lead to errors and inefficiencies. Second, a strict timeline can also limit the essential discovery and exploration phases of the project, potentially leading to a system that doesn't meet the organization's actual needs. Third, it's unrealistic to assume that you'll start the project with a perfect understanding of its scope. A rigid end date makes it difficult to accommodate unexpected changes or new requirements that emerge as the project progresses, which can cause delays or incomplete deliverables. Finally, an inflexible end date can restrict essential stakeholder collaboration, resulting in a product that doesn't adequately serve all users.

Don't make deadlines and schedules inflexible. Accept that schedules may need to change as new circumstances arise.

Pitfall: Structuring the Data Warehouse to Reflect the Source Data Rather Than the Business's Needs

Source data is derived from operational systems that aren't typically designed for comprehensive data analysis or business intelligence tasks, which can limit your MDW's usability. Those systems aren't aligned with the business's strategic goals and KPIs, either, which can mean missing out on valuable insights (which, in turn, has a negative impact on decision making). Modeling your system after the source data also means that changes in operational systems, which are common as businesses evolve, will necessitate major modifications in your warehouse, leading to instability and increased maintenance.

Structure your MDW (or data lakehouse) according to the needs of your business. Don't just mindlessly mirror the structure of the source data.

Pitfall: Presenting End Users with a Solution with Slow Response Times or Other Performance Issues

A surefire way to get inundated with complaints from end users is to give them a solution that is slow to produce the reports, dashboards, or queries they need—especially if the previous solution did it faster. Just like with incorrect data, if slow response times give users a poor first impression, they lose confidence and trust in you and the solution, which will be very difficult to win back.

Don't wait for complaints before you make performance improvements. Measure the response times from the migrated reports and tune the new reports to be *at least* equal. If these reports haven't been migrated, ask users to determine an acceptable baseline level of performance for report creation and interaction.

Pitfall: Overdesigning (or Underdesigning) Your Data Architecture

If you spend too little time on designing the data architecture for your solution, you risk building something that can't handle data sources of a certain size, type, or speed; lacks scalability; performs poorly; or introduces security risks. On the other hand, too *much* architecture design can lead to overcomplexity, lack of flexibility, analysis paralysis, and increased costs.

It's essential to strike a balance when creating a data architecture. The design should be comprehensive enough to provide a robust, scalable, and secure structure but flexible and simple enough to be easily understood, implemented, and adapted to changing needs.

Pitfall: Poor Communication Between IT and the Business Domains

These two critical groups often use different language, have different priorities, and see things from different perspectives, so rifts between them aren't unusual. IT personnel typically focus on technical aspects and system implementation, while business professionals concentrate on strategic objectives and profitability. Poor communication can lead to critical problems such as misaligned objectives, inefficient resource use, missed opportunities, and decreased morale.

A data project's success heavily relies on these two groups working collaboratively. IT must comprehend the business needs, while the business team must appreciate the potential and limitations of the IT infrastructure. It's crucial to foster a culture of open dialogue and mutual respect. Roles such as business analyst can help bridge this gap by translating business requirements into technical specifications and vice versa. The two groups should meet regularly, hold transparent discussions, and clearly document requirements. Effective collaboration can make a big difference to whether the project succeeds or fails.

Tips for Success

After having navigated the minefield of potential challenges and pitfalls that can derail even the most promising projects, it's essential to balance your perspective. As much as it's vital to be aware of what can go wrong, it's equally crucial to understand what drives a project toward its goals. These tips will help you harness proven strategies, best practices, and insightful wisdom, steering you clear of potential missteps and toward success.

Don't Skimp on Your Investment

Sometimes it's better to take twice as long and spend twice the money to build a solution that provides 50 times the value of your old solution. Emphasize the long-term value of investing time and resources in building high-quality, robust, scalable data solutions that support advanced analytics capabilities. This is crucial to fostering a data-driven culture that encourages innovation and operational efficiency.

Rushing projects or skimping on resources can lead to system flaws, inaccurate results, and compliance issues. Ultimately, dealing with constant maintenance or overhauling a flawed system can end up being more expensive than just investing in the best tools to begin with. Investing more time and resources up front allows for better planning, better people, and better tools, all of which contribute to creating reliable, accurate, and scalable systems.

Getting the right expertise and technical knowledge on the team might mean paying more in salaries, but building a data solution requires a priceless combination of business understanding, technical skills, and management capabilities. Furthermore, you need *at least one* person on the project who is well versed in data architectures. They should lead the process of deciding which data architecture to use. This is a huge decision. If you leave it to nonexperts, the resulting solution is likely to be off the mark, resulting in performance problems, inability to ingest data from certain sources, incorrect results, and other issues. Involve people who know what they're doing. This also goes for reporting tools and any other tools you're using; make sure you have people who understand their features and function so you can get the most out of your investment.

Overall, the initial costs and time investment will be offset by a substantial long-term return on investment, which includes reduced long-term operational costs as well as strategic advantages and valuable insights.

Involve Users, Show Them Results, and Get Them Excited

Get end users involved early so they're working with you instead of against you. Early in the project, invite them to help decide questions like which data sources to use and how to clean, aggregate, and validate the data. If they feel involved, they'll cheer the project on and will want to help solve any problems that arise rather than complain about them. If you don't get them involved, they will feel like the changes are being forced upon them. They'll be quick to complain about the solution and push back against using it.

If your solution will require users to work with unfamiliar new technologies (such as reporting tools), train them! Participating in training is a great way for users to prepare for the new solution and even learn faster, better ways to do their jobs. Help them understand any helpful new features and functionality the new tool offers so that they'll look forward to a successful rollout of the new solution.

To that end, show results quickly and often. Don't let months of project work go by without showing users and stakeholders any results. Use an interactive, agile approach to project delivery, with frequent releases. Break the project into phases and go for a quick win that shows lots of benefits you can promote. For example, when you begin ingesting sources, start with one that's high priority but also small and easy. Then repeat the process. This builds a solid foundation and helps developers create best practices for building the solution.

Add Value to New Reports and Dashboards

If you are doing a migration—say, from on-prem to the cloud—don't just re-create your existing reports; add value by giving users new features and functionality. Create dashboards with KPIs they haven't seen before; show them the art of the possible and new ways to get insights into their data. Find ways to help them do their jobs faster and more easily. If the new solution isn't better than the old one, they'll ask, "Why did we spend all this money to re-create what we already have?" Convince them that building a new solution is money well spent.

Ask End Users to Build a Prototype

The only part of the data solution most end users will see and use is the reporting tool. You want to make sure they are all familiar with most, if not all, of its features. Many users aren't even aware of features that could be saving them time and helping them gain insights. It's like driving a Lamborghini in first gear because you don't know it has other gears! Train them on the reporting tool and have an expert demonstrate it using their own data.

Engaging end users in prototype creation plays a key role in this understanding. As you determine the project's business requirements and train people on the reporting tool, have the end users build a prototype. This prototype should consist of sample reports that include all the information they need. By crafting this hands-on representation, users can better grasp the enhanced capabilities of new reports and dashboards. Today's sophisticated reporting tools have become so easy to use that you need only minimum technical skills to build a prototype. They say a picture is worth a thousand words; having a working prototype is a great way for end users to firsthand see the added value and insights the new solution offers.

Find a Project Champion/Sponsor

A *project champion* is a senior executive or influential individual who supports and advocates for the project. Their role is essential and multifaceted. First, they serve as an internal advocate, communicating the long-term benefits of a well-constructed data architecture, including enhanced decision making, operational efficiency, and strategic planning. Second, they are instrumental in securing the necessary resources and funding. Given that data projects require substantial investments in technology, human resources, and time, a project champion who can marshal these resources can be pivotal.

Third, the project champion plays a vital role in facilitating cross-functional collaboration between departments with different interests, aligning everyone's priorities toward the common project goal. Finally, they manage resistance to change—a significant challenge in most data projects—by helping to engage employees and addressing their apprehensions about new systems and processes. This helps ensure smoother transitions and increases the project's likelihood of success.

Make a Project Plan That Aims for 80% Efficiency

The individual responsible for the day-to-day management and execution of the project—often referred to as the *project manager* or *project lead*—should ensure that everyone is optimally engaged. This role is distinct from that of the *project champion* or *sponsor*, who provides strategic support and advocacy from a higher level. The project manager is more "in the trenches," coordinating tasks, timelines, and resources. Ideally, each team member should be utilizing about 80% of their work hours on the project. (Reserve the other 20% for things such as vacation or sick time, non-project meetings, learning, and so on.) You'll need a well-thought-out project plan geared toward minimizing the time each person has to wait for someone else to finish some dependent task. It also means ensuring the right people are performing the right tasks and that everyone is trained before the project begins. Anything less than 80% efficiency could lead to missed deadlines and cost overruns.

Summary

In this chapter, we've journeyed through the pivotal role of the human element in data architectures. While tools and technology might dazzle and inspire awe, they serve as mere instruments in the hands of their human wielders. How organizations harness these tools, and how they navigate cultural shifts in the process, can make or break their architectural endeavors. As you've learned, setting the right team structures, fostering clarity in roles and responsibilities, and having a deep understanding of potential pitfalls and success markers are indispensable to a project's success.

Take a moment to internalize that the most intricate and advanced technology will be only as powerful as the people using it and the processes governing its use. A perfectly designed data lakehouse or a robust data mesh can have an impact only when complemented by a well-organized, informed, and empowered team. The true success of data transformations lies in this delicate balance between humans and technology.

However, while this human-centric perspective is foundational, we cannot ignore the technological marvels that have reshaped the landscape of data architectures in recent years. The next chapter dives deep into the technological realm, exploring the innovations and intricacies of open source movements, the groundbreaking capabilities of Hadoop, the transformative benefits of the cloud, and the offerings of major cloud providers. Additionally, I'll take you into the world of multi-cloud strategies and familiarize you with game changers like Databricks and Snowflake.

People and technology aren't an either-or choice. They need to be a harmonious blend, with each elevating the other. Let's continue our exploration, understanding that our technological efforts are truly realized only when complemented by the right people and processes.

CHAPTER 16

Technologies

As you delve into this chapter, your first crucial decision is choosing between open source solutions and cloud provider offerings. However, there's more to consider. I'll guide you in thinking about the scale of your data needs and your organization's agility requirements.

Beyond this, we'll explore the landscape of cloud service models, from major providers to the complexity of multi-cloud solutions. The chapter ends by introducing you to three essential software frameworks: Hadoop, Databricks, and Snowflake.

Your answers to the questions in this chapter will profoundly shape your data architecture. It's not just open source versus proprietary; it's about crafting the perfect technology mix to suit your unique needs in the world of data architecture.

Choosing a Platform

The decision to use open source software or software from a cloud service provider (CSP) depends on various factors, including specific requirements, budget, expertise, data sensitivity, and control preferences. Evaluate your organization's needs carefully and consider the trade-offs between the advantages of CSP software and the flexibility and customization offered by open source software (OSS).

Open Source Solutions

Open source software refers to software that is distributed for free with its source code openly available for anyone to view, modify, and distribute. It is typically developed collaboratively by a community of programmers who contribute their knowledge and expertise to create and improve the software.

OSS has a rich history that spans several decades. It originated from the Free Software Movement (*https://www.fsf.org/history*) in the 1980s, led by Richard Stallman, which advocated for software freedom. The Open Source Initiative (*https://opensource.org*) (OSI), founded in 1998, created the Open Source Definition and established criteria for OSS licenses, which ensure that the software remains free and open for anyone to use. Linux played a significant role in popularizing OSS. Adopting open source solutions became popular in the 2010s because of their flexibility and low cost. Collaborative platforms like GitHub facilitated OSS development, and the movement has expanded beyond software into open data and hardware initiatives. Some of the top OSS projects include MySQL, PostgreSQL, MongoDB, Apache Hadoop, Apache Spark, Apache Kafka, Presto, and Apache Airflow.

Many data architectures use OSS, but few are built entirely with it. Most architectures use OSS in combination with cloud provider products. Including OSS is well worth considering for your data architecture.

Some of the main reasons you might want to use OSS over cloud provider products include:

Cost savings
OSS is typically free to use. This makes it an attractive option for organizations looking to optimize their budgets.

Flexibility and customization
OSS provides the freedom to modify and customize the source code to suit specific needs. This allows you to tailor the software to your organization's requirements, adding or removing features as necessary.

Transparency and trust
OSS source code is openly available, and anyone can review it for security vulnerabilities, bugs, and potential back doors. This transparency promotes trust and fosters a collaborative environment for code review and improvement.

Rapid innovation and collaboration
OSS benefits from a global community of developers who contribute their expertise and improvements. This collaborative environment fosters rapid innovation, accelerates software development cycles, and results in more reliable and feature-rich solutions.

Vendor independence
With OSS, organizations are not tied to a specific vendor or locked into proprietary software. They have the freedom to switch service providers or customize the software as needed.

There are also a few potential disadvantages to consider:

Limited support
Unlike cloud provider software, OSS may not have dedicated customer support or service-level agreements. Relying on community support can mean varying response times, so critical issues may take longer to address. To avoid this problem, companies often purchase a support contract from a vendor. Additionally, some hardware and software vendors prioritize compatibility and support for cloud-provider solutions over OSS. This can result in limited hardware driver availability or lack of support for certain software applications.

Learning curve and user experience
Working with OSS solutions often requires skilled developers or technical staff to effectively implement, customize, and maintain them. This can result in additional training or hiring costs. OSS projects also vary in terms of documentation quality, user-friendliness of interfaces, and ease of installation. Some projects may lack comprehensive documentation or intuitive user interfaces, making initial setup and configuration more challenging.

Fragmentation, standardization, and compatibility
Due to the distributed nature of OSS development and the vast number of OSS projects and versions, there is little standardization in coding styles, conventions, or approaches. This can lead to fragmentation, making it challenging to choose the right solution or ensure compatibility between different OSS components. Integrating with existing systems may require additional effort. (To learn more, see "Hadoop" on page 235.)

Security and liability
Even under the scrutiny of a global community, vulnerabilities and bugs still exist in OSS. If you use it, you must stay vigilant in applying security patches and updates. Additionally, if your organization modifies the OSS code, it assumes responsibility for maintaining the security and integrity of the customized version.

Uncertain project maintenance
Not all OSS projects are actively developed or offer long-term maintenance. Sometimes projects may become stagnant, with few updates or security patches. Assess the level of activity and community support before adopting an OSS solution.

Intellectual property considerations
When using or contributing to OSS, organizations must navigate intellectual property rights and licensing obligations. It is crucial to understand the terms and conditions of the OSS licenses to ensure compliance and avoid legal issues.

On-Premises Solutions

If your company has an on-prem data warehouse solution, you may be looking at migrating it to the cloud, or at least building new greenfield projects in the cloud. However, there are still a few situations where you might want to have your data warehouse solution on-prem:

- If your internet connection is slow or nonexistent, such as in a deep mine or on a submarine, an offshore oil rig, or a cruise ship.

- If you require millisecond performance, such as for servers in a high-volume mail-processing facility.

- If moving your applications to the cloud would break a third-party support contract.

- If you have a long-term locked-in lease with your datacenter or have just made a very large equipment purchase.

- If you have a very large amount of on-prem-born data that would need to be moved to the cloud and your pipeline to the cloud is too constrained to meet users' reporting needs. Your reports may not reflect the most current data, potentially delaying decision making.

- If you plan to replace or retire your applications and databases in the near future.

- If your data is extremely sensitive (though this no longer prevents many organizations from putting data in the cloud—most CSPs now have top-secret clouds).

If any of this applies to databases at your company, you'll want to keep those databases on-prem, but you can still move others to the cloud. I've talked to hundreds of companies about this over the last few years, and nearly every one of them is at least partially in the cloud. Most have already shut down all of their on-prem data centers. And for any new company, it's a no-brainer to be in the cloud.

If your data warehouse is on-prem, you should be aware of the constraints:

Limited scalability
> Your ability to scale your infrastructure is limited by what hardware you can purchase. Your hardware may be a constraint if you have to use certain vendors, if there are compatibility issues with existing hardware, or if hardware vendors are experiencing production delays. Likewise, datacenters have only so much physical space. When you run out of room to add more servers, you are left with two very expensive options: expanding your datacenter or building another one. Both can take many months.

Up-front costs

Purchasing the hardware for on-prem solutions incurs a very large up-front capital expenditure. Hardware includes server hardware, datacenter space to house the hardware, additional storage devices, firewalls, networking switches, a high-speed network (with redundancy) to access the data, the power and redundant power supplies needed to keep the system up and running, and the costs of securing and backing up the data.

If your warehouse is mission critical, then you'll also need to configure a disaster recovery site, effectively doubling the cost.

I often tell companies that if they have their own on-prem datacenter, they are in the air-conditioning business, because they have to keep all that hardware cool. Wouldn't you rather focus all your efforts on analyzing data? Most companies prefer the yearly operating expense of working with a cloud provider.

Personnel costs

You'll need to pay employees or consultants with the specialized expertise to set up, manage, administer, and support the hardware and software, tune the products for performance, and deploy products and solutions into production. This creates a potential bottleneck when issues arise and keeps responsibility for the system with the customer, not the vendor.

Software costs

Organizations frequently pay hundreds of thousands of dollars in software-licensing fees for data warehouse software and add-on packages, as well as licensing fees to give additional end users, such as customers and suppliers, access to the data. Annual support contracts for such software can easily run to 20% of the original license cost.

Now let's look at the cloud.

Cloud Provider Solutions

The cloud is like a massive, invisible storage room that exists somewhere out there in the ether. It allows us to store, access, and share data from anywhere, while saving us from running out of space or losing valuable data. Its influence spans all the architectures described in this book, reshaping how we work with data. Cloud computing provides on-demand access to shared computing resources such as servers, storage, and applications over the internet, so you no longer have to buy, own, and maintain physical datacenters and servers. This makes for scalable, flexible, and cost-efficient computing.

There are many benefits to having a data-warehousing solution in the cloud:

Scalability and elasticity
> CSP software is designed to scale seamlessly. You can dynamically provision storage and compute resources on the fly to meet the demands of changing workloads in peak and steady usage periods. Capacity is whatever you need whenever you need it.

Cost
> In the cloud system, the complexities and costs of capacity planning and administration (such as sizing, balancing, and tuning the system) are built in, automated, and covered by the cost of your cloud subscription. CSPs also offer flexible pricing models, so you can optimize costs by paying only for the resources you actually use. You can reduce hardware as demand lessens or use serverless options.
>
> This means that you can build a solution quickly, and if it doesn't work out, you can simply delete all the cloud resources the project used. The cost of failure is greatly reduced, which means you can take chances and try new things.
>
> It's also important to consider indirect cost savings: you're not paying for hardware, power, the staff who build and maintain the datacenter, or development of your own upgrades.

Easy deployment and management
> CSP software often comes with integrated deployment and management tools that simplify the setup and configuration processes. These tools streamline the provisioning of resources and scaling, monitoring, and maintenance tasks, reducing operational overhead. You can create all the cloud resources you need (such as compute, storage, and networking) in hours, if not minutes—whereas starting a solution on-prem can take weeks or even months.

Vendor support and service-level agreements (SLAs)
> CSPs offer dedicated support and SLAs, providing assistance, troubleshooting, and guaranteed service availability.

Integrated ecosystems
> Typically, a CSP's software integrates seamlessly with that provider's other services. This can enable easier integration and interoperability between different services and help you leverage the provider's broader capabilities.

Managed services

CSPs often handle specific aspects of software infrastructure, such as managed databases, machine learning services, or serverless computing. These managed services can offload operational complexities, allowing organizations to focus on their core business rather than managing the underlying infrastructure. This also saves you from having to find and pay for services from third-party vendors.

Continuous innovation and feature updates

CSPs regularly introduce new features, services, and updates to their software offerings. You benefit from their innovation without having to invest in upgrading or integrating new features yourself.

Easier hiring

Huge numbers of people use products from CSPs; OSS can have a much smaller user base. Therefore, it can be much easier to find job candidates who know the cloud products your organization uses.

Global availability and high availability

CSPs' datacenters are distributed worldwide, which lets you deploy your software closer to your target audience or leverage multi-region redundancy for high availability. CSPs use load balancing to distribute traffic evenly across multiple servers, ensuring that no single server gets overloaded and causes downtime.

This global infrastructure ensures low latency services and is fault tolerant. In case of a hardware or software failure, the service will automatically failover to a secondary instance, ensuring uninterrupted and reliable access. Also, you can set up disaster recovery for storage in a matter of minutes.

Security and compliance

CSPs invest heavily in security measures such as encryption, access controls, and regular audits to protect data and ensure compliance with industry standards and regulations.

Total Cost of Ownership

All of the CSPs offer a total cost of ownership (TCO) calculator that you can use to estimate the cost savings you could realize by migrating your application and database workloads to the cloud. Simply provide a brief description of your on-premises environment to get an instant report from Microsoft Azure (*https://oreil.ly/UlvtP*), Amazon Web Services (*https://calculator.aws*), or Google Cloud (*https://oreil.ly/e7_uF*).

Cloud Service Models

There are three basic service models for delivering and managing IT resources in the cloud:

Infrastructure as a Service (IaaS)
> The CSP hosts and manages the hardware infrastructure. It offers virtualized computing resources, such as servers, storage, and networking, which can be easily scaled up or down as needed; the customer manages the operating system, applications, and data. Most services are housed within a virtual machine (VM) that the end user will access remotely. This model offers more flexibility and scalability than on-prem, but managing its operating system, applications, and data architectures still requires some level of IT expertise.

Platform as a Service (PaaS)
> The CSP offers a platform for developers to build, test, and deploy applications and databases, as well as an underlying infrastructure (similar to IaaS). It also includes development tools, database management systems, and business intelligence services. The CSP controls the runtime, middleware, and O/S environments—there are no VMs. This allows developers to focus on coding and managing the applications without worrying about managing the platform and underlying infrastructure. This model is even more abstract and easier to use than IaaS, but it is limited in its flexibility and customizability.

Software as a Service (SaaS)
> The CSP hosts and fully manages both the software and infrastructure; customers access the software over the internet having to manage any hardware or software themselves. This is the simplest and easiest-to-use model, but it may have limited flexibility in terms of customization and control. Some CSPs offer data architecture tools that are "SaaS-like": that is, they're not quite as fully managed as a true SaaS tool like Salesforce, requiring just some minor application management.

With any of the cloud service models, you get the latest version of whatever database product you are using. For example, Azure's cloud database, SQL Database, is a newer version of an on-prem database product called SQL Server 2022. Think of SQL Database as SQL Server 2022+. New features are added every few weeks—you can choose to use them or not. Every couple of years, those new features are gathered up and added to the boxed version of SQL Server, but you get them right away with SQL Database. And your code won't break when there is an upgrade.

All of the CSPs offer built-in advanced threat detection, using monitoring to detect anomalous activities that could indicate unusual and potentially harmful attempts to access or exploit databases; assessments that help you to discover, track, and remediate potential database vulnerabilities; and advanced capabilities for discovering, classifying, labeling, and reporting the sensitive data in your databases.

Overall, as Figure 16-1 shows, these four models represent different levels of abstraction and control over the IT infrastructure and software stack. On-prem offers complete control but requires significant investment and expertise, while IaaS, PaaS, and SaaS offer increasing levels of abstraction and ease of use—at the expense of control and customization.

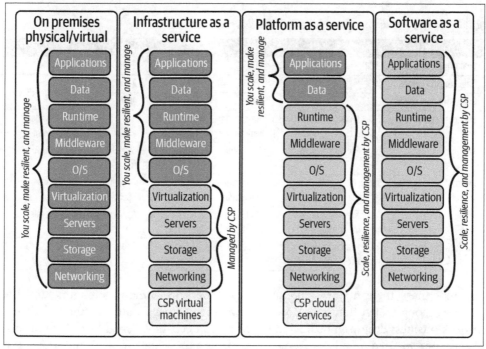

Figure 16-1. Comparison of service models

Which service model you choose will depend on your organization's needs and goals. However, I personally prefer PaaS for data warehouses where possible, for a few reasons. First, you don't have to deal with a virtual machine (VM). It exists somewhere and hosts the databases, but you never have to remote into a server or manage it in any way—you do everything via the CSP portal or third-party tools. Nor are you responsible for patching or upgrading: most CSP databases are patched with no downtime. You get database backups out of the box—no more setup and monitoring.

Finally, PaaS makes disaster recovery (DR) a lot simpler. Most IaaS DR solutions are a pain to set up and monitor, but with PaaS, you basically just have to click which area of the country you want the DR database to reside in. The CSP takes care of setting it up and keeping it working.

Major Cloud Providers

The three major CSPs, Microsoft Azure (*https://azure.microsoft.com*), Amazon Web Services (*https://aws.amazon.com*) (AWS), and Google Cloud Platform (*https://cloud.google.com*) (GCP), have the majority of the market share (estimated at 65% (*https://oreil.ly/oOIx-*) in Q2 2023). For more detailed and up-to-date information on each provider's offerings, I encourage you to visit their respective websites. Table 16-1 compares their major features to give you a comprehensive overview.

Table 16-1. Comparison of the big three cloud service providers

Criteria	Azure	AWS	GCP
Year announced	2008	2006	2008
Data center regions	60	31	24
Global market share	23%	32%	10%
Services offered	200+ services across various categories	Around 200+ services across various categories	100+ services, known for data analytics and machine learning
Pricing	Cost benefits for Microsoft users	More options for instance types	Straightforward and customer friendly
Integration/open source	Strong integration with Microsoft products	Wide variety of open source integrations	Good integrations with various open source platforms
Learning curve	Easier for those familiar with other Microsoft products	Wide range of services leading to steeper learning curve	User-friendly interface, easier learning curve
Analytic products	Azure Synapse Analytics, Microsoft Fabric	Amazon Redshift	Google BigQuery

Each of these three major cloud service providers has unique strengths, and the choice among them often boils down to your specific needs and existing infrastructure. A business deeply embedded in the Microsoft ecosystem might gravitate toward Azure, one focused on advanced data processing might opt for GCP, and a business requiring a broad range of services might lean toward AWS. Ultimately, the decision involves balancing technical requirements, cost, and the strategic direction of the business.

Multi-Cloud Solutions

Many organizations find themselves deliberating between adopting one of the big three CSPs or employing services from more than one, which is often called a *multi-cloud approach*. Some companies feel like relying on just one CSP is "putting all their eggs in one basket" or fear that the CSP might become a competitor to their business. (This happened, for instance, when Amazon bought Whole Foods, becoming a competitor to other supermarket businesses.)

This approach does have some major benefits, mostly because it leverages each CSP's strengths and weaknesses. If one CSP has lower latency and another has better availability or disaster recovery, using both could improve the organization's ability to meet its SLAs. You can do similar comparisons for cost, capacity, and various features and products; if one CSP doesn't have everything you want, you can lean on another to make up for it. However, this is less relevant than it used to be; today, all three CSPs now have very similar offerings, with few unique features or products.

Data sovereignty is also a factor. Not all CSPs have the same cloud regions, which can be very important for regulatory compliance. For example, if you are using MongoDB in Azure but Azure does not have a region in Taiwan, your Taiwan operations could use MongoDB in AWS.

Imagine a fictional global ecommerce giant we'll call TechTreasures Inc. TechTreasures is based in the United States—specifically Ponte Vedra, Florida—but operates around the world, including in North America, Europe, and Asia.

To ensure optimal performance, reliability, and compliance with regional data regulations, TechTreasures adopts a multi-cloud approach. It leverages Microsoft Azure for its North American operations due to Azure's robust low-latency network and data centers in the region. In Europe, it utilizes GCP for its advanced data analytics capabilities and strong presence in European cloud regions. For its Asian operations, TechTreasures relies on AWS, which offers cloud regions in key Asian markets, including Taiwan.

This multi-cloud strategy allows TechTreasures to provide fast, reliable services to its global customer base while ensuring compliance with data sovereignty regulations. It's a strategic choice that enables the business to harness the unique strengths of each major CSP to optimize business operations.

But there are plenty of drawbacks to multi-cloud. Since these clouds aren't designed to work together, moving data and compute back and forth can be slow and clunky. Interoperability is an issue too; products from one CSP don't always work well with those from different CSPs. Moving data and applications from one CSP to another and launching another product could be very costly, especially if you have to re-engineer applications to support multiple clouds. CSPs also charge egress fees if you move data from their cloud to a competitor's cloud, and they don't make it easy to migrate to another CSP. And if you've invested in a larger internet pipeline, like Azure's ExpressRoute, you'd need to make a similar investment with any other CSPs you use. Moreover, storing your data in multiple clouds increases its exposure to security threats.

If you want to make it easy to move from one cloud to another, you will have to use an IaaS service model instead of PaaS, which takes away many of the higher-value services that each CSP offers—a big opportunity cost.

In terms of personnel, you'll need to hire and/or train your people to understand two or more clouds, greatly increasing costs. Managing an additional CSP; handling security; and creating policies, standards, and procedures for it also requires more people and skill sets. You'll also have to get different types of security to get to work together, and you'll have two places to add, delete, or update users; two places to monitor; and two sets of billing statements, adding significant administrative complexity (and cost).

Finally, having two cloud providers is not likely to save you from an outage. The CSPs have specifically designed their networks so that an outage at one region doesn't impact other regions. Your disaster recovery solution should be to failover to another region within the same CSP, not to another CSP.

Many people believe that using the multi-cloud approach forces CSPs into a competitive situation, allowing you to negotiate a better deal. However, this is mostly a myth. For enterprise license agreements (ELAs), the CSPs give higher discounts based on how much consumption you can commit to on their cloud—the more you use, the bigger your discounts.[1] When you add in tier-based pricing and sustained usage discounts, you will likely save more by sticking with just one CSP. However, some companies will threaten to jump to another CSP to control their pricing. Going with just one CSP can also allow for partnership benefits if your company is a large enterprise. For example, Microsoft has a collaboration with Ernst & Young to drive a $15 billion growth opportunity and technology innovation across industries.

I don't expect the multi-cloud approach to gain wider adoption. In time, I think most companies will choose one CSP and stick with it, to go deeper and fully leverage its services, PaaS and SaaS, and ecosystem. Some very large companies will settle on a couple of clouds if the CSPs offer different things that are beneficial to the workload. That makes sense if the company is big enough to invest the time and people to go deep on both and take advantage of each provider's PaaS services.

We now move from a discussion of cloud service models to software frameworks, transitioning from establishing the foundation of data architecture to exploring the tools that leverage this foundation. In the upcoming section, we'll delve into key software frameworks that harness cloud infrastructure to unlock the full potential of your data.

---

1 CSPs use different names for these commitment-based discounts; you might see them called "reserved instance pricing," "pre-commit discounts," "commercial pricing discounts," or "volume-based discounts."

Software Frameworks

In the world of data architecture, your choice of software frameworks can make all the difference in how effectively you process, analyze, and derive insights from your data. These frameworks serve as the engines that power your data operations, allowing you to extract valuable information and drive data-driven decisions. In this section, we will journey into the realm of software frameworks, exploring three prominent players: Hadoop, Databricks, and Snowflake. Each of these frameworks brings unique strengths to the table, and understanding their capabilities is essential for building a data architecture that meets your specific needs and objectives.

Hadoop

Hadoop is an OSS framework created in 2005 by the Apache Foundation. It's designed to harness the power of distributed computing. Various tools and libraries extend Hadoop's capabilities, making it a popular choice for organizations that deal with massive volumes of data and are seeking cost-effective scalability.

At its core, Hadoop consists of two main components. First, the Hadoop Distributed File System (HDFS) can store and process big data workloads efficiently by splitting data into smaller blocks and distributing it across multiple nodes and clusters of computers, as pictured in Figure 16-2. This enables high fault tolerance and tasks such as batch processing, data integration, and analytics. HDFS enables high-throughput access to data and provides reliability even when hardware fails.

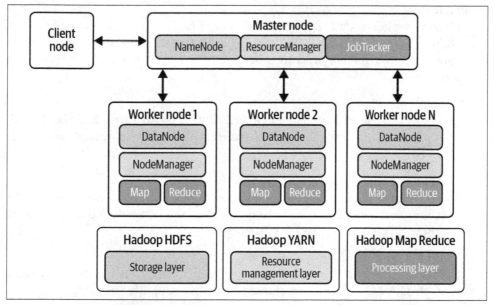

Figure 16-2. Hadoop's cluster architecture

Second, the MapReduce framework is a programming model used for processing and analyzing large datasets in parallel across a cluster, again by dividing the workload into smaller tasks and distributing them across multiple nodes in the cluster. It breaks down large, complex computations into multiple tasks and assigns those tasks to individual worker nodes, which coordinate and consolidate the results. The MapReduce framework automatically handles parallelization, fault tolerance, and data distribution. A MapReduce program is composed of a `Map()` procedure that filters and sorts (such as sorting students by first name into queues, one queue for each name) and a `Reduce()` procedure that summarizes the data (such as counting the number of students in each queue, yielding name frequencies). MapReduce libraries have been written in many programming languages (usually Java), with different levels of optimization.

Hadoop offers several benefits that make it a popular choice for handling big data:

Scalability
Hadoop provides a scalable architecture that can handle large volumes of data. It allows you to scale your storage and processing capabilities easily by adding more commodity hardware to the cluster, making it cost-effective and flexible.

Distributed computing
Hadoop distributes data and processing tasks across a cluster of machines, enabling parallel processing. Dividing the work across multiple nodes allows it to process large datasets faster.

Fault tolerance
Hadoop replicates data across multiple nodes in the cluster, ensuring that data endures and remains available even if hardware fails. If a node fails, Hadoop automatically redirects tasks to other available nodes, ensuring uninterrupted processing.

Cost-effective storage
HDFS allows you to store large amounts of data on standard, affordable hardware that you can buy off the shelf, rather than expensive, specialized storage systems.

Data locality
Hadoop optimizes data processing by moving computation closer to where the data is stored instead of transferring data over the network, reducing network overhead and improving overall efficiency.

Flexibility and compatibility
Hadoop is compatible with various data formats and can process structured, semi-structured, and unstructured data. It supports a wide range of

programming languages and tools, allowing developers to work with their preferred languages and integrate different components into their data pipelines.

Ecosystem of tools

Hadoop has a rich ecosystem of tools and frameworks that extend its capabilities and provide higher-level abstractions, data-processing languages, and analytics. These include:

- YARN (*https://oreil.ly/xGJCB*), for resource management and job scheduling
- Hive (*https://hive.apache.org*), for data warehousing
- Pig (*https://pig.apache.org*), for data analysis
- HBase (*https://hbase.apache.org*), a NoSQL database
- Spark (*https://spark.apache.org*), for in-memory processing
- Presto (*https://prestodb.io*), for distributed SQL

Hadoop vendors sell platforms that incorporate, test, and pre-integrate several OSS products together, saving you the time and effort of integrating and testing various components yourself.

Community support

Hadoop has a large and active open source community that contributes to its development, improvement, and support and provides a wealth of resources, documentation, and expertise to users.

Hadoop's potential disadvantages include:

Complexity

Hadoop has a steep learning curve and can be complex to set up and manage. It requires specialized knowledge and expertise in distributed systems, which may pose a challenge for organizations without prior experience or dedicated resources.

Latency

MapReduce, Hadoop's core processing framework, is based on batch processing, which introduces latency, so it may not be suitable for real-time or interactive data-processing scenarios. Hadoop is most effective for large-scale data-processing tasks, such as batch analytics and processing massive datasets. If you need immediate or near-real-time insights, alternative solutions or frameworks like Apache Kafka or Apache Flink might be more suitable.

Hardware requirements

Hadoop's distributed architecture requires a cluster of machines to function efficiently. Setting up and maintaining such a cluster, including hardware and network infrastructure, can involve significant costs and complexity.

Data management overhead
> While Hadoop's HDFS provides fault tolerance and replication, replicating data across nodes consumes storage space. This introduces additional data storage overhead.

Complex ecosystem
> While the Hadoop ecosystem is rich and wide-ranging, it's also complex, so managing and integrating its components can be challenging. It requires understanding the capabilities and compatibility of each tool and maintaining the tools' configurations and dependencies.

Data security and governance
> Hadoop's distributed nature and data replication can introduce unique challenges in terms of data security, privacy, and governance. Unlike traditional data storage systems, Hadoop's distributed nature requires organizations to go beyond standard security practices and adopt specialized security measures and access controls tailored to its intricacies. These measures are essential to ensure data protection and maintain compliance with Hadoop-specific requirements and best practices.

Hadoop gained significant adoption in the early 2010s, but as the big data landscape and cloud computing have evolved, introducing technologies like serverless compute, cloud data warehouses, and data-streaming platforms, use of Hadoop has waned. Today, cloud infrastructure can replace Hadoop clusters and cloud object storage can replace HDFS. Its core principles, such as distributed storage and processing, remain relevant, but its specific components and tools have seen varying degrees of adoption. For example, technologies like Apache Spark have gained popularity as alternatives or complements to MapReduce.

Databricks

Databricks is a cloud-based platform for running workloads in Apache Spark, an open source data analytics–processing engine. Spark was originally developed at UC Berkeley's AMPLab in 2009 as a way to deal with the limitations of MapReduce.[2] It was designed to be faster and easier to use and to handle both batch processing and real-time data streaming.

Some of Spark's original creators were among Databricks' founders in 2013. Databricks has continued to work to commercialize Spark, providing a Unified Data Analytics Platform, a fully managed service that offers a comprehensive, simplified platform for big data analytics, integrating data science, engineering, and business. It

---

2 Spark was open sourced in 2010 under a Berkeley Software Distribution license, and it became an Apache Software Foundation project in 2013.

is designed to make it easier for businesses to use Spark without having to worry about setting up and maintaining their own infrastructure, making advanced analytics and machine learning accessible to a broader set of users.

Since its inception, Databricks has been a significant contributor to Apache Spark, working to improve its processing speed through Project Tungsten, a series of optimizations aimed at leveraging modern CPU architectures to increase efficiency. It has also developed an optimized autoscaling system that dynamically adjusts the number of machines allocated to a job in response to computational demands, improving both cost-efficiency and performance.

Databricks has introduced various libraries to expand Spark's capabilities, such as MLlib (for machine learning), GraphX (for graph computation), and Spark Streaming (for real-time data). It has also played a crucial role in training and supporting the Spark community, which has accelerated adoption and enabled users to better leverage Spark's capabilities.

Databricks also focused on making Spark easier to use, introducing high-level APIs in Python, Java, and Scala to make writing Spark applications more accessible. It also developed Databricks notebooks, interactive environments where data scientists and engineers can write Spark code, visualize their results, and build models. This platform allowed data scientists and data engineers to work together more effectively by unifying data science, data engineering, and business analytics.

To address the limitations of data lakes and improve reliability and data quality, Databricks also introduced Delta Lake (see Chapter 12), an open source storage layer that runs on top of existing data lakes. It enhances Spark's big data capacities with ACID transactions, scalable metadata handling, and unified streaming and batch data processing. Delta Lake addresses traditional data lakes' challenges with data quality, reliability, and performance. Databricks made Data Lake open source in 2019, contributing the project to the Linux Foundation to allow the broader community to contribute. Today, Delta Lake has been widely adopted.

In 2020, Databricks introduced a novel data architecture, the data lakehouse (also covered in Chapter 12). This innovation represented a significant shift in data management paradigms. Instead of being forced to choose between data lakes and data warehouses, organizations can opt for a hybrid architecture that fuses data lakes' scalability and cost-effectiveness with the robust structure, reliability, and performance of data warehouses.

In Databricks' view, modern data architectures should be open, collaborative, and able to handle all types of data and advanced analytics use cases. The company thus supports architectures that allow businesses to scale as they grow and change over time.

With its Unified Data Analytics Platform and tools like Delta Lake, Databricks could provide the underlying infrastructure for each data product or domain within a data mesh (see Chapters 13 and 14). Its platform can handle a variety of data types and supports both batch and real-time data processing, making it versatile enough to serve the needs of different data domains. The key features of Delta Lake, such as ACID transactions, schema enforcement, and versioning, can ensure data quality and consistency within each data domain. Moreover, it offers the ability to "time travel" (access previous versions of data). This can be particularly useful in a data mesh, where teams may need to audit or revert changes in their respective domains. Databricks' collaborative environment can also enable cross-functional teams within a data mesh to work together more efficiently, aligning with the principle of enabling domain-oriented, decentralized teams.

Snowflake

Snowflake is a fully managed, cloud-based data-warehousing solution for storing, organizing, and analyzing large amounts of data and, uniquely, can serve as a data lake in addition to providing traditional data-warehousing functionalities.

The company was founded in 2012 to address the limitations of traditional data-warehousing solutions. Its founders developed a unique architecture that separates compute and storage, allowing efficient data analytics and workloads that can scale independently and automatically based on demand. The platform, launched in 2014, gained recognition for its ability to handle diverse data types and ability to store and process a wide range of data formats, including CSV, JSON, Parquet, and Avro. Its cloud-native approach and architecture have attracted a wide range of customers across industries. It offers pay-per-use pricing, robust security, flexibility, and reliability.

You can load data in various formats directly into Snowflake as you would with a data lake, eliminating the need to transform or preprocess data before ingestion. Snowflake further simplifies the process by automatically inferring the schema of the ingested data. Once the data is loaded, Snowflake provides a structured and scalable environment for organizing and cataloging it, allowing users to create tables, define schemas, and apply metadata tags. This ensures efficient organization and easy accessibility.

Using Snowflake as a data lake provides the benefits of a unified data platform, eliminating the need for a separate data lake infrastructure and reducing complexity. It offers a scalable and performant environment for storing, managing, and analyzing diverse data types, making it an attractive choice for organizations looking to leverage the power of a data lake within a unified ecosystem.

Snowflake's strength lies in its highly optimized data-warehousing capabilities and efficient querying and analysis within its platform. However, if you require specific computations or specialized processing that can be better served by other compute engines, exporting the data from Snowflake and utilizing those engines is the common approach. While Snowflake provides seamless data export capabilities, it does not directly support running external compute engines or tools on data stored within its platform.

Snowflake aligns well with the data mesh principles (covered in Chapter 13). The company acknowledges the importance of empowering domain experts and teams to take ownership of their data. With Snowflake, different business units or domains can have separate accounts or virtual warehouses, enabling them to manage and control their own data assets. This decentralized approach promotes agility and autonomy, allowing domain teams to make data-driven decisions and take responsibility for the quality and usability of their data.

Snowflake's robust data management capabilities, including schema management, metadata tagging, and cataloging, let you treat your data as a valuable asset that can be accessed and consumed by other teams within the organization, promoting data product thinking. Snowflake also aligns with the scalability and elasticity aspects of the data mesh concept: its cloud-native architecture allows for independent scaling of compute resources, helping teams adapt to changing requirements and handle data processing and analytics efficiently. In summary, Snowflake empowers organizations to adopt a data mesh approach that promotes collaboration, autonomy, and agility in their data ecosystems.

Summary

The decisions you make about data architecture technologies will be pivotal to the success of your data initiatives. This chapter guided you through the fundamental choices that lay the foundation for your data infrastructure.

We explored three essential software frameworks: Hadoop, Databricks, and Snowflake, each offering a unique approach to data processing and analytics. Whether you opt for open source solutions, embrace the offerings of cloud providers, or combine the two, consider the scale of your data needs and your organization's agility requirements.

Moreover, remember that the world of data technology is not binary. It extends to the landscape of cloud service models, where major providers offer a diverse array of services and multi-cloud solutions add a layer of complexity to your decision making.

As you move forward in your data architecture journey, keep in mind that the choices made in this chapter are not isolated; they are interconnected and will shape the landscape of your data environment. It's not merely about selecting open source or proprietary solutions; it's about crafting a harmonious blend of technologies that align with your organization's goals and challenges. With these considerations in mind, you are well equipped to navigate the ever-evolving world of data architecture technologies.

Happy deciphering!

Index

integrated layer (data lake), 64

About the Author

James Serra works at Microsoft as a big data and data warehousing solution architect where he has been for most of the last nine years. He is a thought leader in the use and application of big data and advanced analytics, including data architectures such as the modern data warehouse, data lakehouse, data fabric, and data mesh. Previously he was an independent consultant working as a Data Warehouse/Business Intelligence architect and developer. He is a prior SQL Server MVP with over 35 years of IT experience. He is a popular blogger (*https://www.jamesserra.com*) and speaker, having presented at dozens of major events including SQLBits, PASS Summit, Data Summit and the Enterprise Data World conference.

Colophon

The animal on the cover of *Deciphering Data Architectures* is a blue discus fish (*Symphysodon aequifasciata*), a freshwater fish found in the tributaries of the Amazon River. The wavy markings and coloration make blue discus fish popular for aquariums, but their natural habitat can be difficult to replicate and maintain.

Blue discus fish eat worms and small crustaceans and grow up to 9 inches long. The young feed off of the secretions of their parents. Many of the animals on O'Reilly covers are endangered; all of them are important to the world.

The cover illustration is by Karen Montgomery, based on a black-and-white engraving from *Akademie der Wissenschaften*. The series design is by Edie Freedman, Ellie Volckhausen, and Karen Montgomery. The cover fonts are Gilroy Semibold and Guardian Sans. The text font is Adobe Minion Pro; the heading font is Adobe Myriad Condensed; and the code font is Dalton Maag's Ubuntu Mono.